A BATTLE OF HOSTS:
THE CONTROVERSY OF THE SIXTH SEAL

LINWOOD JACKSON, JR.

PUBLISHED BY FIDELI PUBLISHING, INC.

© Copyright 2018, Linwood Jackson, Jr.

All Rights Reserved.

No part of this book may be reproduced, stored in a retrieval system, or transmitted by any means, electronic, mechanical, photocopying, recording, or otherwise, without written permission from the author.

ISBN: 978-1-948638-71-5

Cover created by artist Darko Hristov
@hristov_darko

For information, email the author at
LinwoodJackson@hotmail.com

Published by
Fideli Publishing, Inc.
www.FideliPublishing.com

Contents

1	Discerning The Nations	1
2	The Kindreds Of The Nations	4
3	The Anger Of The Nations	11
4	The Opening Of The Sixth Seal	15
5	The Pattern Of The Seals	28
6	The Tremors Of The Great Earthquake	35
7	The Coming Of The Son Of Man	43
8	A Quaking To Appear	53
9	A Prepared Host And Fury	64
10	The Sects Of The Controversy	71
11	The Stage Of The Controversy	77
12	The Year Of Commotion	87
13	An Unfolding Vengeance	98
14	A Quaking Line	107
15	Establishing Judgment's Line	115
16	The Philis'tines, Saul, And Jonathan	123
17	E'dom's Appointed End	132
18	A Time Of Change	140
19	A Running Fever	148
20	The Impact Of His Revelation	153
21	An Appointed Meeting	160
22	A Blessed Movement	168
23	A Pot Of Flesh	179
24	Places Of Wonder	187
25	The One Hundred Forty-Four Thousand	195
26	Love's Factor	202
27	The Last Trump	214
28	Heaven's Eminent Reign	226
29	The Earth's Sorrow	232
30	A Judgment Of Deliverance	238
31	In Righteousness	246
32	The Figure Of His Impression	256
33	A Thoughtful End	266
34	He Will Come	275

Introduction

1. If E'noch, who is "the seventh from Adam,"[1] prophesied, "saying, Behold, the Lord cometh with ten thousands of his saints,"[2] and "Noah the eighth person, a preacher of righteousness,"[3] witnessed the LORD "bringing in the flood upon the world of the ungodly,"[4] then we have, through the events of the flood, the fulfillment of the saying, "The Lord Jesus shall be revealed from heaven with his mighty angels."[5] E'noch prophesied of that flood, but Noah caught it, allowing us to understand that the "waters" of the flood are but an illustration of heaven's anticipated appearing. When thinking on a flood of "waters," it is well to remember how it says, "The voice of a great multitude, and as the voice of many waters,"[6] and, "The rushing of nations, that make a rushing like the rushing of mighty waters,"[7] and, "The waters...are peoples, and multitudes, and nations, and tongues."[8] "Waters" represent religious tribes and denominations. To hear of a "flood" upon the ungodly is to hear of "waters" upon the ungodly, which is to hear of a specific religious band united "against the rulers of the darkness of this world,

---

1 Jude 1:14
2 Jude 1:14
3 2 Peter 2:5
4 2 Peter 2:5
5 2 Thessalonians 1:7
6 Revelation 19:6
7 Isaiah 17:12
8 Revelation 17:15

against spiritual wickedness in high places."[9] This "flood" that Noah witnesses typifies the vision that E'noch prophesied of, allowing us to understand that this vision is no literal apocalyptic prognostication, but is simply a premonition of a reformatory movement perfectly executed by the Spirit's then human host.

2. Why did the LORD sanction a flood? It is written, "The earth also was corrupt before God, and the earth was filled with violence."[10] Violence warranted a flood, but what kind of violence? It says, "Her priests have polluted the sanctuary, they have done violence to the law,"[11] and, "It is time for thee, LORD, to work: for they have made void thy law."[12]

3. Because the earth had anciently violated and committed violence against the law of the LORD's Spirit, a flood of His wrath was deemed necessary, for, concerning His "wrath," it says, "The wrath of God is revealed from heaven against all ungodliness and unrighteousness of men, who hold the truth in unrighteousness."[13] Because the antediluvians held the LORD's name in national religious error, a flood was necessary, and because the then Egyptian Babylon of the Revelation will equally do the same, a great flood awaits her chief men, and their supporters, "to give unto her the cup of the wine of the fierceness of his wrath."[14] Now, if all joined to her "have been made drunk with the wine of her fornication,"[15] and this "fornication" being no literal physical intercourse, but rather spiritual and mental "wine"; as it says, "They are mad upon their idols,"[16] and, "Repented not of the works of their hands";[17] then it is fair to conclude that the "wine" of the Spirit's wrath is no physical or natural deluge, but is according to the saying, "He did

---

9   Ephesians 6:12
10   Genesis 6:11
11   Zephaniah 3:4
12   Psalm 119:126
13   Romans 1:18
14   Revelation 16:19
15   Revelation 17:2
16   Jeremiah 50:38
17   Revelation 9:20

good, and gave us rain from heaven, and fruitful seasons, filling our hearts with food and gladness."[18]

4. "Wine" is, in Scripture, figurative language denoting a judgment of doctrine, as it says, "They are swallowed up of wine, they are out of the way through strong drink; they err in vision, they stumble in judgment."[19] To hear of a devouring "wine" is to hear of a devouring doctrine; "wine" of "fornication" is a spiritual doctrine of religious error against the living God's name. For priests and ministers of the spirit of error to commit fornication, it is that they must fulfill saying, "God also gave them up to uncleanness through the lusts of their own hearts, to dishonour their own bodies between themselves,"[20] which is speech pointing to the act of ministers having intercourse with the philosophies of other ministers to satiate their heart for molesting not only their own faith's personal body, but the faith of every member within their assemblies by their amalgamating "every wind of doctrine, by the sleight of men, and cunning craftiness, whereby they lie in wait to deceive."[21] This is why the Spirit, when speaking on the ministers of the religious world, and their institution, says, "All tables are full of vomit and filthiness, so that there is no place clean."[22] "Their fear toward me is taught by the precept of men,"[23] says the Spirit concerning "false apostles, deceitful workers, transforming themselves into the apostles of Christ";[24] the serpent's product only knows, and preaches, satisfaction "through philosophy and vain deceit, after the tradition of men, after the rudiments of the world."[25]

5. When such a manner of worship and service through the pen of priests and elders becomes nationally accepted and globally endorsed as the rule of life, heaven's host will then pray, "It is time for thee, LORD, to work: for they have made void thy law."[26] Why is it that this prayer is

---

18	Acts 14:17
19	Isaiah 28:7
20	Romans 1:24
21	Ephesians 4:14
22	Isaiah 28:8
23	Isaiah 29:13
24	2 Corinthians 11:13
25	Colossians 2:8
26	Psalm 119:126

made? Paul tells us that, due to priests and elders holding the Word's name in unrighteousness, wrath must fall upon them; "The wrath of God is revealed from heaven against all ungodliness and unrighteousness of men, who hold the truth in unrighteousness,"[27] he says. Since the earth is destroyed because of "unrighteousness," them that forward this "unrighteousness" must receive that wage for "unrighteousness," wherefore, concerning "unrighteousness," it is well to know that "all unrighteousness is sin."[28] Whatever "sin" is, it is all of what "unrighteousness" is, and since "whatsoever is not of faith is sin,"[29] it is an eternal and indisputable fact that because "the law is not of faith,"[30] it is that "the strength of sin is the law."[31] The "law" here mentioned by Paul is "the law of commandments contained in ordinances";[32] "the handwriting of ordinances"[33] "after the commandments and doctrines of men."[34] When the Spirit says, "Their fear toward me is taught by the precept of men,"[35] He is informing us of what "sin" priests and elders commit against His Faith. The religious law of ministers is today that "sin" against heaven's will and doctrine, for which cause His "Christ hath redeemed us from the curse of the law."[36]

6. The former will, or the old covenant, was based upon obedience to the pen of priests and elders for blessing; the passing flesh of the LORD's Christ on the tree has made this manner of devotion obsolete; when "he saith, A new covenant, he hath made the first old."[37] "The strength of sin is the law,"[38] therefore to hear a priest preaching a *Christ* encouraging obedience to the pen and judgment of a religious law is to hear religious error, for the Word's Christ appeared "to redeem them

---

27	Romans 1:18
28	1 John 5:17
29	Romans 14:23
30	Galatians 3:12
31	1 Corinthians 15:56
32	Ephesians 2:15
33	Colossians 2:14
34	Colossians 2:22
35	Isaiah 29:13
36	Galatians 3:13
37	Hebrews 8:13
38	1 Corinthians 15:56

that were under the law."[39] The LORD's Christ was considered a transgressor against *God* because He not only refused the philosophies of priests, He also instructed against it, moving them to say of Him, "Why do thy disciples transgress the tradition of the elders?"[40] He preached against "sin's" *God* not to be stubborn or petty, but because His LORD and Father taught a contrary doctrine, namely, a perfect personal religion, and "perfect, as pertaining to the conscience."[41] The religious laws and ordinances of priests and elders only *bless* the conversation's outward appearance without nourishing the conscience of the conversation, which is why He repeatedly told them, "Ye Pharisees make clean the outside of the cup and the platter; but your inward part is full of ravening and wickedness."[42] To bless the conscience, more is demanded than lifeless traditions and a confidence in doctrines, for our mind is to be "written not with ink, but with the Spirit of the living God."[43]

7. Isn't this the doctrine that the Word's Christ teaches? Doesn't He say, "Ye are clean through the word which I have spoken,"[44] and, "If a man love me, he will keep my words,"[45] and, "That which is born of the Spirit is spirit"?[46] To be written of the Spirit means to have the impression of the Spirit's Word made upon the spirit of the mind, which is why we are counseled, "Be renewed in the spirit of your mind."[47] The LORD's manner of sanctification occurs only within the spirit of the mind through mentally and spiritually discerning His words. By "rightly dividing the word of truth,"[48] and by acting out that knowledge retained by investigation, a clearer understanding of the Spirit's voice will move us to confess, "The law of the Spirit of life in Christ Jesus hath made me free from the law of sin and death."[49] Because the legal

---

39 Galatians 4:5
40 Matthew 15:2
41 Hebrews 9:9
42 Luke 11:39
43 2 Corinthians 3:3
44 John 15:3
45 John 14:23
46 John 3:6
47 Ephesians 4:23
48 2 Timothy 2:15
49 Romans 8:2

religious law is made "sin" by the passing of this Christ on the tree, it is become our assignment, through the Spirit's law and judgment, to know a resurrection from dead religious manners, and "the sting of death is sin; and the strength of sin is the law."[50] The LORD's Christ on the tree is a figurative illustration of a conversation forwarded by the pen of priests and elders come under condemnation. Because "he that is hanged is accursed of God,"[51] when observing His Christ on the tree, we are witnessing "the handwriting of ordinances"[52] officially accursed of the Word.

8. Therefore, "having abolished in his flesh the enmity, even the law of commandments contained in ordinances,"[53] such manners are become "sin" to the Word's Faith. To hear of priests and elders holding the LORD's name in unrighteousness is therefore to hear of a *Christ* preaching *blessing* through what is accursed and abolished. Such a *Christ*, and his host, will experience a "flood" for their spiritual negligence, and this flood will swallow up their institution and strike through their inward parts. E'noch prophesied of this flood, but Noah's age foreshadowed the movement to appear, for that ancient flood did "serve unto the example and shadow of heavenly things."[54] Literal waters did plague the earth, but John, upon receiving vision of the Spirit's great revelation, beheld the throne pronouncing this vision, and of this throne he writes, "And there was a rainbow round about the throne, in sight like unto an emerald."[55] This rainbow is the same covenant that the Spirit made with the earth's host, saying, "Neither shall all flesh be cut off any more by the waters of a flood; neither shall there any more be a flood to destroy the earth."[56] This rainbow represents the fact that no natural disaster or calamity will ever again ruin priests and ministers by the LORD's throne, allowing us to understand that the wrath pronounced upon them practicing unrighteousness in

---

50   1 Corinthians 15:56
51   Deuteronomy 21:23
52   Colossians 2:14
53   Ephesians 2:15
54   Hebrews 8:5
55   Revelation 4:3
56   Genesis 9:11

the Revelation, and upon them taking unrighteousness to be for *righteousness*, is wholly spiritual.

9. The flood of waters that Noah witnessed typifies the "angels" that E'noch witnessed; "angels" are human messengers of spiritual understanding, as it says, "Who maketh his angels spirits, and his ministers a flame of fire."[57] When hearing, "In flaming fire taking vengeance,"[58] the vision is not literal, but is imagery pointing to a work accomplished by them that are likened to a flame of fire, who are those ministers of the Word's Spirit. Thus, because this vengeance is accomplished by the Spirit's creation, it is well to understand "the Lord" that is joined to them, for Paul says, "The Lord Jesus shall be revealed from heaven with his mighty angels."[59] Because John's vision, along with E'noch's, is not a literal vision, we must not fail to understand that "the Lord Jesus Christ our Saviour"[60] is, in right context of language, "the commandment of God our Saviour."[61] What the Spirit's men do prophesy of is no literal warfare of any celestial event against human flesh, but rather the greatest reformatory movement ever known among priests and ministers within the religious world, even as it says, "There was a great earthquake, such as was not since men were upon the earth, so mighty an earthquake, and so great."[62] Such an earthquake occurs because the doctrine of the Lamb has appeared before the eyes of men and is correcting their conversation's inwards. And isn't this the fact of the vision? Doesn't it say, "To execute judgment upon all, and to convince all that are ungodly among them of all their ungodly deeds"?[63]

10. The "judgment" that is executed is that understanding after the saying, "A law shall proceed from me, and I will make my judgment to rest for a light of the people."[64] Heaven's angels fully "give the light of the knowledge of the glory of God in the face of Jesus Christ";[65]

---

57 Hebrews 1:7
58 2 Thessalonians 1:8
59 2 Thessalonians 1:7
60 Titus 1:4
61 Titus 1:3
62 Revelation 16:18
63 Jude 1:15
64 Isaiah 51:4
65 2 Corinthians 4:6

the Spirit's sanctified host preaches "the law of the Spirit of life"[66] in omnipotent glory to error's host, for it says of His horse, "In righteousness he doth judge and make war."[67] "Righteousness" is no physical act, seeing as how "though we walk in the flesh, we do not war after the flesh."[68] To "war" in the flesh is to perform a manner of devotion through that which "sanctifieth to the purifying of the flesh,"[69] which baptism is contrary to the Word's intention, whose will is to "purge your conscience from dead works to serve the living God."[70] Whosoever unlawfully chases the flesh or body of their faith seeks to beautify the body of their faith at the expense of the conversation's center, which center is the conversation's conscience. Whatsoever halts the growth and development of our faith's mind is "sin," for it stops the person from exercising faith on the Spirit's will and law for right knowledge of heaven's name and science to live by. Therefore "whatsoever is not of faith is sin,"[71] and we have every right to conclude, by the testimony of the LORD's Christ on the tree, that "the law is not of faith."[72]

11. While priests and elders preach *righteousness* by the legal religious law, the Word defines righteousness by the edification of the mind to bless and govern our faith's body, which edification appears by examining and doing the Word's judgment. Whosoever preaches *righteousness* by the religious law and tradition does not know the Word and has never seen "the Lord Jesus Christ our Saviour,"[73] which "Lord" and "Savior" is "the commandment of God our Saviour."[74] The religious law is condemned as "sin" by the passing flesh of the LORD's Christ on the tree, therefore to say, and to hear, that the religious law is of the Word's commandment, is to hear propaganda supporting "sin," "and the strength of sin is the law."[75] Herein is the reason why John

---

66	Romans 8:2
67	Revelation 19:11
68	2 Corinthians 10:3
69	Hebrews 9:13
70	Hebrews 9:14
71	Romans 14:23
72	Galatians 3:12
73	Titus 1:4
74	Titus 1:3
75	1 Corinthians 15:56

is compelled to write to Christian elders, "In him is no sin. Whosoever abideth in him sinneth not: whosoever sinneth hath not seen him, neither known him."[76]

12. The doctrine of the Lamb is a doctrine exchanging "sin" for faith's higher learning to "know him, and the power of his resurrection, and the fellowship of his sufferings, being made conformable unto his death."[77] When we hear of the Lamb's wrath, we are hearing of a doctrine coming to vengefully defend the name of its LORD and Word, cruelly ripping "sin's" confidence from the eyes of error's assembly. The Lamb is a doctrine taking away sin; which "sin" is all reliance upon handwritten religious laws and doctrines; and when the wrath of the Lamb is preached, it will "convince all that are ungodly among them of all their ungodly deeds which they have ungodly committed, and of all their hard speeches which ungodly sinners have spoken against him."[78]

13. There is no greater injustice against the LORD's name than turning His doctrine upside down, which is why He says, "Woe unto them that call evil good, and good evil; that put darkness for light, and light for darkness; that put bitter for sweet, and sweet for bitter!"[79] His "Christ hath redeemed us from the curse of the law, being made a curse for us: for it is written, Cursed is every one that hangeth on a tree";[80] are we to now called what is cursed *blessed*? The tree is a sign of abominable religious habits, and what is nailed to the tree is accursed of heaven's will and learning; are we to take what is accursed for being honored? Isn't it written, "He whom thou blessest is blessed, and he whom thou cursest is cursed"?[81] Being "made under the law,"[82] when found on the tree, this Christ, through His flesh, has blotted out and abolished the religious law from His LORD's Faith, cursing it as "sin" to that Faith. But seeing as how, upon passing away, He said, "Father, into thy hands

---

76   1 John 3:5,6
77   Philippians 3:10
78   Jude 1:15
79   Isaiah 5:20
80   Galatians 3:13
81   Numbers 22:6
82   Galatians 4:4

I commend my spirit,"[83] we have, through His passing, regenerating, and high priestly appointment, a spirit of mind to claim. Through this Christ is preached the passing away of a flesh-based conversation for regeneration within the conversation's conscience, which is why we are counseled, "Put off concerning the former conversation the old man... and be renewed in the spirit of your mind."[84]

14. What E'noch prophesied of took place in Noah's age, and what Noah's age witnessed will take place when priests and ministers again openly mishandle heaven's confidence. This flood will be no natural disaster; this "Lord" will be no physical thing; but the saying will be fulfilled, "I will bring strangers upon thee, the terrible of the nations: and they shall draw their swords against the beauty of thy wisdom, and they shall defile thy brightness."[85] For this cause, the Spirit says, "I will also make the multitude of Egypt to cease by the hand of Nebuchadrez'zar king of Babylon. He and his people with him, the terrible of the nations, shall be brought to destroy the land: and they shall draw their swords against Egypt, and fill the land with the slain. And I will make the rivers dry, and sell the land into the hand of the wicked: and I will make the land waste, and all that is therein, by the hand of strangers: I the LORD have spoken it. Thus saith the Lord GOD; I will also destroy the idols, and I will cause their images to cease out of Noph; and there shall be no more a prince of the land of Egypt: and I will put a fear in the land of Egypt. And I will make Path'ros desolate, and will set fire in Zo'an, and will execute judgments in No."[86]

15. We should not connect any of the figures here mentioned to their literal person. When speaking on Nebuchadrez'zar, the Spirit says, "Nebuchadrez'zar the king of Babylon, my servant."[87] Nebuchadrez'zar and his host, because of their mission against a company willingly contrary to the LORD's name; as He says, "I will give the land of Egypt unto Nebuchadrez'zar";[88] figuratively represents the doctrine of His

---

83   Luke 23:46
84   Ephesians 4:22,23
85   Ezekiel 28:7
86   Ezekiel 30:10-14
87   Jeremiah 25:9
88   Ezekiel 29:19

Son and the stewards preaching that judgment. Through heaven's host, fear will find itself within the then Egyptian Babylon, even according to how the LORD says, "I will put my fear in their hearts, that they shall not depart from me."[89] This "fear" engraved upon their heart, it is His Spirit's law and judgment engraved upon their heart in omnipotent fury, fulfilling the saying, "I will put my law in their inward parts, and write it in their hearts; and will be their God, and they shall be my people."[90] Thus, through the Spirit's wisdom, the saying is fulfilled, "In that day shall there be an altar to the LORD in the midst of the land of Egypt, and a pillar at the border thereof to the LORD. And it shall be for a sign and for a witness unto the LORD of hosts in the land of Egypt: for they shall cry unto the LORD because of the oppressors, and he shall send them a saviour, and a great one, and he shall deliver them. And the LORD shall be known to Egypt, and the Egyptians shall know the LORD in that day."[91]

16. When hearing, "Behold, he cometh with clouds; and every eye shall see him, and they also which pierced him,"[92] it is that we are hearing, "Behold, the LORD rideth upon a swift cloud, and shall come into Egypt: and the idols of Egypt shall be moved at his presence, and the heart of Egypt shall melt in the midst of it."[93] These "clouds" are no literal entity, for it says, "He shall come up as clouds, and his chariots shall be as a whirlwind: his horses are swifter than eagles."[94] These "clouds" are "chariots," even chariots of "horses" according to how it says, "The chariots of God are twenty thousand, even thousands of angels,"[95] and, "The LORD of hosts hath visited his flock the house of Judah, and hath made them as his goodly horse in the battle."[96] These "clouds" are ministers of heaven's will, whose conversation displays a character as white as the clouds, for they "have washed their robes,

---

89 Jeremiah 32:40
90 Jeremiah 31:33
91 Isaiah 19:19-21
92 Revelation 1:7
93 Isaiah 19:1
94 Jeremiah 4:13
95 Psalm 68:17
96 Zechariah 10:3

and made them white in the blood of the Lamb."[97] Being of the Lamb, there is no "sin" in their devotion, for they are partakers of the Word's righteousness. Through their voice, all who have pierced the law of heaven's mediation will finally comprehend their wrong through their own eyes, that is, "the eyes" of their understanding.[98] Through the avenging praise of the Word, that Pharaoh of the then religious age; "who opposeth and exalteth himself above all that is called God, or that is worshipped";[99] will "come to his end, and none shall help him."[100]

---

[97] Revelation 7:14
[98] Ephesians 1:18
[99] 2 Thessalonians 2:4
[100] Daniel 11:45

1

Discerning The Nations

1. Says Scripture, "And the nations were angry, and thy wrath is come."[101]

2. The "nations" mentioned cannot be literal civil or political entities. Because the Revelation is no secular vision, these "nations" must be understood as religious denominations, ecclesiastical factions, religious kindreds, religious assemblies, religious people and tribes; as it says, "Nations, and kindreds, and people, and tongues,"[102] and, "Peoples, and multitudes, and nations, and tongues."[103] The nations being "angry" are best likened to the seas raging, therefore the angry nations cannot be literal secular nations, but are the denominations of the "sea." Such a link between the sea and Gentile religious denominations is witnessed by the saying, "The abundance of the sea shall be converted unto thee, the forces of the Gentiles shall come unto thee."[104] The "sea," through Isaiah's speech, is herein understood to represent "Gentile" religious denominations.

---

101   Revelation 11:18
102   Revelation 7:9
103   Revelation 17:15
104   Isaiah 60:5

3. An example of proof that political powers are not ultimately at war in this prophecy of the Revelation is that the wrath afterwards mentioned does not fall as the nations are "angry," but rather during a time of pretended spiritual progression through a false religious movement. It should be remembered that the war it seems "Satan" is after is not a political war. The spirit of his erroneous religion is after a religious revolution against heaven's will and doctrine, even a spiritual battle to seat error's mind above the LORD God's throne religion, and the only war that can be forwarded in such a manner is one that pays ultimate homage to a State ordained theocracy, even as it says of this faith's ambition, "I will ascend into heaven, I will exalt my throne above the stars of God: I will sit also upon the mount of the congregation...I will be like the most High."[105]

4. Again, another proof that political nations are not in play is that in the second division of the Revelation, verses twenty-six and twenty-seven, the Spirit promises, to the angel or messenger of the church of Thyati'ra, that the one who should remain in His name's understanding would be given power over the nations, to rule them. Such an angel of these times should be "a ruler and a deliverer,"[106] and this one who should rule would be as Moses, and only men of religion at this time fulfill the vision, who did not rule the political world, but who shook every religious denomination by the voice of that message found in the fourteenth division of the Revelation. To rule the nations is not to rule the political world, but rather to rule the isles of the religious world, for it says of the doctrine of the Spirit's Christ, "The isles shall wait for his law."[107] Herein it is well to understand that the angry nations are religious institutions that are wroth against the Spirit's host for some reason, and that reason is because "the altar of Ba'al was cast down, and the grove was cut down that was by it."[108]

5. It says, in the eleventh division of the Revelation, that the nations were angry, wherefore when hopeful to further understand the definition of a "nation," we observe, in the sixty-sixth division of

---

105 Isaiah 14:13,14
106 Acts 7:35
107 Isaiah 42:4
108 Judges 6:28

Isaiah, in the eighth verse, that the earth is called a "nation," and when observing the fourth division of the book of Micah, the second verse, we are counseled that many nations shall come to the Spirit's House and City to learn of His name's law and doctrine. For we also see in the sixtieth division of Isaiah, verses three to five, that the nations who should come to the Spirit's name are in reality Gentiles, a sea of pagans professing service to the *Creator* of the Bible, and that they are to be converted to the living God's name by the testimony of His then regenerated and reformed assembly. Of old it says, "Two nations are in thy womb, and two manner of people,"[109] for these nations in the Revelation are various tribes and kinds of people of faith that do not know the Faith of heaven's new covenant will. The nations being angry are the many Gentile religious groups of the religious earth; who are the many religious families of the sea; enraged at or excited over some thing transpiring within the earth. These denominations are angry or wrathful at some thing or some one, or they are outraged and offended about some thing or some one, or they are intoxicated with some thing, or some one.

6. It appears that a season of events should exist from the angry denominations until heaven's appointed wrath. When the world collectively desires a *moral* voice to order it, when the world longs after the justice and favor of *God* for whatever has befallen it, this should be the time when the denominations decide to act for themselves to take spiritual matters into their own hands, and by the power of their State. The result will leave a peculiar group of people hated by the established spurious ecclesiastical government for their stance against the new Republic, for the new beast of the earth grossly violates heaven's LORD and Word by his policy.

---

109   Genesis 25:23

2

The Kindreds Of The Nations

1. Scripture says, "And the nations were angry,"[110] and it is not that literal nations should be wroth, but rather it should be as it is said, "People and kindreds and tongues and nations."[111] Thus, in the eighteenth verse of the eleventh division of the Revelation, religious "kindreds, and tongues, and nations,"[112] were wroth, even as it says concerning "kindreds" and "nations," "In thy seed shall all the kindreds of the earth be blessed,"[113] and, "In thy seed shall all the nations of the earth be blessed."[114]

2. It should be remembered that, unlike the book of Daniel, the book of the Revelation is not a vision of secular history, but rather of church history; it is written, "To testify unto you these things in the churches."[115] Literal nations do not have a mind to naturally care for the religious preference of any one, but it is that when religiously perverse minded individuals desire an end for their own dogmas and beliefs, that

---

110 Revelation 11:18
111 Revelation 11:9
112 Revelation 13:7
113 Acts 3:25
114 Genesis 22:18
115 Revelation 22:16

then they may work the hand of the State for advantage. The "nations" here mentioned in the Revelation are not royal kingdoms, but they are kindreds of religious faiths, people of religious denominations, even as it was once said, "Whence comest thou? what is thy country? and of what people art thou?"[116] What is the correct answer to these questions? The Spirit's man says, "I am an Hebrew."[117] The kindred or people or country that Jonah belonged to was a religious tribe of people, a nation or denomination of people called Hebrews. Thus, the reality of what the Spirit admits in the eighteenth verse of the eleventh division of the Revelation is that "all the kindreds of the nations"[118] were wroth.

3. The fact that it says, concerning these nation, "Were angry,"[119] and not, "Are angry," witnesses to the fact that what is being spoken of is a past event in the time that it is mentioned, for at this particular time in vision, "the Lord God omnipotent reigneth."[120]

4. "All kindreds of the earth,"[121] all families and denominations of people, all "clusters of the vine of the earth,"[122] were angry. In order for these, "after their families, after their tongues, in their countries, and in their nations,"[123] to be angry, it is that as anger has levels, so there should be stages of anger until it is fulfilled, "The dragon was wroth."[124] Notice that the nations were angry, but that it is the dragon that goes out to make war. The dragon goes after the Spirit's host and assembly because his host and assembly is disrespected by them, for, the creature of this "disrespected" sect has power "over all kindreds, and tongues, and nations."[125] For this cause, the angry nations are prominent force when the dragon is wroth, for both; the angry nations and the vengeful dragon; appear to be one entity fulfilling the same vision, even as it

---

116   Jonah 1:8
117   Jonah 1:9
118   Psalms 22:27
119   Revelation 11:18
120   Revelation 19:6
121   Acts 3:25
122   Revelation 14:18
123   Genesis 10:20
124   Revelation 12:17
125   Revelation 13:7

says, "The prince asketh, and the judge asketh for a reward; and the great man, he uttereth his mischievous desire: so they wrap it up,"[126] and, "There was none like unto Ahab, which did sell himself to work wickedness in the sight of the LORD, whom Jez'ebel his wife stirred up."[127]

5. It is because the then "woman Jez'ebel"[128] is disrespected that *Ahab* will be stirred up to act on her behalf. Yet as one must have a reason to give place to anger, it must be observed as to where the anger of these churches derives its agitation. We lightly touched on this issue in the fourth paragraph of the previous chapter, for such anger of the denominations cannot fail of finding place by how it was said of old, "There is a certain people scattered abroad and dispersed among the people in all the provinces of thy kingdom; and their laws are diverse from all people; neither keep they the king's laws: therefore it is not for the king's profit to suffer them."[129] It is evident that, at this time in the Revelation, the dragon's host "made an image of gold,"[130] saying, "Whoso falleth not down and worshippeth shall the same hour be cast into the midst of a burning fiery furnace."[131] When a few who will not honor the image are found out, then the dragon; a symbol in prophecy of a State; will find a reason for violence against them, even as was "Nebuchadnez'zar full of fury, and the form of his visage was changed against Sha'drach, Me'shach, and Abed'-nego."[132]

6. It should be clearly observed that this is an image test not brought against the religious world, but on "children in whom was no blemish,"[133] "certain of the children of Israel,"[134] even them that "be of the seed of the Jews."[135] This is a trial specifically ordained for the Spirit's household to fulfill the saying, "I will cause you to pass under

---

126 Micah 7:3
127 1 Kings 21:25
128 Revelation 2:20
129 Esther 3:8
130 Daniel 3:1
131 Daniel 3:6
132 Daniel 3:19
133 Daniel 1:4
134 Daniel 1:3
135 Esther 6:13

the rod, and I will bring you into the bond of the covenant: and I will purge out from among you the rebels, and them that transgress against me."[136] This is a purging that has nothing to do with them that violate the LORD God's Faith, for the religious world is already willingly subject to the State's religious order. What heaven's assembly should today begin to prepare themselves for; or what them that presently profess to dwell within the Spirit's heavenly Sanctuary should currently study after; is a living experience in that Faith of the doctrine of that Temple's LORD and High Priest to know no harm by the test that is to first fall on them. The Spirit's congregation is to be purified before mercy's last message extends to the religious world, for, at this later time of investigation, the saying will be fulfilled, "Judgment must begin at the house of God."[137]

7. "Before the decree bring forth"[138] "a time of trouble, such as never was,"[139] something must happen to change the complexion of the earth's history, for it must first be fulfilled, "He shall enter into the glorious land,"[140] and this vision signifies the fulfillment of how it says, "They should make an image to the beast."[141] There will not be a literal entrance of the king of the north into the glorious land per se, but rather a spiritual. The *north's* spirit and dominion will indeed enter into the then *Jerusalem*, for his spirit and mind will flourish by way of an erected image, which image "should both speak, and cause that as many as would not worship the image of the beast should be killed."[142] It was because the LORD's faithful refused to honor the image of old that such disobedience procured wrath against them. When it is that the earth's current frame should officially become an apostate *Roman* and *Egyptian* faction subscribing to a church and State government, it is then that heaven's right host will begin to stand out, fulfilling the saying, "Thou makest us a reproach to our neighbours, a scorn and a

---

136 Ezekiel 20:37,38
137 1 Peter 4:17
138 Zephaniah 2:2
139 Daniel 12:1
140 Daniel 11:41
141 Revelation 13:14
142 Revelation 13:15

derision to them that are round about us. Thou makest us a byword among the heathen, a shaking of the head among the people."[143]

8. The Spirit's house will become a hated people to the countries or kindreds or denominations of the then popular State religion. Such disregard for the image of the earth beast; which image fulfills the vision, "I saw a woman sit upon a scarlet coloured beast,"[144] or rather, saw a church upheld and supported by State power; will molest and persecute "the daughter of Zion."[145] It will be fulfilled, "The Lord covered the daughter of Zion with a cloud in his anger, and cast down from heaven unto the earth the beauty of Israel,"[146] and this will continue until the Spirit says, "I will no more make you a reproach among the heathen."[147]

9. Such events carry the mind back to that vision given to John of the seals, wherein he records, "The stars of heaven fell unto the earth, even as a fig tree casteth her untimely figs, when she is shaken of a mighty wind."[148] Now, "the Lord hath a mighty and strong one, which as a tempest of hail and a destroying storm, as a flood of mighty waters overflowing, shall cast down to the earth with the hand,"[149] and such an agent will be permitted a space of time to "purify" His professed, even as He says, "I will sift the house of Israel among all nations."[150]

10. It was because His people served other gods that the LORD was constantly at odds with them, as He says, "Ye provoke me unto wrath with the works of your hands, burning incense unto other gods in the land of Egypt."[151] These nations of the eleventh division of the Revelation are angry over the same issue. Because His host refuses to worship any other doctrine than that put forth by the Spirit of His Son's mediation, the denominations of the earth will be full of wrath and fury against them, yet it is not the churches of the earth that execute their fury, but rather the earth's dragon does their bidding. The frustration

---

143 Psalms 44:13,14
144 Revelation 17:3
145 Lamentations 1:6
146 Lamentations 2:1
147 Joel 2:19
148 Revelation 6:13
149 Isaiah 28:2
150 Amos 9:9
151 Jeremiah 44:8

of the earth's kindreds against heaven's daughter will grow and build up in strength until they have had enough with this peculiar group of individuals.

11. When the earth beast should speak as a dragon, when a church and state government should openly rule the land of the serpent's spiritual persuasion secularly, there is enough proof that, after this time of an established pagan apostate religious State, the nations, or the kindreds, should be "angry." From this point in time, until it should be fulfilled, "The cities of the nations fell,"[152] the word will be fulfilled that the nations were angry, and then that great judgment of the Spirit's wrath will come. It is understood that the wrath spoken of after the nations' agitation is of the LORD's Spirit because the elders recounting this history say, "Thou hast taken to thee thy great power, and hast reigned."[153] The plagues do not pronounce the living God's complete reign, for ministers are still alive to error against His throne during their outpouring, and are even cursing His name because of them. Yet the cities of the nations must now be understood to be "the kingdoms of the countries,"[154] or "the families of the countries,"[155] and it will be that all associated with the vine of the earth will fall by that Spirit saying, "I am the true vine."[156]

12. It is for this reason that it is written, "He shall judge among the heathen, he shall fill the places with the dead bodies; he shall wound the heads over many countries."[157] Because this judgment is based upon the saying, "Out of his mouth goeth a sharp sword,"[158] because this is that "sword of the Spirit, which is the word of God,"[159] it is herein evident that the wound these heads or chief priests should suffer is not literal or physical, but is a vengeance ordained to devour their conversation's inwards, as it says, "My heart is like wax; it is melted in the midst of my

---

152   Revelation 16:19
153   Revelation 11:17
154   1 Chronicles 29:30
155   Ezekiel 20:32
156   John 15:1
157   Psalms 110:6
158   Revelation 19:15
159   Ephesians 6:17

bowels,"[160] and, "My bowels are troubled; mine heart is turned within me,"[161] "for the wrath of God is revealed from heaven against all...who hold the truth in unrighteousness."[162] Such an event; due to the fact that the Spirit's wrath is born for spiritual injustice against His name; allows us to learn that it is fair to mark the beginning of the angering of the nations at that point in time when the image of the beast is established. At no other time before should it be placed, and even no other time after. The nations being "angry," or the kindreds being wroth, lead to the dragon being wroth, for it is because the dragon's religiously erroneous "wife wept before him, and said, Thou dost but hate me, and lovest me not,"[163] that "the heathen rage."[164]

13. "These shall make war with the Lamb, and the Lamb shall overcome them: for he is Lord of lords, and King of kings: and they that are with him are called, and chosen, and faithful."[165]

---

160   Psalm 22:14
161   Lamentations 1:20
162   Romans 1:18
163   Judges 14:16
164   Psalm 2:1
165   Revelation 17:14

3

The Anger Of The Nations

1. Other words or terms for "angry" is bitter, hostile, nasty, or irreconcilable, for, at this time, the families of the earth are rebellious against the LORD's voice, which rebellion is shown and understood through them receiving correction by the wrath of His Spirit's Word. The result of a new *Papal* State is seen when there is a rejection of the LORD's Faith and Ten Commandments; the ones within this Egyptian institution have become reprobate to heaven's will, to then receive the end of their stubbornness. For, as a matter of fact, in another aspect of thinking, to be "angry" means that one is intoxicated, which is why it is written, "They are mad upon their idols,"[166] and, "Babylon hath been a golden cup in the LORD's hand, that made all the earth drunken: the nations have drunken of her wine; therefore the nations are mad."[167]

2. The nations being "mad" may, in one sense, mean that they are belligerent and drunk, that is, drunken from the doctrines and policies established by the woman of the then nationally enforced religion, as it says, "All nations have drunk of the wine of the wrath of her fornication, and the kings of the earth have committed fornication with her,

---

166 Jeremiah 50:38
167 Jeremiah 51:7

and the merchants of the earth are waxed rich through the abundance of her delicacies."[168] The nations are not angry at first; literal anger is not the first rung of wrath's ladder; but rather they are spiritually drunk and deluded by a particular spiritual understanding, and are therefore become irritable to heaven's host and doctrine. The nations being angry should then cover the formation of a church and state government until that government joins hands with she who should be healed, to give birth to a new phase of that government religion. When this new dominion is formed, and when every spirit has had the full opportunity to conscientiously reject or accept this dominion over their heart, when every conscience has made their decision to either stand for the living God or to stand for this counterfeit ministry of *healing*, then the Spirit's wrath will fall on the earth after her wrath is fulfilled on the earth.

3. The summary recorded in the eleventh division of the Revelation, verse eighteen, cannot be anything before New Pagan and Papal *Jerusalem* is formed, or anything before the new *Roman* and *Egyptian* State is judicially established. If the nations are "angry" then they are, in every way, contrary to what is written in the first division of Titus, verses seven and eight. They are become self-willed, soon angry, given to wine, a striker, given to filthy lucre, are haters of right hospitality, are haters of good and benevolent ministers, are intoxicated, self-righteous, ungodly, and intemperate; this is the character that advances the anger of the denominations.

4. Because of this spirit flourishing within their camp, they will fulfill the saying, "The kings of the earth set themselves, and the rulers take counsel together, against the LORD, and against his anointed,"[169] and this is done because of how it is says, "Ye perish from the way."[170] What more can be done for them that willingly perish from the fact and science of the Spirit's doctrine? Therefore indeed the next scene that John should see is the falling wrath of the Spirit. Nothing in the eleventh division of the Revelation, verse eighteen, should be found before the movements to establish a pagan *Jewish Roman-Egyptian* State, or

---

168 Revelation 18:2,3
169 Psalm 2:2
170 Psalm 2:12

before the establishment of a pagan apostate *Christian* State under the direct influence of that ancient spirit within Papal Rome, is born.

5. Another interesting thing to note is that to be "mad" does not just mean to be raging or angry, or to be drunk or inebriated, but it also means to wonder, to marvel, or to have in great admiration. The denominations, in order to own the state of mind that they are in, are mentally wondering at some thing to have that thing in great admiration. It is after the fallen leopard beast is healed that the religious world becomes "mad"; as it says, "The world wondered after the beast,"[171] and again, "I wondered in great admiration."[172] When John sees that woman of the two-horned earth best persecuting heaven's faithful, he too also wonders, or is fallen mad for her with great mystifying admiration.

6. The nations cannot begin to be angry until within the then earth the then *Jerusalem*; a spiritually foul and apostate church and State government contrary to the heavenly Sanctuary; is formed, and they will not be fully angry until this pagan State joins hands and uplifts that spirit of the first beast before it. So again, nothing before the newly established pagan-apostate *Christian* government should be linked to the angry nations. John wondering after the woman is not representing the actions of the faithful, but of them that fulfill the saying, "They that dwell on the earth shall wonder, whose names were not written in the book of life from the foundation of the world,"[173] and, "All that dwell upon the earth shall worship him, whose names are not written in the book of life."[174] The nations are drunk with the established religious policies, doctrines, customs, laws, and traditions of the enforced one world ecclesiastical dominion.

7. John sees the nations angry and then writes, "Thy wrath is come,"[175] not, "Thy wrath came." John sees order. Only blatant madness against the LORD's name warrants heaven's immediate wrath, as it says, "If any man worship the beast...the same shall drink of the wine

---

171 Revelation 13:3
172 Revelation 17:6
173 Revelation 17:8
174 Revelation 13:8
175 Revelation 11:18

of the wrath of God."[176] There is therefore conclusive proof that, by the time the nations are angry, the image of the former religious age; as represented by the leopard beast; is set up, even the dominion of a pagan apostate *Jewish-Egyptian* State. So then the nations are in fact "angry" and "mad" by the time Pagan *Papal Jerusalem* enforces their name and mark under their three-fold union, which act secures the Spirit's wrath to her and her supporters.

---

176 Revelation 14:9,10

4

The Opening Of The Sixth Seal

1. It is quite interesting to note that, in the eleventh division of the Revelation, verse fifteen, the seventh angel sounds and then John is taken into the future. We know that it is the future because of certain key words. Verses fifteen through seventeen of the same chapter are a fulfillment of the nineteenth division of the Revelation, verses four through six. The same elders of the eleventh chapter of the Revelation are observed in the nineteenth as falling down and worshipping at LORD's throne, for the same words and spirit are expressed in both chapters, allowing us to understand that the scenes are synonymous. With that being said, the eleventh division of the Revelation, verse fifteen, does not break character from them that pronounce victory in the ninetieth. In chapter eleven of the Revelation, verse fifteen, the elders of the LORD's throne are talking, and their voice appears to break only in verse nineteen, leaving it to be understood that what they are saying is a continuous stream of revealed events, events that lead up to the ultimate reign of His Christ's law and doctrine over the earth's stout members.

2. If this is so; and it is; then the elders are voicing what leading events forward their LORD's reign by His Word. The tenth division of the Revelation, verse seven, speaks on the sounding of the seventh

trumpet in its beginning tones; the eleventh chapter of the Revelation, verses fifteen through nineteen, not only bring in those beginning tones of the seventh trumpet, but extend to its final note. Both chapters and verses express different periods of events for the same incident; chapter eleven of the Revelation expressing that which is joined to and succeeds the tenth chapter of the Revelation, in that before His reign appeared, His wrath is manifested, and before His wrath is come, the nations are angry, which angering is a witness to the fact that, within heaven's household, the will and mystery of the Spirit is finishing during a great reformatory movement. For this cause, the wrath spoken of by the elders in the eleventh chapter of the Revelation cannot simply be that of the seven last plagues, for the elders are blessing their LORD after the plagues are fallen, and after heaven's Faith has reigned.

3. In addition to verses four and five of the nineteenth division of the Revelation being an exact fulfillment of verses fifteen through seventeen of the eleventh chapter of the Revelation, in Revelation nineteen we read about that wrath the elders speak of, which wrath then leads in to the time of the dead, which year is spoken of in the twentieth division of the Revelation, verses eleven and twelve. This wrath is not solely the plagues, but it is as revealed in the fifteenth verse of the nineteenth chapter of the Revelation, and in the sixteenth verse of the sixth chapter of the Revelation, and in the seventh verse of the first chapter of the Revelation, even the wrath of the Word's Lamb, the day of the vengeance of the LORD's Spirit. We know that this is certain because, in the second half of the nineteenth verse of the eleventh chapter of the Revelation, there is a true fulfillment of verses seventeen through twenty-one of the sixteenth chapter of the Revelation. The seventh plague brings forth a great earthquake, which language is used in the thirteenth verse of the eleventh chapter of the Revelation to depict the French Revolution and the fall of Papal Rome, symbolizing that the earthquake in thirteenth verse of the eleventh chapter of the Revelation, and the great earthquake in the eighteenth verse of the sixteenth chapter of the Revelation, are of the same spiritual substance, for in this earthquake exists the warring of religious denominations and spiritual factions by the Word's impression.

The Opening Of The Sixth Seal • 17

4. The angry nations are a fulfillment of verses thirteen through eighteen of the sixteenth division of the Revelation, for within the next line of events; "Thy wrath is come,"[177] says the elders; and in the nineteenth verse of the sixteenth chapter of the Revelation, that fierceness of wrath is administered against the then Babylon, or as is seen in the second verse of the nineteenth chapter of the Revelation, the great whore and her members, the seed of the pagan *Jewish* apostate *Christian* union. This Babylon the great is divided into three parts, expressing that the union between apostate *Protestant Rome* and the spirit of Papal Rome is here long since complete. The nations being angry cannot happen before the new *Papal* pagan religion flourishes throughout the then religious world, and it appears that its anger occurs throughout the plagues, and it must.

5. The wrath spoken of by the elders in the eleventh chapter of the Revelation cannot simply be the Spirit's seven last plagues, for, no period of an investigative judgment appears after the plagues, but rather another wrath administered by the face of the Spirit's High Priest. As the elders are speaking from a point of view of events finalized and sealed to perfect completion, the events must only relate to that leading up to a complete spiritual reign of the LORD's throne and doctrine. Notice that the elders speak from heaven and are not on earth, and that as they say these things, they are before the LORD and His Word in heaven, and are not on earth. The events the elders are mentioning are those that not only affect earth's elements, and the members within the earth, but also literally involve heaven's assembly, and the power of heaven's voice. The seven last plagues against the earth's spirit and religious dominion does not disturb what is in heaven, neither do the first three plagues before these seven; which three will be against the Spirit's professed by the dragon of these nations; for these things are done on earth against them that have no right knowledge of heaven's course, and that are stout against that course. The nations being angry therefore call heaven's authority into the realm of action. In verse nineteen of the eleventh division of the Revelation, the imagery depicted expresses an apparent uproar against what is observed in the second

---

177   Revelation 18:11

room of the LORD's heavenly Temple, which is His Ten Commandments along with the Faith of His Son. The nations are bitter against a commandment-keeping people, for when the plagues fall, only them that know the living God, and that worship at His throne within His heavenly Building, and that reverence His Son's name and face, will not be affected by them.

6. Scripture says, "And every Island fled away, and the mountains were not found,"[178] and this is in direct reference to how it is said, "Every mountain and island were moved out of their places."[179] If this is so; and it is; I see no reason why the sixth seal should be divided by time, seeing as how none of the other seals are; each of the first five seals are fulfilled in their time and are never partially accomplished. Therefore, the great earthquake of the twelfth verse of the sixth chapter of the Revelation must be related to the great earthquake of the seventh plague, for both are synonymous; both lead up to the wrath of the Lamb and speak on the end of error's secular and religious reign. The sun becoming black and the moon becoming as blood, and with the stars falling, are, as in the twelfth verse of the eighth chapter of the Revelation, a vision of ecclesiastical power being overthrown and removed. The heaven departing is as it says in verses ten through twelve of the first chapter of the book of Hebrews, even a change in power and in spiritual dispensation, and the law of His Christ's priestly operation administers this change by the woe of the seventh trumpet, which woe is captured by the sixth seal.

7. That end revealed by the sixth seal sends the mind to the first verse of the twelfth chapter of the Revelation, which is a vision revealing a church clothed with the sun and standing on the moon while wearing a crown of twelve stars on her head. The garment that this woman wears is as bright as the sun, but now, by that great earthquake, it is black. The moon that this woman stands on is white and bright, but now the ground of her feet is as red as blood. The angels of her head are the messengers of her thoughts and feelings, and her falling stars may also denote the ninth and tenth verses of the eighth chapter of the book of

---

178   Revelation 16:20
179   Revelation 6:15

Daniel, along with the third and fourth verses of the twelfth chapter of the Revelation. A new woman is found destroying the angels of that woman of heaven; whose angels in heaven lawfully subscribe to the name of the Father and His Son; and by that red moon she is standing on, as it says, "I saw a woman sit upon a scarlet coloured beast."[180]

8. The moon derives its light from the sun, so this red moon shone bright by the black sun that it upholds, and such a scene of the sixth seal must be the fulfillment of the seventeenth chapter of the book of Isaiah. So then it makes sense why John should hear, in the eleventh verse of the sixth chapter of the Revelation, that others should be killed as they were by Papal Rome, for in verses five and six of the seventeenth chapter of the book of Isaiah, and verse thirteen of the sixth chapter of the Revelation, we see the fulfillment of a final scattering and gathering.

9. The sixth seal is a full vision, as are the other seals one entire vision that is not divided. Therefore when the sixth seal is opened up, we are made to find an apostate church sitting on a great red dragon. The church and doctrine of the *Sun of righteousness* is born with a new black garment of hair to cover the earth's right woman; it is not even a garment of fine linen; for heaven's bright doctrine must be banned and not tolerated, creating a division between the true woman, and the false, on earth. The moon being red doesn't only denote this false woman's failing power and foundation, but also her spiritual death for ignoring the voice of that right woman in the earth, for the dragon "persecuted the woman."[181] The stars of heaven; in one application; are those ministers whose eyes dwell in heaven and not in the established earth on earth. The sixth seal, then, is one vision expressing the union between the Pagan *Jewish* Republic of *Egyptian Jerusalem* and the spirit of Papal Rome, her works, and the destruction of them that are joined to her through the Lamb's wrathful doctrine.

10. The vision of the sixth seal shows that this corrupt religious economy will vanish at the end of the great day of the Word's wrath; which wrath is that wrath of the Lamb's name and face; yet before this

---
180 Revelation 17:3
181 Revelation 12:13

day, there should be an anger to wonder at, anger which is as madness and drunkenness put forth on behalf of that healed force joined to the new pagan *Jewish-Roman* Republic. Therefore, in one sense, and in one stream of thought, the sixth seal must open to John with a great earthquake and then move from that quaking to express the reason for that earthquake. An earthquake is a commotion or a tempest, and a tempest is a violent windy storm. John beholds a terrible commotion taking place within the earth's religious denominations, and more terrible than that within any of the previous seals, for, a part of the great commotion he sees are powers amalgamating to shake and cast down heaven's true stars like as by a tremor born of a mighty wind, or by their doctrine greatly fallen away from the doctrine of heaven's High Priest, as it says of this "wind," "With every wind of doctrine."[182]

11. Herein we learn that the sixth seal opens up with the saying, "Babylon the great is fallen, is fallen";[183] with the complete union of pagan apostate *Jerusalem* to the spirit and career of the first beast before it; and the only thing that should warrant the casting down of the Spirit's messengers is a challenging of the authority of this government's Egyptian doctrine, for heaven's right stars say, "Come out of her, my people,"[184] which is the full message of that third angel within the fourteenth division of the Revelation. Therefore, within the sixth seal, we have a fulfillment of the forty-third and forty-fourth verses of the eleventh chapter of Daniel, which are a fulfillment of the twelfth and thirteen verses of the sixth chapter of the Revelation. So then this great earthquake is the same earthquake as that within the seventh plague of the sixteenth chapter of the Revelation, but within the line of events concerning this earthquake within the sixth seal is the record of apostasy and perdition, until that record is visited and blotted out.

12. The seals have, from the beginning of their revelation, dealt with an apostate Christian church history, and this great earthquake of the sixth seal will be no thing less than important apostate Christian church history, even the final movement of that great apostasy against

---

182 Ephesians 4:14
183 Revelation 18:2
184 Revelation 18:4

the LORD's throne until it is quenched by His Faith in terrible fury. The seventh angel of the seventh trumpet must finish the Spirit's mystery among the hardhearted within the ark of the spirit of their mind, sealing that conscience within their soul's temple to His LORD by the knowledge of His High Priest's name, and in a time of great agitation. Apostasy will take place within the earth's glorious land, and that apostasy will internally devour the earth's organs to fall even further into apostasy with the spirit of the leopard beast, and this appears to be the opening of the sixth seal, which opening marks the purging of the clean and sincere worshipper from the unclean by this new State creature, as it says concerning His professed host, "I will send the sword, the famine, and the pestilence, among them, till they be consumed from off the land that I gave unto them and to their fathers."[185]

13. A message, after the earth's first disturbance is evident, should go forth by the Spirit's host, growing in strength at the time of the earth's first apostasy, and then swelling in power at her second and final wrong against the heavenly Sanctuary. After the message has spread and the entire religious world has consciously made their decision to stand by the LORD's Word, or by the established doctrine of the religious world's church, death should fall to the troublers and violators of the kingdom of the beast while the seven last plagues fall on the kingdom of error; the first three plagues before the final seven falling in right order to advance the movement of perdition. Thus, the thirteenth verse of the sixth chapter of the Revelation; portraying the fig tree casting her untimely or unripe figs; are them shaken out of error's household at this time, and by the impression of the third woe, which is a direct fulfillment of verses twenty-five to twenty-seven of the twelfth chapter of the book of Hebrews. The shaking of this people means the purification of an assembly, which is a repetition of history as found in the record of Smyrna, except this time the persecutor is the Word. That great earthquake embraces His mighty wind; which quaking is a great commotion of doctrinal conflict between the seed of error and the stewards of truth; and at this time, every impostor will know the power of spiritual death and regeneration.

---

185   Jeremiah 24:10

14. John sees six seals relaying the decline of spiritual purity and the rise of accepted religious obscurity, along with the means this church's rise and the spirit of her heart, but it seems that the Spirit would not have John without hope and comfort. John doesn't just see heaven's true reformed assembly on earth destroyed by false dwellers; the Spirit brings him to not only see those who are victorious over the apostasy, but he is also shown that the Spirit's Faith will be victorious in earth as in heaven, and that the saying will be fulfilled, "Zion shall be redeemed with judgment, and her converts with righteousness,"[186] for it is written, "In righteousness he doth judge and make war."[187] Thus, the sixth seal is truly diverse from the others. The fourth church of the fourth seal had power, but not full power. The second and third seals reveal that the same religious institution had power also, but not as that of the fourth seal, yet the future apostate church of this same institution; that institution within the sixth seal; is not seen in the same light.

15. The seals must not stray from their root. The seals contain the history of that fraudulent church on the Spirit's earth and her treasonous movements; it is for this reason that no thing in the sixth seal should exclude this trait of her character. The description of horse and rider should not be necessary for the sixth seal, for the pattern is drawn, but the vision terrible. The sun and the moon are honestly out of the way. The same horse and rider of the fourth and fifth seals reign in the sixth, for the seals are her career. Concerning her career, in one sense of the imagery put forth by the seals, that great earthquake of the sixth seal, in addition to manifesting her end, is but a revelation of the religious world taken hostage by the same ecclesiastical spirit of the previous seals, which spirit governs the red moon under her feet, even the religious foundation of Egypt; as it says, "Pharaoh king of Egypt, the great dragon";[188] which scene is a direct fulfillment of the forty-second verse of the eleventh chapter of Daniel. At this time in prophetic history, *Egypt*; the then *Jerusalem*; and the glorious land, are one and the same entity, even an apostate church and State govern-

---

186 Isaiah 1:27
187 Revelation 19:11
188 Ezekiel 29:1-3

ment joined to the spirit of that former Papal regime. Such a union means the creation of a new universal religious dominion within the *earth*, and within this denomination there will be no place for the living God.

16. The great commotion recorded in the sixth seal cannot be any thing but the complete fulfillment of the saying, "Babylon the great is fallen, is fallen."[189] Ultimate power will be given to this empire that the true end of its spirit and character may reach the conscience of every spirit willingly and unwillingly under its dominion. In the twelfth chapter of the Revelation, the stars of heaven fell to the earth only when Roman paganism supremely ruled within the Christian camp, and what is here presented for the future religious error cannot be any thing different. Like as after that ancient time there was a Protestant reformation, at this later time, the spirit of the first church of the first seal should be joined, in spirit, to the sixth church of Philadelphia to form the Word's new and living protesting assembly against error's three-fold union. It is impossible for the sixth seal to fall out of context from the first five, for what should happen after the fifth seal is a combination of every seal in one, and that combination is given full power for a time; the LORD's Spirit will afterwards vanquish it. The sixth seal cannot be any thing but the unsealing of a further apostate church. This church will be even more diverse and grotesque than the one before it, for her spirit will be even viler. This new religion and family will be the combination of a pagan apostate *Jewish* tribe joined to the spirit of Papal Catholicism.

17. The nations being angry cannot therefore happen at any time outside of the context of the ones who even introduce the subject of anger. The fulfillment must carefully follow the line from which it originates. The sixth seal appears to be that time when spiritual bitterness, wonder, madness, and drunkenness, have reached their height, and it is at this time when the apostasy of ages commences. Nothing within the seals have been literally accomplished as it is written, meaning that all things spiritually mentioned under the first five seals are literal moments of history to be fulfilled in their own way and order, and so

---

189   Revelation 18:2

under the sixth seal, a spiritual moment of history, and not some literal thing made spiritual, should take place.

18. The seals are direct, and the language of the Revelation is sure and strong, and the sixth chapter laying a foundation for events that should not be disturbed by any thing, for they are wrought by the Spirit's voice and His way of delineating. As verses fifteen through nineteen of the eleventh chapter of the Revelation is a summation of events beginning at a fixed point and ending at a fixed point, so the sixth seal is a vision unsealing a set of historical events fixed for a certain time for ending at a fixed point, which point comes to an end after the nations are "angry" or "mad," to then have the vision of the praise of the elders continue into its next phase of fulfillment. So then, the nations being angry, and the appearing of the Spirit's wrath, may simply be a shorter way of saying that from the time of the first great earthquake opening the sixth seal, to the second great earthquake of the seventh plague; which second quaking is also, in context, included within the line of the sixth seal's commotion; an air and spirit of madness governed the earth, leading up to its inevitable decline by the Lamb's wrath after the Spirit's plagues are fallen.

19. That new church born of unholy union needs no description in the sixth seal. The seals make plain the essence of what religious institution is within them, and what will come to be through that institution. What will exist should be a clear repetition of history, but this time with a more *perfect* foe against the Word than has ever been established, for she is indeed, and will be, the last to be established.

20. How can it be said that she will be the worst? It should be understood that with each of the first four seals, a beast tells John to come and see. Now, this beast is of one body bearing four heads, and for each seal, one of the heads counsels John to come and see, although we are not told which.

21. The first beast of the first seal is doubtless the voice of the head of the lion, for the lion conquers with honest power. The second beast that spoke to John is doubtless the calf, for at this time the church of Smyrna became known as a willing servant to the State of Rome, even as a calf is a servant to the owner of the field. The third beast that spoke was the head of a man, for the mind of a man, of Adam, is

a mind of compromise, and so the Christian church degraded herself even further by compromising divine principles for foreign policies to advance her secular ambitions. Therefore the fourth beast that spoke to John cannot be any thing but the voice of the head of the eagle,[190] denoting that work and institution of iniquity officially as head of the Christian religious world.

22. It should then be observed that, after the fourth seal, the beasts stop talking to John. The head of the voice that spoke to John represents each phase of the Christian church, but eventually John would not be called by any of the beasts, for what should come after the fourth seal should remain in a form similar to that entity within the fourth seal, for the pattern is set. As before John was called to see, now all things were opened to him; now the character of the marred beast of Daniel should be made plain to the beholder. As the fifth seal opens up, John plainly saw; he didn't need to be called to see; the work of the dreadful beast of Daniel, which is the same leopard beast that he later sees in the thirteenth chapter of the Revelation.

23. In the sixth seal, John is again not called to see, but again he saw and beheld. As before the heads were separate when speaking on the different events of the church, the heads should now be joined as one entity in one mind governing one body and established upon one and the same powerful policy as before. Indeed such a scene warrants, in vision, a great earthquake taking place, which quaking cannot be found outside of the previously established seals leading up to this one, for then it would make no sense to John or us. The beast that should govern the earth until the revelation of the Word in glory is a dreadful institution ruling by law and religion, bearing within it the spirit of that same beast Daniel saw and had no words for.

24. Under the fifth seal, John saw souls under the altar that had been slain for the Word and for their confidence and experience in the Word's name. The altar that John saw was doubtless that altar before the first veil of the Temple, the altar outside of the Holy Place used for burnt offerings. This seal is in fulfillment of the second verse of the eleventh chapter of the Revelation. The court without the temple is

---

190   Hosea 8:1; Hosea 7:1; Daniel 11:14; Daniel 8:23-24

the outer court, and this place was given to the Gentiles; who at this time in history are the ministers of Papal Catholicism; for 1260 years. Them that were slain by her are slain on this altar, and them that will be again killed in like manner will die also on this same altar. If the ones of the future should die as them that died of old, doubtless them that slew them there will again slay those that should come after, allowing us to understand that the earthquake of the sixth seal will repeat the history of the thirteenth and fifteenth verses of the twelfth chapter of the Revelation. The events of the sixth seal cannot happen until she who slew of old is resurrected in spirit, for that slaying did not occur until after her first universal ordination on the governmental throne of the earth and the religious world

25. Concerning the earth, in the first and second verses of the sixteenth chapter of the Revelation, the vials of wrath are to fall on the earth, that is, on them that have the mark of the beast and worship his name's image. The earth, in context, is as it is revealed in the tenth verse of the sixteenth division of the Revelation, even the seat and kingdom of this dreadful union of pagan apostate *Christianity* to the spirit of Papal Catholicism, and all joined to her fellowship. When this union should commence, then the scenes of the sixth seal should forward. The formation of this dominion must be the first great earthquake. The New *Roman* Republic of Pagan Apostate *Christianity* is that State joined to the image of the beast before it, and bearing sway in the earth by the union of law and religion; such an error occurring within the earth will terribly divide it.

26. Herodias; the spirit of the Papacy; and her daughter; a further pagan apostate *Christian* religion; will court Herod; the then Pagan Republic of *Jerusalem*; to bring her the head of *John*, who is a representative of the Word's true and living assembly keeping His LORD's name and ten laws, who also give the light of the knowledge of His glory in the face of His Son's name. Again, this final beast is and will be dreadful, for he will be given error's full mind to exercise the vision of his will on earth through her and her faith's mediator, even through that man or minister of "sin" against the LORD's new covenant will. So again, the sixth seal appears to have, within the history of its earthquake,

the record of the first to eighth verses of the twenty-ninth division of the book of Isaiah.

27. Another fair note to mention is that the first four seals are attached to the noise of thunder, for when the first is unsealed, there is a sound of thunder, leaving it that thunder should follow the opening of every seal. The tenth verse of the second chapter of the first book of Samuel, and the tenth verse of the seventh chapter of the first book of Samuel, teaches that thunder is a symbol of judgment and of overthrowing. Each of the seals must open with thunder because a spiritual character is passing away within the Christian church to give rise to a new spirit, or an old phase of the church is being overthrown and re-introduced by a new mind of religious error. Under the fifth seal, the noise of thunder exposes persecution, under the fourth, an apostate church receiving power over the world; the third brought the noise of compromise; the second the sound of murder from unjust spiritual ambition; the first of *pure* conquest. The sixth seal should also open with the noise of judgment, with the sound of a new decreed phase of character within the church of the seals for roaring a new church sentence, for it is that a new dominion will be unsealed to the world for a great quaking within it.

28. This seal cannot be unsealed on earth until the wound of the first beast of the thirteenth division of the Revelation is healed and conversing with that two-horned earth beast. Then, and only then, can it be possible for the great earthquake and terrible tempest of commotion to occur. Again, the seals denote a new phase of Christian church history that is beginning. The great earthquake of the sixth seal should conceal the movements to begin that great and renewed Babylon, and also the full career of such a tragedy.

5

The Pattern Of The Seals

1. To "seal" means to stamp with a signet or private mark for security or preservation; a seal is a stamp impressed for a mark of privacy or genuineness. The first verse of the fifth chapter of the Revelation lets us know that the seals are as locks of security on a book written within and without, and surely these seals are for the purpose of keeping secure the events of history within a church on earth. For no other reason does this book exist but to hold the history of a church most important to the ultimate reign of the LORD's name in the earth, and so the book is sealed with seven seals, denoting that this book contains the perfect history of a specific erroneous church, with each seal respecting a specific set of events to bring into harmony the vision written on its pages.

2. Now, as the seals contain church history that is to be fulfilled, they should not be expected to go beyond that word and order given them of the LORD's Spirit, and should not be held to any standard lower. The One who wrote and ordained these things in this book is not His Christ and High Priest. The One who first holds the book is not His Chief Minister, or any other messenger. The things in this book contain the structure of events that are to occur within and against one church on the earth's surface contrary to the Author, and that is it. The

seals are likened to that vision of the statue given to Babylon's king, but instead of seeing kingdoms and nations, the vision is of a church, and the various stages or ages of that church removing herself from the Faith of the LORD's Son to grow strong in apostasy, until she is swept away by the vengeance of His Spirit's Word. The vision of the seals is of a flesh-based church superpower growing strong in spiritual frailty, securing to her conversation a power not of heaven's throne to accomplish the sensual ambitions of her heart. To leave the foundation of what the seals are, to forget the purpose and order of the seals, is to do an injustice to the Spirit's Revelation, accepting misinterpretation as fact.

3. With these things being said, each seal cannot abandon its intended purpose. If the first five seals blatantly expound upon a certain period of ecclesiastical history, the sixth and the seventh should be treated with no less respect. To take the seals out of context does harm to what the Revelation is trying to convey and establish in the other portions of its vision; every division of the Revelation is ordained to fit one solid and intelligent delineation. And this is indeed the issue that must be remembered, namely, that this is a sealed vision of the inward circulation of the blood of a church as the living Father sees it should be, and as He has beforehand written it to be according to His own will and purpose. His Spirit has contained, in the first five seals, the script of His own enemy church ascending to and reigning in supposed supremacy, and seeing as how He has never written of her fall in the first five seals; even though that fall did happen at the end of the fifth; it is that the sixth seal should continue to voice that supremacy until she should be completely taken out of the way. It is for this reason that literal and natural happenings on the earth cannot fulfill one piece of the vision of the seals, for the seals are not created of the Spirit to speak on natural happenings in the earth, but are rather a detailed sketch of Christian church history, and of only the history of this one spirit. Herein we confirm this point by how it says, "To testify unto you these things in the churches."[191]

---

191 Revelation 22:16

4. The church of the fourth seal received a deadly wound after the fifth seal, but it is not mentioned of the Spirit in the book of the seals. John never confesses, when observing the events of the seals, to a deadly wound of any church, even though John wrote of this same church at a later period in vision, saying, "I saw one of his heads as it were wounded to death."[192] He never says that he saw power stripped away from the church he sees advancing in strength within the seals. The horse and rider of the fourth seal, and the spirit following them, are not depicted as ever being slowed down, and for this reason it is fair to continue to see them in existence at the sixth seal. The Spirit said to them in the fifth seal, "Thy brethren shall pass as thou."[193] These souls of the fifth seal were seen under an altar, and doubtless the altar outside of the temple for animal sacrifices, which altar was given to Papal Rome for 1260 years, from 538AD to 1798AD. This work is observed in the fourth and fifth seals, and the same spirit that fulfilled the vision of old is to fulfill it again within the sixth seal, but they cannot fulfill the vision unless some great earthquake should take place, for the spirit of the horse and rider does presently sleep. Every seal is plainly centered on the career of Satan's church, and the sixth seal should speak on the same career, although, in the sixth seal, we now find ourselves embracing the end of her spirit in the earth.

5. It may seem well to place a literal earthquake at the sixth seal, along with other natural events, but this is incorrect and unjust to do. The Spirit's Christ was indeed correct when saying, "Immediately after the tribulation of those days shall the sun be darkened, and the moon shall not give her light, and the stars shall fall from heaven, and the powers of the heavens shall be shaken: and then shall appear the sign of the Son of man in heaven: and then shall all the tribes of the earth mourn, and they shall see the Son of man coming in the clouds of heaven with power and great glory."[194] And again, "And there shall be signs in the sun, and in the moon, and in the stars; and upon the earth distress of nations, with perplexity; the sea and the waves roaring; men's

---

192   Revelation 13:3
193   Revelation 6:11
194   Matthew 24:29,30

hearts failing them for fear, and for looking after those things which are coming on the earth: for the powers of heaven shall be shaken. And then shall they see the Son of man coming in a cloud with power and great glory. And when these things begin to come to pass, then look up, and lift up your heads; for your redemption draweth nigh."[195]

6. The coming of the Son of man is the LORD's Faith and High Priest coming not to the physical earth, but to the LORD and Father of the second apartment within the Most Holy Place of the heavenly Sanctuary. This Christ, being the Son of man, denotes one thing and one thing only, that He is the Minister and High Priest of spiritually negligent individuals against His LORD's new covenant will, and that is all; this is why His doctrine is Savior to the religious world and Captain of His Father's manner of deliverance. This doctrine, at that anticipated time, will perform no literal physical descent, but we are rather told to understand that, at this great time in ecclesiastical history, "His name is called The Word of God,"[196] for this name will appear "to execute judgment upon all, and to convince."[197] The "judgment" to appear for execution is the LORD's Word, for, seeing as how the vision speaks of convincing, of persuading, of convicting, of educating, of teaching, it is that the omnipotent vengeance of the Spirit will, by the law and judgment of the Lamb, fulfill the saying, "By sound doctrine both to exhort and to convince the gainsayers."[198]

7. The history of the spirit of Papal Catholicism is concealed within the seals. The seals contain the makeup of the events of that foreign religious institution, and not once is this institution reported as being taken away in the vision of the seals; even though it later says of her, "He that killeth with the sword must be killed with the sword";[199] but it is revealed that only the Spirit will personally wipe her away. The word that our Priest spoke to His disciples fulfilled the prophecy of the Lisbon earthquake and the well known darkening of the sun and moon, leading to the literal fulfillment of the falling of the stars and the

---

195   Luke 21:25-28
196   Revelation 19:13
197   Jude 1:15
198   Titus 1:9
199   Revelation 13:10

shaking of the civil dominion of Papal Rome. Indeed after this point, the tribes of Catholicism; the Protestant denominations of her religious persuasion; did mourn for disappointment not once or twice, but then afterwards they beheld the Spirit's High Priest coming with heaven's angels to His Father so that redemption's science should enter a new phase. Thus, at this time it is fulfilled, "The Lord, whom ye seek, shall suddenly come to his temple."[200]

8. The Spirit's final product should know creation at this time of His entrance into the second Room of the heavenly Temple, and His Christ spoke perfectly for our understanding this year by the signs in the earth, which signs speak to His name coming to and entering "the temple of the tabernacle of the testimony in heaven."[201] Therefore with that being said, the prophecy of Christ to the disciples, and the vision given John of the sixth seal, are not the same vision, for the seals cannot escape the stipulation placed on them by the Spirit, even as the prophecy spoken of by His Christ cannot escape the word in which it was uttered. Remember, this revelation given to John is that vision the Spirit gave to His resurrected High Priest, for again, this is the counsel of the Father relaying events that He Himself designed, and because "God is a Spirit,"[202] we cannot take what is of and given by the Spirit to be fleshy or natural, "for a spirit hath not flesh and bones."[203] To confess the sixth seal as representing a natural earthquake with natural movements of the heavens is to cast a shadow on a vision that is as light, and that is wholly spiritual. By interpreting the vision literally, we render the vision incapable of being read. If the vision should be read in such a manner, then there is a break in the vision's fulfillment that does not follow the pattern of the other seals.

9. The seals flow and speak without any break in the time of their vision; why should the Spirit now break the spiritual pattern of church history in the sixth seal to insert natural events? And from inserting these natural events, why should the vision be left to dry out, being partially fulfilled? What benefit should be drawn from inserting natural

---

200 Malachi 3:1
201 Revelation 15:5
202 John 4:24
203 Luke 24:39

ecological, geological, and astronomical events, to then somehow reinstate the underlining spiritual theme and order of the seals? The events spoken of by the LORD's Christ to His disciples are those that fulfill the sign for taking knowledge of Him entering in to the second phase of His heavenly mediation. The signs given; in the age in which they were witnessed; were to push a sleeping Christian tribe to further study His voice that they may discern the times in which they lived. Yet they would remain a sleeping church and fail to do the counsel, "Be watchful, and strengthen the things which remain, that are ready to die,"[204] which is why the Spirit says of them, "I know thy works, that thou hast a name that thou livest, and art dead";[205] only a few would join the LORD's Priest in His new phase of mediation. The seals do not reveal this Christ coming to His Father to begin the second and final phase of His priestly office. The seals have nothing to do with natural earthly events, but the language given to us within the seals is speech revealing an ascending secularly empowered religious institution falling by the fury of the LORD's Spirit through the speech of His assembly.

10. It makes no sense for the sixth seal to leave the order ordained within the previous five seals. Each seal opens with a new phase of apostate Christian church history under a newly formed apostate power and hierarchy, and the sixth seal opens as such; the seventh opens with its own specific order relating to the right establishment of the living God's heavenly Temple before the eyes of all. These things are true and are not misconstrued, for there is no gain, but rather a plague, against one who would not carefully study to honestly expound upon heavenly things. The seals cannot escape the nature of which they are created, and there is no reason why the sixth seal should go away from what the Spirit has decreed the seals to be, namely, a spiritual revelation of a spiritually negligent church. For this cause it is written, "The word of our God shall stand for ever,"[206] and the Spirit says, "My words shall not pass away,"[207] and His host says, "Thou hast created all things, and

---

204   Revelation 3:2
205   Revelation 3:1
206   Isaiah 49:8
207   Mark 13:31

for thy pleasure they are and were created."[208] This is the living God's vision, and its interpretation should be by the voice and order of the living God. For "whatsoever God doeth, it shall be for ever: nothing can be put to it, nor any thing taken from it: and God doeth it, that men should fear before him."[209]

11. That of the sixth seal fulfills the saying, "The sun shall be turned into darkness, and the moon into blood, before the great and the terrible day of the LORD come,"[210] for it says, "His countenance was as the sun shineth in his strength."[211] That which the sixth seal presents before the student is a great commotion by the same institution of the fourth seal to fulfill the saying, "The stars of heaven fell unto the earth,"[212] even as of old it was said of her, "It cast down some of the host and of the stars to the ground, and stamped upon them,"[213] which is why it says, "Reward her even as she rewarded you, and double unto her double according to her works."[214] If it is true that them that should be the Word's new and right voice should suffer as their brethren of old; and it is; since the fifth seal speaks of no break in power from the fourth seal, then the same spirit of those two seals; which force is observed throughout the seals; will be reinstated at the beginning of the sixth seal to finish the work of purifying the Spirit's household of the erroneous, only to usher in a reason for the LORD's complete reign by His Son's then wrathful voice.

---

208 Revelation 4:11
209 Ecclesiastes 3:14
210 Joel 2:31
211 Revelation 1:16
212 Revelation 6:13
213 Daniel 8:10
214 Revelation 18:6

6

The Tremors Of The Great Earthquake

1. It is completely evident that the sixth seal should follow after and open with ecclesiastical history, even as the five previous seals do. The nature of what should occur at this point in history draws John's attention to an earthquake, for he sees a great earthquake occur when the sixth seal is unsealed. An earthquake is a commotion, and this commotion cannot be any thing less than what is written and says, "The noise of the bruit is come, and a great commotion out of the north country, to make the cities of Judah desolate,"[215] and, "He shall stretch forth his hand also upon the countries: and the land of Egypt shall not escape."[216] Now, as it says, "He shall enter also into the glorious land,"[217] it is not that, at this time, a physical entrance or appearance should take place, for it says, "They should make an image to the beast."[218] The king of the north does not physically enter into the world's then *Jerusalem* at first, but he rather enters by way of the image of the creature before it,

---

215 Jeremiah 10:22
216 Daniel 11:42
217 Daniel 11:41
218 Revelation 13:14

which image is a national government joined together by law and religion. After that image is reproduced and this *Jerusalem* should become that Pagan Apostate Republic, then should the great commotion of the sixth seal occur, even that great and final marriage of *the Word's earth* to the spirit of the leopard beast.

2. Why should such an alliance not be an earthquake of commotion? Here we have, in the fourth and fifth seal, the souls of the reformation, and the souls of the fathers of the reformation, crying out for justice, only to observe their brethren falling to their same fate, and most likely over the same plague by the same beast and spirit with the same gross ambition of old.

3. Says Scripture, "Their brethren, that should be killed as they were,"[219] for, "death" does not begin physically, even as Eve tasted the fruit of the cursed tree inwardly before she did any physical thing with it. "Death" for that church within the seals began at the saying, "Thou hast left thy first love,"[220] and this death found itself inflicted upon her heart and mind, which death would lead to "that woman Jez'ebel, which calleth herself a prophetess, to teach and to seduce...to commit fornication, and to eat things sacrificed unto idols."[221] Should any disagree with her persuasion, it was ordained for her "to kill with sword, and with hunger, and with death, and with the beasts of the earth."[222] The spirit of this woman will again rise in power to cause a great commotion in the earth, for she joins into a relationship with another woman's husbands to take her and him and their companions captive, as it says, "All nations have drunk of the wine of the wrath of her fornication."[223]

4. The seals contain the history of the labors of the Christian church, and the opening of the sixth seal should handle the origins of its revitalized apostate spirit. One portion of the great earthquake John beholds points to a terrible happening among the religious denominations of modern Jerusalem by the spirit of first five seals. There can be no other word to describe this time of commotion except by that said

---

219 Revelation 6:11
220 Revelation 2:4
221 Revelation 2:20
222 Revelation 6:8
223 Revelation 18:3

of old: "And it came to pass, when king Hezeki'ah heard it, that he rent his clothes, and covered himself with sackcloth, and went into the house of the LORD. And he sent Eli'akim, which was over the household, and Sheb'na the scribe, and the elders of the priests, covered with sackcloth, to Isaiah the prophet the son of Amoz. And they said unto him, Thus saith Hezekiah, This day is a day of trouble, and of rebuke, and blasphemy: for the children are come to the birth, and there is not strength to bring forth."[224] But it is written, "Thus saith the LORD, Be not afraid of the words which thou hast heard, with which the servants of the king of Assyria have blasphemed me. Behold, I will send a blast upon him, and he shall hear a rumour, and shall return to his own land; and I will cause him to fall by the sword in his own land."[225] "I will defend this city, to save it, for mine own sake, and for my servant David's sake."[226] "Out of Jerusalem shall go forth a remnant, and they that escape out of mount Zion: the zeal of the LORD of hosts shall do this."[227]

5. We have before us the event that will push the sixth seal into motion. That which should lead up to a change in the sun and the moon should occur at a time when the religious world is self-complacent, and when the religion and laws of the doctrine of the LORD's Christ are openly violated, for this is how it happened of old within the Christian church, which then led to a controversy over the LORD's name within His fourth commandment, which, for them that should be slain as their former brethren, will be that storm dividing the earth. There is none other time that the laws of the Faith of heaven's High Priest are openly violated other than when the image of the leopard beast is established, for the first law of His mediation; sanctification by an experimental faith on His voice; and the second law of His Faith; free indiscriminate godly benevolence due to faith's exercise; will cause further apostasy in already erroneous Christian denominations, and again the times will

---

224 2 Kings 19:1-3
225 2 Kings 19:6,7
226 2 Kings 19:34
227 2 Kings 19:31

warrant the counsel, "Thou hast left thy first love,"[228] and, "Remember therefore from whence thou art fallen."[229]

6. Because these two precepts of heaven's Faith were violated by Christian elders, the apostle was compelled write, "Whosoever transgresseth, and abideth not in the doctrine of Christ, hath not God."[230] Because the church left the understanding secured to her by them that knew the LORD's Word, and that did mature in conversation by His Son's name, deviation from heaven's will was given free reign to continue. If the sun became black, and if John, at the beginning of the Revelation, noticed, of the Spirit's Priest, that "his countenance was as the sun shineth in his strength,"[231] and if the Spirit's doctrine is "the light of the glorious gospel of Christ,"[232] then at this time of the sun dressed in sackcloth; in one train of thought; the history will be repeated, "My two witnesses...shall prophesy a thousand two hundred and threescore days, clothed in sackcloth."[233] That sun of error is, in reality, wearing sackcloth because she is made to eventually embrace sorrow and lamentation through the Spirit's voice, but error's earthquake will first cause heaven's will and name to mourn until "they shall have finished their testimony."[234]

7. We cannot forget that these two witnesses mentioned by the Spirit represent the oppressed will and counsel of the Spirit by Papal Rome from 538AD to 1798AD. Such a period of history kept the Spirit's will and knowledge in gross obscurity, and the sixth seal presents to us the same history repeated. There is enough proof to show that the great earthquake of the sixth seal cannot take place but after the time of such an official apostasy as was anciently accomplished. An apostate creed founded upon transgressing the Spirit's will and knowledge forsook the power and wisdom of His ministry to take hold of the Roman State for executing her ambition. Without the Spirit's wisdom blessing her

---

228 Revelation 2:4
229 Revelation 2:5
230 2 John 1:9
231 Revelation 1:16
232 2 Corinthians 4:4
233 Revelation 11:3
234 Revelation 11:7

congregation and purifying her ministers, she would have the State act as a conscience for the people to bring them to appreciate her religious philosophy. The Christian church would teach, "Righteousness come by the law,"[235] openly violating the fact of righteousness by a knowledgeable faith, and because of her spirit, murder flourished within her elders and rested in her house, which is why the apostle wrote to her men, "This commandment have we from him, That he who loveth God love his brother also."[236] This he wrote because it was him who was shown in vision that a church feigning loyalty to his LORD and High Priest of the Bible should "take peace from the earth, and that they should kill one another."[237]

8. The sun becoming as sackcloth is a representation of the history of the Protestant reformation repeated. "When the Assyrian shall come into our land: and when he shall tread in our palaces...the remnant of Jacob shall be in the midst of many people as a dew from the LORD... the remnant of Jacob shall be among the Gentiles in the midst of many people as a lion,"[238] it is written. The time of purifying the Gentiles cannot come before the time of sanctifying the Spirit's house, for it is that the Spirit's house must first know baptism, and this purification taking place during and after that greatly anticipated earthquake of an established union between law and religion in spiritual *Jerusalem*, and lasting until the final resurrection of the spirit of the seals, which spirit suffered a terrible wound to its legislative head. It is this earthquake of the sixth seal that gives rise to "a day of trouble, and of rebuke, and blasphemy"[239] against the living God's throne. As it was of old, that the king of Assyria spoke against the LORD's name and voice, so again it will happen, and again the LORD will protect His sealed inheritance by a mighty revelation "upon the men which had the mark of the beast, and upon them which worshipped his image."[240]

---

235   Galatians 2:21
236   1 John 4:21
237   Revelation 6:4
238   Micah 5:5-8
239   2 Kings 19:3
240   Revelation 16:2

9. As the illustrations of the Revelation are not literal, but are as a figure of the description of the times in which that vision should come to pass in, as the sun covered in sackcloth is a symbolic representation, so is the moon that became as blood. The first five seals are an allegorical representation of a literal institution that should foully dominate the pure religion of the LORD's Sanctuary on earth, and the institution of the sixth seal should not be expected to stray from that course.

10. Now, the moon, in one application; because the sixth seal, in addition to referencing the fall of religious error, also depicts the criminal activity of a foreign institution; is as it says, "It shall be established for ever as the moon, and as a faithful witness in heaven."[241] The moon is a testimony of the light of the sun. If the moon became as blood, if the testimony of the sun became as blood; remembering that the sixth seal conveys both the triumph and end of error; then it is known, "The blood of Jesus Christ his Son cleanseth us,"[242] and, "Have washed their robes, and made them white in the blood of the Lamb,"[243] for it is written, "Slain for the word of God, and for the testimony which they held."[244] It should follow that as the doctrine of Christ and the commandments of His LORD are preached by heaven's then messengers, *death* and *oppression* by the institution of the previous five seals will follow them; both literal and spiritual; for they go against the then institution of the times. The sun becoming as sackcloth; in one train of thought, and not the whole; is the light of heaven's tidings prophesying in spiritually troublous times, and if its faithful witness became as blood, then the testimony of those who stand for truth at this time will not be without physical and spiritual terror.

11. Looking further at what such an earthquake should be, we see how it is written, "As it began to dawn toward the first day of the week, came Mary Magdale'ne and the other Mary to see the sepulchre. And, behold, there was a great earthquake: for the angel of the Lord descended from heaven."[245]

---

241 Psalms 89:37
242 1 John 1:7
243 Revelation 7:14
244 Revelation 6:9
245 Matthew 28:2

12. Such events cannot find place outside of where it says, "I saw another angel come down from heaven, having great power; and the earth was lightened with his glory. And he cried mightily with a strong voice, saying, Babylon the great is fallen, is fallen."[246] Herein we here have a replica to the resurrection of the Spirit's Christ, even as it is said, "The beast that was, and is not, even he is the eighth, and is of the seven, and goeth into perdition."[247]

13. That birth of the eighth and final religious government will be a great commotion in the earth, and that commotion must absolutely follow the same pattern as that witnessed in Matthew. The angel descended and a great earthquake took place on the first day of the week; Sunday; at the resurrection of the Spirit's wisdom, and it should follow that at the resurrection of the false institution of *Christ*, the perdition of that church should indeed be marked by an earthquake revolving around the first day of the week, even as it occurred through Constantine by a Sunday law 321AD. Indeed at this later year, the Spirit's messages will be fully empowered by His wisdom within them that have withstood the test of the beast's image. Herein the Gentiles are permitted to receive the Word's doctrine with the light of the knowledge of the LORD's glory through heaven's new protesting reformers, yet the times will be draped in sackcloth with much pain and sorrow in and by understanding.

14. As during the 1260 years of Papal dominion the light of the sun was only as bright as the rays of Catholic darkness, so again the eighth kingdom; the Pagan *Papal* Republic of spiritual *Egypt* and *Jerusalem*; will look to cast down the stars of heaven to the earth. Again, the pattern of the seals is evident, and the consistency of a new dominion erected per seal cannot be avoided or overlooked. The images of the vision are not literal, nor should they ever fall to a literal platform, for then the other seals must be literally observed, and such an interpretation will destroy the message to be relayed. John sees a great earthquake and then is brought to notice that the sun became black and the moon became as blood, while the stars of heaven fall unto the earth. This

---

246 Revelation 18:1,2
247 Revelation 17:11

vision does pronounce the fall of this erroneous spirit and her religious institution, but, by the illustration used, we may also discern that, and without forcing or strangling Scripture, a year of trouble awaits them who would stand by the LORD's ten laws through the doctrine of His Spirit. What will break out on the *earth* will be the spirit of a gruesome religious State, and by this State will distress and anxiety; both literally and spiritually; devour the inhabitants of the then religious world.

15. The first five seals do not touch on light events. They do not deal with any thing but persecution in all of its forms. It is absurd to believe the sixth seal should stray from this character; every seal depicts the heinous acts of a Christian institution drawn from a spirit of error.

7

The Coming Of The Son Of Man

1. To the church of Sar'dis, the counsel given them of the Spirit was, "If therefore thou shalt not watch, I will come on thee as a thief, and thou shalt not know what hour I will come upon thee...He that overcometh, the same shall be clothed in white raiment; and I will not blot out his name out of the book of life, but I will confess his name before my Father, and before his angels."[248]

2. We here have before us the history of the events of the church from 1798AD to 1833AD. The members of the Protestant church had come out from Papal captivity and were to handle certain messages that were to lead up to the hour of the appearing of the LORD's Son. Although many remained hot for the Spirit's doctrine; as it says of this time, "Many shall run to and fro, and knowledge shall be increased";[249] seeing into the future, the Spirit would remind this people, "Be watchful, and strengthen the things which remain, that are ready to die."[250] Such a message is as of a similar tone to that which the LORD's Christ uttered when on earth: "Watch ye therefore: for ye know not

---

248 Revelation 3:3,5
249 Daniel 12:4
250 Revelation 3:2

when the master of the house cometh,"[251] and, "Watch therefore, for ye know neither the day nor the hour wherein the Son of man cometh."[252] To this church was given a message warning of the inevitable coming of the Son of man, yet because they failed to fully separate themselves from the lore of their mother, they failed to strengthen that understanding which would have perfectly secured their faith.

3. In His message to the church of Sar'dis, the Spirit's Christ indeed makes the fact of His appearing clear. At the end of the Spirit's counsel and observation of this church, the LORD's Spirit says of them that should remain faithful, "I will confess his name before my Father, and before his angels."[253] At no other time should Christ Himself confess the names of any of His faithful than that which should be during an investigation. Scripture cannot be referencing that time when John "saw thrones, and they sat upon them, and judgment was given unto them,"[254] as it says, "To execute upon them the judgment written: this honour have all his saints."[255] Our High Priest is not going to be confessing names to His Father at this time, for there will be no confession at all, as the spiritually redeemed of His congregation will share His throne and make sure the judgments and sentences already written by the Father are good for execution, for they are the ones who will execute those things written against them that refused mercy's course for the route of ungodliness. It is therefore well to know that the confession of names before the Father happened when "one like the Son of man came with the clouds of heaven, and came to the Ancient of days."[256]

4. At this time, the saying is fulfilled, "The hour of his judgment is come,"[257] and to John is given the instruction, "Measure the temple of God, and the altar, and them that worship therein";[258] the illustration

---

251 Mark 13:34
252 Matthew 25:13
253 Revelation 3:5
254 Revelation 20:4
255 Psalms 149:9
256 Daniel 7:13
257 Revelation 14:7
258 Revelation 11:1

of this age is of an investigative judgment, therefore it is fulfilled, "And the Ancient of days did sit; thousand thousands ministered unto him, and ten thousand times ten thousand stood before him: the judgment was set, and the books were opened."[259] Herein are the "angels" before the Father that the Spirit spoke of in vision to John, and herein is the seat of confession before the LORD our Father. The Son of the Word is the High Priest of the Spirit for them that err against His LORD and Father's name. This Christ is the living God's High Priest over His heavenly Temple, and we know that this is true from the figures established of old, which figures uttered the reality that was to exist after His resurrection, seeing as how they did "serve unto the example and shadow of heavenly things."[260]

5. When John observed this Christ after His ascension, he saw "one like unto the Son of man, clothed with a garment down to the foot, and girt about the paps with a golden girdle."[261] Where may one see this type of clothing in Scripture, and for whom is it ordained? It is written, "Thou shalt make holy garments for Aaron thy brother for glory and for beauty...that he may minister unto me in the priest's office...These are the garments which they shall make; a breastplate, and an e'phod, and a robe, and a broidered coat, a mitre, and a girdle...And the curious girdle of the e'phod, which is upon it, shall be of the same, according to the work thereof; even of gold."[262]

6. Today, the body of the knowledge of the Spirit's Christ wears the same clothes that Aaron anciently wore, for "Christ glorified not himself to be made an high priest; but he that said unto him, Thou art my Son, to day have I begotten thee."[263] Christ being the Son of God is the doctrine of His Christ being the High Priest and Minister over the Spirit's House in "the city of the living God, the heavenly Jerusalem."[264] John didn't simply see the outfit of this Man, he saw His location to bear witness to the fact that this Faith of the heavenly Sanctuary is

---

259   Daniel 7:9
260   Hebrews 8:5
261   Revelation 1:13
262   Exodus 28:1-8
263   Hebrews 5:5
264   Hebrews 12:22

indeed not dead, but is in fact a living Minister over a living church for every one willing to learn of and do the will of His mediation.

7. John writes, "I turned to see the voice that spake with me. And being turned, I saw seven golden candlesticks; and in the midst of the seven candlesticks one like unto the Son of man."[265] Where was our Priest at the time John received this Revelation? It says, "There was a tabernacle made; the first, wherein was the candlestick, and the table, and the shewbread; which is called the sanctuary,"[266] for the Spirit had said, "The vail shall divide unto you between the holy place and the most holy,"[267] and, "Set the table without the vail, and the candlestick over against the table."[268]

8. Now, the LORD God's Temple has two veils, therefore Paul confessed that Christ "entereth into that within the veil."[269] There is a veil to enter the Temple and there is a veil within the Temple. Within the first veil, which veil can be looked at as a door to an apartment, is the Holy place, and that apartment which comes after the first apartment, that is the second apartment of the temple, and it is called the Most Holy place, or "the second veil, the tabernacle which is called the Holiest of all."[270] From the time God's Christ was resurrected and took His place next to His Father, until the words should become relevant, "I will come on thee as a thief,"[271] Christ ministered from within the Holy place of the heavenly Sanctuary. This appearing of "Christ" indeed came upon Protestants as a thief, for while they believed a physical person was coming to the earth to execute vengeance on them that they understood to be contrary to *Him*, the saying was fulfilled, "The Lord, whom ye seek, shall suddenly come to his temple."[272]

9. This coming of "Christ" is not a man coming to the earth, but is rather an appearance after the saying, "The Son of man came with

---

265   Revelation 1:12,13
266   Hebrews 9:2
267   Exodus 26:33
268   Exodus 26:35
269   Hebrews 6:19
270   Hebrews 9:3
271   Revelation 3:3
272   Malachi 3:1

the clouds of heaven, and came to the Ancient of days."[273] The Word's Christ today currently bears "a more excellent name"[274] for us given Him of His LORD, for it says, "Him hath God exalted with his right hand to be a Prince and a Saviour, for to give repentance to Israel, and forgiveness of sins,"[275] and this name or praise or eminence fulfilling the promise, "We have an advocate with the Father"[276] "who is consecrated for evermore,"[277] "who is even at the right hand of God, who also maketh intercession for us."[278] When His form will come to receive His faithful who have passed the investigative judgment that is currently underway, His name will appear in a glory that is born to mercilessly penetrate the inward parts of man. When we hear of His appearance before His LORD, and for the purpose of confessing names, we may understand that His office as merciful and faithful High Priest in things concerning the Spirit's Word is still open to forward His Father's will.

10. When John received the Revelation, it was given in a day when he confessed, "It is the last time."[279] Now, John believed that at the end of these times, heaven should find itself moved to execute a judgment, for he wrote, "Abide in him; that, when he shall appear, we may have confidence, and not be ashamed before him at his coming,"[280] and, "That we may have boldness in the day of judgment."[281] John knew a judgment was set to occur at the end of the times, that is, at the fulfillment of the years that said, "Blessed is he that waiteth, and cometh to the thousand three hundred and five and thirty days."[282] The times were to last until the revelation of the Spirit's Man should come as a thief not to the earth, but to His Father within the second apartment of the Spirit's Temple, for the Spirit would then declare, "There should be

---

273 Daniel 7:13
274 Hebrews 1:4
275 Acts 5:31
276 1 John 2:1
277 Hebrews 7:28
278 Romans 8:34
279 1 John 2:18
280 1 John 2:28
281 1 John 4:17
282 Daniel 12:12

time no longer."[283] The period of time allotted to prophetic events to run its course with men would finish when our High Priest would begin the second and final phase of His heavenly ministry.

11. Seeing as how the disciples who were alive at the time of Christ's expected coming misunderstood the instruction relating what exactly the LORD's Temple was, and to the complete fact of His Son's mediation, it is fair to believe that the faithful of old also had no idea of what the next phase of Christ's heavenly ministration should be, for, to them also, it must mean the end of all temporal things on earth. This is why it says, "Who may abide the day of his coming?"[284] Understanding what pain and disappointment many would experience when He should not manifest physically, the Spirit counseled, "Be watchful, and strengthen the things which remain, that are ready to die."[285] The things that were ready to die made up the property or possessions, the goods and the substance, that had been stripped from them by the church of Rome. From searching the scriptures with an empty, humble, and penitent spirit, and with an hungry soul, they would not only receive light to cast away the darkness of Catholic lore, but they would receive knowledge on the precepts of the Word's manner of justification, to the end they would know the shadow of that sanctification, as it is revealed by the ancient priesthood of Aaron, to discern that which currently stood in heaven.

12. But the disciples of Sar'dis did not strengthen their understanding of the Spirit's counsel. To them came the report, "I know thy works, that thou hast a name that thou livest, and art dead."[286] These were called Protestants because their fathers had not just protested the doctrines of the church of Rome, but they had shed their blood for the Spirit's truth in their age. But it is written for our learning, "She that liveth in pleasure is dead while she liveth,"[287] for the Protestant church carried their conversation in sensual spiritual pleasure, therefore she was spiritually dead with her that fulfilled the character, "Thou

---

283 Revelation 10:6
284 Malachi 3:2
285 Revelation 3:2
286 Revelation 3:1
287 1 Timothy 5:6

that art given to pleasures";[288] this rebuke is against that "daughter of Babylon."[289] Because Protestants did not turn away from their inherited pillars of Catholicism, it was that they were indeed a sleeping tribe needing mental and spiritual blessing, therefore the Spirit said, "Thou hast a few names even in Sar'dis which have not defiled their garments; and they shall walk with me in white."[290] If this church had searched the scriptures with more of a fervent innocence that marked their powerful movement, it would not have been fulfilled, "Then shall all the tribes of the earth mourn."[291]

13. Because they failed to understand the subject of the Sanctuary, the many Christian denominations that came together as one band wept for disappointment when the Word's Christ did not literally appear in the clouds of the sky, and then soon fainted to fall back into the obscure religion from whence they came. The nominal Christian institution was at this time shaken out of fellowship with heaven's Son and Spirit, for when His Christ did "send his angels with a great sound of a trumpet,"[292] only His faithful stood still when they saw "the Son of man coming in the clouds of heaven,"[293] therefore these were told, "Thou hast kept the word of my patience,"[294] and those that apostatized, "Them of the synagogue of Satan, which say they are Jews, and are not."[295]

14. That message told to the disciples; concerning the signs of the end; is a twofold prophecy in one, for the Word's Christ mingled events together, events that would leave every spirit wailing and mourning because of His Faith's name. He told us, "Immediately after the tribulation of those days shall the sun be darkened, and the moon shall not give her light, and the stars shall fall from heaven, and the powers of the heavens shall be shaken: and then shall appear the sign of the

---

288 Isaiah 47:8
289 Isaiah 47:1
290 Revelation 3:4
291 Matthew 24:30
292 Matthew 24:31
293 Matthew 24:30
294 Revelation 3:10
295 Revelation 3:9

Son of man in heaven: and then shall all the tribes of the earth mourn, and they shall see the Son of man coming in the clouds of heaven with power and great glory. And he shall send his angels with a great sound of a trumpet."[296] There is plainly one vision here put forth by Christ, yet the vision is split in two and, at the same time, representing a whole.

15. The tribulation that Christ spoke of is that "given unto the Gentiles: and the holy city shall they tread under foot forty and two months."[297] Such a tribulation fulfills the saying, "The woman fled into the wilderness...a thousand two hundred and threescore days,"[298] for such times were "to continue forty and two months."[299] The time that the Spirit puts forth is the Dark Ages, and from 538AD to 1798AD, the Catholic Church was to oppress heaven's Faith until she would be overthrown, and she would be overthrown, as it says, "A great earthquake, and the tenth part of the city fell,"[300] which is why the Spirit said, "I gave her space to repent of her fornication; and she repented not."[301] The space given the Christian church for repentance was the same 1260 years allotted for her reign.

16. After the tribulation should occur, there should be signs in the heavens to awaken His people of His coming, that is, to inform them of the revelation of His words, as it says, "If a man love me, he will keep my words."[302] The events surrounding the sun, moon, and stars, did take place as spoken, for writers have left us with what occurred during the year of 1780AD for our observation. After these things should conclude, then should many on earth look for the Word's appearance, yet He should appear by angels with the sound of a great trumpet; or with the sound of a message by voices pronouncing heaven's Faith; and indeed the angels of the fourteenth division of the Revelation entered into church history. No man came to the earth from the sky, but the Spirit's Christ rather came to His Father to receive the hand of His

---

296 Matthew 24:29-31
297 Revelation 11:2
298 Revelation 12:6
299 Revelation 13:5
300 Revelation 11:13
301 Revelation 2:21
302 John 14:23

bride, even that City of the Spirit called New Jerusalem, for one said to John, "I will shew thee the bride,"[303] and John said, "He carried me away...and shewed me that great city, the holy Jerusalem."[304] This is why, when He should enter the second apartment, He tells us, "Ye yourselves like unto men that wait for their lord, when he will return from the wedding."[305]

17. The Son of man coming to the Father in the clouds, or with angels, is not the same as "when he cometh in the glory of his Father with the holy angels"[306] "in flaming fire taking vengeance on them that know not God, and that obey not the gospel."[307] The first appearance is related to Him leaving the first apartment to receive and accept what He should in the second, and to do the work that is there prescribed in the second room, namely, "of reconciling the holy place, and the tabernacle of the congregation, and the altar."[308] The appearance of God's Man; as recorded in the nineteenth chapter of the Revelation; will indeed be the revelation of His name in terribly omnipotent glory, and when this appearing should occur, a great reformatory gathering will commence to bring every eye of faith to the name of His Father.

18. All of these things are herein mentioned to prove how absurd it is to link the vision of the seals, and the intelligently flowing material contained within them, to that which does not even demand a general likeness or thought of being synonymous. It is wrong to place the interpretation of the vision of the seals outside of the frame from which they are pictured and ordained. Indeed there is a great earthquake of the French Revolution portrayed to us within the eleventh division of the Revelation, and after this event, the sun and the moon literally became dark, and the stars did fall to the earth, but what is the next scene of the sixth seal? Is it the revelation of God's Man in the second apartment of the heavenly Sanctuary, or is it the appearing of the Lamb to fulfill His LORD's vengeance? It is not good to pull and place spiritual

---

303   Revelation 21:9
304   Revelation 21:10
305   Luke 12:36
306   Mark 8:38
307   2 Thessalonians 1:8
308   Leviticus 16:20

things without bringing the thought to the Author, for although the words may appear to fit an application, the LORD's Spirit is deep, and His operation and voice is orderly and consistent, and the consistency of His counsel in the seals cannot break that consistency because He spoke the events. For this cause it is well to hear how it is written, "Whatsoever God doeth, it shall be for ever: nothing can be put to it, nor any thing taken from it."[309]

19. The accounts of the discourse that Christ had with His disciples would have to be forced in to an application in order to fit an interpretation for the sixth seal. The Spirit's visions are a vision within a vision that is a vision of a reality, and based on the evidence of the flow and structure of the first five seals, it is impossible that the sixth seal should deviate from a spiritual and figurative application, to then find place on a literal ground.

20. Should the stars of the sixth seal literally fall to the earth, as it says that they should? If we believe they should, then when did a pale horse ever travel the earth? The sun and the moon became dark; so then a red horse and a black horse also happened to literally appear among us? Somehow, the sixth seal is made to be literally spiritual, yet the first five seals are accepted as spiritually literal: where is consistency? Why would the living God deviate from the order with which He Himself establishes? Each seal contains the ecclesiastical history of the same spirit within the same church, and the sixth seal is no different, except here we see the second rise and work and fall of this church and her spirit. The images of the seals describe an established religious economy, and the great earthquake of the sixth seal should be the formation of that final orthodox economy and religious kingdom on earth, along with her time in power, until her demise by the unmerciful Word of the LORD's Spirit.

---

[309] Ecclesiastes 3:14

8

A Quaking To Appear

1. Concerning the unveiling of the sixth seal, John writes, "I beheld when he had opened the sixth seal, and, lo, there was a great earthquake."[310] The use of the word, "lo," denotes an element of surprise from the beholder. For some reason, John was taken back by what he saw, and said, when observing what should shake the earth, "I wondered with great admiration."[311] An earthquake is a violent storm, a commotion, a tempest, and at the opening of the sixth seal, there occurs, there comes to pass, there transpires, a very great earthquake.

2. Scripture records, "The Lord hath a mighty and strong one, which as a tempest of hail and a destroying storm, as a flood of mighty waters overflowing, shall cast down to the earth."[312] Such a mighty one undoubtedly fulfills the saying, "The stars of heaven fell unto the earth"[313] as "of a mighty wind,"[314] for it says, "His tail drew the third part of the stats of heaven, and did cast them to the earth."[315] Again it says,

---

310 Revelation 6:12
311 Revelation 17:6
312 Isaiah 28:2
313 Revelation 6:13
314 Revelation 6:13
315 Revelation 12:4

"Woe to A'riel, the city where David dwelt!"[316] "Thou shalt be visited of the LORD of hosts with thunder, and with earthquake, and great noise, with storm and tempest, and the flame of devouring fire,"[317] for He promises "burning instead of beauty"[318] to this apostate assembly. Against the house of *God* will come a great storm and tempest, and this marks the living God's visitation upon *His* professed household, as He says, "I will bring evil upon them, even the year of their visitation, saith the LORD."[319] "A whirlwind of the LORD is gone forth in fury, even a grievous whirlwind,"[320] says Scripture, and of this "whirlwind" it says, "His chariots shall be as a whirlwind."[321] Herein "the lion is come up from his thicket, and the destroyer of the Gentiles is on his way"[322] "to make thy land desolate."[323]

3. Again, concerning this season of visitation against them "which are called by the name of Israel, and are come forth out of the water of Judah, which swear by the name of the LORD, and make mention of the God of Israel, but not in truth, nor in righteousness,"[324] the Spirit says, "Therefore shall they fall among them that fall: in the time of their visitation they shall be cast down."[325] Now, hear the following language of this scene, for it says, "There shall be no grapes on the vine, nor figs on the fig tree, and the leaf shall fade,"[326] sending one to observe the saying, "Gleaning grapes shall be left in it, as the shaking of an olive tree, two or three berries in the top of the uppermost bough, four or five in the outmost fruitful branches thereof,"[327] for it says, "As a fig tree casteth her untimely figs, when she is shaken of a mighty wind."[328] The fig tree is a "she," a church that is shaken, for it says, "The fortress

---

316 Isaiah 29:1
317 Isaiah 29:6
318 Isaiah 3:24
319 Jeremiah 23:12
320 Jeremiah 23:19
321 Jeremiah 4:13
322 Jeremiah 4:7
323 Jeremiah 4:7
324 Isaiah 48:1
325 Jeremiah 8:12
326 Jeremiah 8:13
327 Isaiah 17:6
328 Revelation 6:13

also shall cease from E'phraim."³²⁹ "I will distress A'riel, and there shall be heaviness and sorrow,"³³⁰ says the Spirit. "I will camp against thee round about, and will lay seize against thee with a mount";³³¹ as it says, "The king of the north shall come, and cast up a mount";³³² wherefore the LORD's Man said, "When ye see Jerusalem compasses with armies, then know that the desolation thereof is nigh,"³³³ for He spoke of the destruction of Jerusalem in 70AD by the armies of Rome.

4. Them that exist by the structure, rule, or organization of the house of *God* on *earth*, they and the house are to be destroyed. While many confess, "See what manner of stones and what buildings are here!"³³⁴ the Spirit's stewards will give the counsel, "Behold what manner of the love the Father hath bestowed upon us,"³³⁵ and, "We have an altar, whereof they have no right to eat which serve the tabernacle."³³⁶ The servants of the tabernacle will perish with the tabernacle, but the servants of heaven's Faith will fulfill the saying, "They overcame him by the blood of the Lamb, and by the word of their testimony."³³⁷ The sixth seal brings to view the situation of them that follow in the footsteps of their brethren from the fifth seal, for it says, "Their brethren, that should be killed as they were."³³⁸

5. This tempest that is to hit the Spirit's house and people, and is to send such terrible vibrations throughout the earth of His doctrine, is doubtless "a defenced city,"³³⁹ "a palace of strangers"³⁴⁰ containing "the strong people,"³⁴¹ "the city of the terrible nations,"³⁴² "the storm"³⁴³

---

329   Isaiah 17:3
330   Isaiah 29:2
331   Isaiah 29:3
332   Daniel 12:15
333   Luke 21:20
334   Mark 13:1
335   1 John 3:1
336   Hebrews 13:10
337   Revelation 12:11
338   Revelation 6:11
339   Isaiah 25:2
340   Isaiah 25:2
341   Isaiah 25:3
342   Isaiah 25:3
343   Isaiah 25:4

and "blast of the terrible ones."[344] As for these strangers, we see, "Strangers of Rome,"[345] for the "stranger" is one not naturally born to the LORD's Faith, but baptized or converted into that faith, as it says, "The strangers that sojourn in Israel,"[346] and, "The strangers which sojourn among you."[347] Such a palace of strangers oppressing heaven's faithful possess a counterfeit religion of heaven's assembly, fulfilling the saying, "Strangers are risen up against me, and oppressors seek after my soul,"[348] for it says, "The throne of iniquity"[349] "frameth mischief by a law,"[350] for "they gather themselves together against the soul of the righteous."[351] There can be no other city of strangers that accomplish this work but those ministers that fulfill the saying, "Through covetousness shall they with feigned words make merchandise of you."[352] Contained within that merchandise is the "souls of men,"[353] for "they speak great swelling words of vanity, they allure through the lusts of the flesh,"[354] "to draw away disciples after them."[355] She who fulfills this work says, "I sit a queen, and am no widow, and shall see no sorrow";[356] her sentiments are, "I am, and none else beside me; I shall not sit as a widow, neither shall I know loss of children."[357]

6. This power of destruction is called, "That great city,"[358] and it was told John, "The woman which thou sawest is that great city";[359] even that woman "upon a scarlet coloured beast";[360] "which reigneth

---

344 Isaiah 25:4
345 Acts 2:10
346 Leviticus 20:2
347 Leviticus 17:8
348 Psalms 54:3
349 Psalm 94:20
350 Psalm 94:20
351 Psalm 94:21
352 2 Peter 2:3
353 Revelation 18:13
354 2Peter 2:18
355 Acts 20:30
356 Revelation 18:7
357 Isaiah 47:7,8
358 Revelation 18:16
359 Revelation 17:18
360 Revelation 17:3

over the kings of the earth."³⁶¹ Such a power is, of old, associated with the prince of Ty'rus, for it says, "Thine heart is lifted up, and thou hast said, I am God, I sit in the seat of God."³⁶² Such a character fulfills the vision: "The son of perdition; who opposeth and exalteth himself above all that is called God, or that is worshipped; so that he as God sitteth in the temple of God, shewing himself that he is God."³⁶³

7. Again, Scripture says of Pharaoh king of Egypt, "Thou hast lifted up thyself in height, and he hath shot up his top among the thick boughs, and his heart is lifted up in his height."³⁶⁴ Egypt is here exhibiting the same character as the prince of Ty'rus, except that for Egypt, "under his shadow dwelt all great nations."³⁶⁵ It appears that Ty'rus, in spirit, is Egypt, and that Egypt will have a chief doctrinal prince sitting in power over the religious world; the entire religious world appears to be the seat of *God*. The two; Egypt and Ty'rus; are one figurative power existing together by one spirit, for John saw the woman seated on a red beast, and concerning Egypt we read, "Pharaoh king of Egypt, the great dragon."³⁶⁶ Egypt is the one carrying the woman. Concerning Ty'rus, we read of all that is in him by how it says, "Thy riches, and thy fairs, thy merchandise, thy mariners, and thy pilots, thy callers, and the occupiers of thy merchandise, and all thy men of war,"³⁶⁷ and such men are synonymous with "the kings of the earth, who have committed fornication and lived deliciously with her,"³⁶⁸ even "the merchants of the earth."³⁶⁹ For, as they say, "What city is like Ty'rus,"³⁷⁰ so they say, "What city is like unto this great city!"³⁷¹

8. As Ty'rus and Egypt are one spiritual power existing by different names, it is seen how both Egypt and Ty'rus share the same spirit of the

---

361 Revelation 17:18
362 Ezekiel 28:2
363 2 Thessalonians 2:3,4
364 Ezekiel 31:10
365 Ezekiel 31:6
366 Ezekiel 29:3
367 Ezekiel 27:27
368 Revelation 18:9
369 Revelation 18:11
370 Ezekiel 27:32
371 Revelation 18:18

prince and king of Ty'rus, for this prince appears to have a seat over the religion and government of this Ty'rus that is Egypt, for, Egypt is that great dragon. The description of Egypt, saying no "tree in the garden of God was like unto him in his beauty,"[372] this fits that rebuke concerning Ty'rus, which says, "Thou hast said, I am of perfect beauty,"[373] and such imagery mirrors the heart of the king of their prince, of whom it is said, "Thine heart was lifted up because of thy beauty."[374] As it is said, "As is the mother, so is her daughter,"[375] so the report against the king of Ty'rus states, "Thou hast corrupted thy wisdom by reason of thy brightness,"[376] and for his son, the prince of Ty'rus; who is that minister of perdition; it says, "Thy wisdom and thy knowledge, it hath perverted thee; and thou hast said in thine heart, I am, and none else beside me."[377]

9. When there should again be a woman upheld by a great dragon, it is that an earthquake should commence. Of old, it was civil power that upheld the impure woman, and it was civil power that was taken away from the woman; as it says, "I saw one of his heads as it were wounded to death."[378] In the age of the sixth seal, the spirit that should come up out of the earth "causeth the earth and them which dwell therein to worship the first beast, whose deadly wound was healed";[379] worship is herein observed to come after her wound is healed.

10. As a "beast" is, in prophetic language, a pagan royal or government "kingdom," we here have, in the thirteenth division of the Revelation, a kingdom, a throne, a civil power, compelling worship to the rule of the first beast before it, which leopard beast, according to history, is openly understood to be the Roman Catholic Church in its Papal form. The fact that the earth beast is acting as a religious conscience for the inhabitants of the earth is evidence that the government of this

---

372 Ezekiel 31:8
373 Ezekiel 27:3
374 Ezekiel 28:17
375 Ezekiel 16:44
376 Ezekiel 28:17
377 Isaiah 47:10
378 Revelation 13:3
379 Revelation 13:12

age will be one of a combined union between law and religion, or it will be a beast framed after the image of the first beast, which image will form the Pagan Republic of Apostate *Judaism*. Therefore if Ty'rus and Egypt bear the same DNA, and if Egypt is known as the great dragon, then as the great dragon is the one who offers himself for service to the woman; as it says of the dragon, "He persecuted the woman which brought forth";[380] it is that the nation from whom the two-horned earth beast arises acts as Egypt in prophecy, even as a powerful civil government under an officially working church and State order who will forward the mind of an impure church, namely, her two equally minded horns. Therefore as John says, "Lo," so it is that "his deadly wound was healed: and all the world wondered after the beast."[381]

11. That image within the seventeenth division of the book of the Revelation is Papal Rome. In verse one, the woman is the great whore; in verse eighteen, she is the great city; the woman is a pagan apostate Roman Christian church carried by the State of Rome to forward the ambition of her heart. In the sixteenth division of the Revelation, verse nineteen, the great city, that great whore, is divided into three parts: the dragon, the beast, and the false prophet; and that two-horned beast, in all that has been discussed, and in all that is observed within thirteenth division of the Revelation, is beast, dragon, and false prophet.

12. The seventeenth division of the Revelation, verses seven and eight, place the woman and the beast that carries her as one entity. The beast in the seventeenth division of the Revelation, although Papal Rome, is a figurative representation of an apostate ecclesiastical faction supported by its government and ran by priests of spiritual error. This woman that is yet to exist is clearly seen in the eighteenth division of the Revelation, verses two and three, for this is not solely that church of Rome or any Protestant church today; these churches are yet fallen from the LORD's Faith in name and in understanding. But the Christian church will fall even further in respect to heaven's science and operation, joining to their State by a most grotesque religious error,

---
380 Revelation 12:13
381 Revelation 13:3

beginning her downward fall to accept governance under the spirit of that institution ascending in to perdition.

13. When considering the Revelation, in chapter seventeen and verse eight, this beast that existed in the time of John was not papal Rome, but pagan Rome; that dragon which had seven heads and ten horns. In the Revelation chapter twelve, verses one through three, the beast that carries the woman is the dragon, the woman is plainly a Christian church under Rome's age of dominion, and the entire vision is Papal Catholicism at the height of her reign for 1260 years, from 538AD to 1798AD.

14. In the Revelation chapter seventeen, verses one and eight, the Spirit teaches, "The beast that you saw"; Papal Rome; "did exist, and does not now currently exist," for the vision of this chapter is of "the judgment of the great whore."[382] And this same beast, or rather, the spirit of this beast, after the judgment here witnessed is accomplished in her, will ascend in to perdition at a later date. This creature of perdition is observed in chapter thirteen of the Revelation, verses two and three, in her active form, and in chapter seventeen of the Revelation, verses three through five, which is another visual of the active leopard beast of Revelation chapter thirteen. This beast is the same entity in every illustration, for which cause this beast of Revelation seventeen is papal Rome on the surface.

15. In John's time, the papacy was not yet in existence, yet in vision he represents future seers, and he saw that for future disciples, the papacy used to be in power, and that it is not currently in power at a particular season, and yet it exists, but without power, but eventually its spirit will reign in full power again, for at the sight of this spirit's resurrection, John fell in awe of her. There is only one spirit that causes wonder, and it is the craft of the Papal beast, and here, the spirit and mind of the Papal beast is to go in to perdition, is to once again seek government authority to compel worship of her and her head Bishop. The dragon, then, at this time, should represent the civil power of the two-horned beast; even as it did of old; and the woman appears to ever be the same spirit or constitution of the church of Rome. Yet,

---

[382]   Revelation 17:1

this church must now be an accepted mixture of two grossly apostate religions professing service to *the LORD of the Hebrews*; for it has two horns; leaving the woman, in reality, to be a new apostate pagan government religion upheld by her State and *blessed* by the spirit of the Catholic religion.

16. At a very future point, the mind of the Papacy will be seated on top of The New Pagan *Jewish* Government, which government is the seventh *kingdom* that is to be for a short space, ordaining a new universal pagan *Jewish* faith of *peace* and *safety*. The height of her empire comes at Revelation chapter eighteen and verse two, for herein is the true and most significant mark of her fall from the living God's will and doctrine, even the combination of two filthy houses: apostate *Christianity* joined to another popular, false, and perverted polytheistic universal religion. It must be that after this establishment, a rule is soon enacted with civil force by the church of the new pagan universal *Jewish* leadership against the name of heaven's LORD's, which name is revealed by His fourth commandment.

17. The announcement of the fall of Babylon the great is the decaying of 3 entities,[383] therefore her most significant fall; which fall is so emphatic that scripture presents a likeness to that uttered as it was of old in the second angel's message; cannot take place within either Catholicism or Protestantism alone, for both institutions are already today fallen from fact and right heavenly science. Babylon the great will be the final product of perdition between a modern pagan religious government and the spirit of Papal Rome, leaving her final act; the newly resurrected church of the religious world; and her error, to be that which aggravates the living name and seal of the Spirit's Word. Indeed such a decree caps a rejection of the Spirit's Faith, and with regard to learning of and keeping His ten precepts by that Faith's course, even as it was so done before of old by the Protestant churches. Herein we see, within chapter eighteen of the Revelation, verses four and five, that the angels of heaven's new reformatory movement will know the sign of error's great fall to give creation's last message with power to the then Gentiles of error's religious institution.

---

383   Revelation 16:13,19

18. When that law against the name of heaven's LORD and High Priest is become a reality, the preaching of the Spirit's intention will go forward in the full and complete measure of the Spirit by them that are known of His Word, and who know His voice. The message will increase in fullness until that strange decree against heaven is formed, and that message will continue under this ecclesiastical establishment until the first of the seven plagues should fall, for then its force will vengefully rage. How long a space from the unlawful decree until the first of seven plagues, or how short, we do not know. The fall, then, of new Babylon, should be when open perdition occurs, for 2 Thessalonians chapter two, verses three and four, mentions an official falling away, or of intercourse between paganism and Christianity, but in this case of that revealed dominion within the sixth seal, it will be between apostate *Christianity* and a pagan universal religion, leading up to the outward show of her moral and spiritual fall by a mark against the worship of the true God.

19. This gross amalgamation will fulfill the vision of a great earthquake, or of a great commotion, within the religious earth. The Catholic church is the main focus of the seals, and the resurrection and perdition of its spirit can only be of a magnitude to have it known as a great commotion, a terrible storm and tempest to break out on the *earth*. Because the Protestant church is not mentioned in the seals; besides the image of them as dead souls pleading for vengeance; there is no reason to deviate from the record established by the seals. As there is an earthquake, and as the beast that came up out of the earth in the thirteenth division of the Revelation is a grossly apostate pagan version of American Christianity, there will be some terrible happening in the earth, both in its government and its church, and that happening will lead up to the true visitation of the Spirit's house, first within error's State, and then throughout the entire world.

20. The same words, "I beheld,"[384] and, "Lo,"[385] as said within the sixth seal, are found also in the third seal. The third seal is a representation of the Christian church under a spirit of compromise, for it

---

384   Revelation 6:5
385   Revelation 6:12

says, "Thou hast there them that hold the doctrine of Ba'laam, who taught Ba'lac."[386] Ba'laam represents an apostate church; Ba'lac represents the chief ruler of a pagan State. This history of compromise will repeat itself, for a pagan church will join herself to the government of the modern glorious land, causing an earthquake by that State openly crucifying the body of heaven's knowledge, and then an even greater earthquake, revolving around a first-day resurrection, will occur, for a terrible storm will break out on the *earth's* inhabitants, as them that are spiritually compromised raise up to health that pale horse with his rider and companion.[387]

---

386 Revelation 2:14
387 Revelation 6:8

9

A Prepared Host And Fury

1. John beheld a great earthquake at the opening of the sixth seal, with the sun and the moon darkening, with the stars falling to the earth, and with the heavens becoming no more. Such a vision finds place in the saying, "All the host of heaven shall be dissolved, and the heavens shall be rolled together as a scroll: and all their host shall fall down, as the leaf falleth off from the vine, and as a falling fig from the fig tree,"[388] for as it says, "Even as a fig tree casteth her untimely figs, when she is shaken of a mighty wind,"[389] and, "The stars of heaven fell unto the earth,"[390] the result will be that "the heaven departed as a scroll when it is rolled together."[391] This is the scene of "the day of the LORD's vengeance, and the year of recompense for the controversy of Zion,"[392] for the Spirit says, "I will shake the heavens, and the earth shall remove out of her place, in the wrath of the LORD of hosts, and in the day of his fierce anger."[393]

2. Such a scene is doubtless the fulfillment of the saying, "Assemble yourselves, and come, all ye heathen, and gather yourselves together

---

388 Isaiah 34:4
389 Revelation 6:13
390 Revelation 6:13
391 Revelation 6:14
392 Isaiah 34:8
393 Isaiah 13:13

round about: thither cause thy mighty ones to come down, O LORD,"[394] for it says, "Come near, ye nations, to hear; and hearken, ye people: let the earth hear, and all that is therein; the world, and all things that come forth of it. For the indignation of the LORD is upon all nations, and his fury upon all their armies."[395] Now, the mighty ones of the LORD are not them that do not know His name, but they are rather "a great people and a strong,"[396] fulfilling the word, "I have commanded my sanctified ones, I have also called my mighty ones for mine anger, even them that rejoice in my highness. The noise of a multitude in the mountains, like as of a great people; a tumultuous noise of the kingdoms of nations gathered together: the LORD of hosts mustereth the host of the battle."[397] These that are of the LORD's Spirit are "the weapons of his indignation,"[398] even as it says, "The LORD hath opened his armory, and hath brought forth the weapons of his indignation"[399] against "the land of the Chalde'ans."[400] "Their day is come, the time of their visitation."[401]

3. These men of the LORD were anciently "the archers against Babylon."[402] These archers were told, "All that she hath done, do unto her,"[403] for they fulfill the word that is gone out, "In the cup which she hath filled fill to her double."[404] Now, these that were sent against Babylon fulfilled the vision, "I will stir up the Medes against them,"[405] for the Spirit said of their king, "Who is a chosen man, that I may appoint over her? for who is like me?"[406] These scenes that anciently took place are to be fulfilled personally by the Spirit through His host. So, then, who is like Him? Scripture says of this time of His ancient

---

394 Joel 3:11
395 Isaiah 34:1,2
396 Joel 2:2
397 Isaiah 13:3,4
398 Isaiah 13:5
399 Jeremiah 50:25
400 Jeremiah 50:25
401 Jeremiah 50:27
402 Jeremiah 50:29
403 Jeremiah 50:29
404 Revelation 18:6
405 Isaiah 13:17
406 Jeremiah 50:44

wrath, "Thou wentest forth for the salvation of thy people, even for salvation with thine anointed,"[407] therefore the Spirit said, "Thus saith the LORD to his anointed, to Cyrus,"[408] "He is my shepherd, and shall perform all my pleasure: even saying to Jerusalem, Thou shalt be built; and to the temple, Thy foundation shall be laid."[409]

4. Cyrus is a figure of the Spirit's Christ, for, in him, the saying is fulfilled, "Who raised up the righteous man from the east, called him to his foot, gave the nations before him, and made him ruler over kings?"[410] Now, the Medes were not alone, for Scripture revealed "a tumultuous noise of the kingdoms of nations gathered together,"[411] therefore it is written, "Set ye up a standard in the land, blow the trumpet among the nations, prepare the nations against her, call together against her the kingdoms of A'rarat, Min'ni, and Ash'chenaz; appoint a captain against her; cause the horses to come up as the rough caterpillars. Prepare against her the nations with the kings of the Medes, the captains thereof, and all the rulers thereof, and all the land of his dominion. And the land shall tremble and sorrow: for every purpose of the LORD shall be performed against Babylon, to make the land of Babylon a desolation without an inhabitant."[412]

5. The events of the rise and fall of Babylon will be repeated and fulfilled once again, but this time its complete fulfillment will end by the fury of heaven's voice. It is for this reason that the same imagery used for the anticipated appearing of the Spirit's vengeance is used for the ancient fall of Babylon, for it says, "The day of the LORD cometh, cruel both with wrath and fierce anger, to lay the land desolate: and he shall destroy the sinners thereof out of it. For the stars of heaven and the constellations thereof shall not give their light: the sun shall be darkened in his going forth, and the moon shall not cause her light to shine. And I will punish the world for their evil, and the wicked for their iniquity; and I will cause the arrogancy of the proud to cease, and

---

407   Habakkuk 3:13
408   Isaiah 45:1
409   Isaiah 44:28
410   Isaiah 41:2
411   Isaiah 13:4
412   Jeremiah 51:27-29

will lay low the haughtiness of the terrible."[413] The sun, the moon, and the stars, are illustratively revealed as "sinners" to heaven's name and will within earth's established religious economy, which are even the ministers "which had the mark of the beast"[414] and "which worshipped his image."[415] Such events begin the day of the LORD's wrath by His Spirit, which day is "a day of darkness and of gloominess, a day of clouds and think darkness."[416]

6. Now, Joel omits a portion of that found in Zephaniah, for that written by Joel takes place after that of Zephaniah. Zephaniah reports: "The great day of the LORD is near,"[417] for it is not yet come in this vision. The day of the LORD begins at the dark and gloomy day; in Zephaniah, we should receive that which will express the nearness to the fulfillment of that great day. Scripture says, "That day is a day of wrath, a day of trouble and distress, a day of wasteness and desolation, a day of darkness and gloominess, a day of clouds and thick darkness, a day of the trumpet and alarm against the fenced cities, and against the high towers."[418] The events of Joel do not find place until after three key events are fulfilled in Zephaniah, and as Joel marks the fourth, fifth, and sixth events to be that of the beginning wrath of the Word's voice, the first three events must fulfill that which leads up to the coming of His salvation's science in omnipotent force, and that indeed is a time of wrath and trouble with distress and violence upon them of His own house that have violated His name and throne, for it says, "The dragon was wroth with the woman."[419] We may understand that terror must first begin against the Spirit's professed by what that king of old uttered when confronted with the then dragon of the then world: "This is a day of trouble,"[420] he said.

---

413 Isaiah 13:9-11
414 Revelation 16:1
415 Revelation 16:1
416 Joel 2:2
417 Zephaniah 1:15
418 Zephaniah 1:15,16
419 Revelation 12:17
420 2 Kings 19:3

7. Joel chapter two opens at the seventh trumpet during the third woe; this is no dispute; and it is therefore evident that the true fulfillment of the Medes; that sanctified and mighty host joined by nations and armies after their mind against Babylon; cannot be any other illustration than that shown to John, who writes, "I saw heaven opened, and behold a white horse; and he that sat upon him was called Faithful and True, and in righteousness he doth judge and make war."[421] "And the armies which were in heaven followed him upon white horses, clothed in fine linen, white and clean. And out of his mouth goeth a sharp sword, that with it he should smite the nations: and he shall rule them with a rod of iron: and he treadeth the winepress of the fierceness and wrath of Almighty God."[422] Again, concerning this event, it is written, "Behold, the Lord cometh with ten thousands of his saints, to execute judgment upon all, and to convince."[423]

8. It may then be fair to view the vision of the sixth seal from two perspectives resulting in one. The great earthquake could very well be the formation of the new Babylon, and the events of that quaking reveal her final reign of terror until a more perfect earthquake permanently dethrones her. Yet Scripture says, "The LORD also shall roar out of Zion, and utter his voice from Jerusalem; and the heavens and the earth shall shake."[424] As it says of old, "The third part of the sun was smitten, and the third part of the moon, and the third part of the stars,"[425] so at this time, heaven's name and judgment will completely obliterate the hierarchy of the established throne of iniquity. The sixth seal is a vision of terrible quaking within the religious earth, beginning with the day of the dragon's wrath and ending with heaven's victory; the LORD's Spirit will fulfill the saying, "Thou hast made of a city an heap; of a defenced city a ruin: a palace of strangers to be no city."[426] "Thou shalt bring down the noise of strangers,"[427] "the branch of the terrible

---

421 Revelation 19:11
422 Revelation 19:14,15
423 Jude 1:14,15
424 Joel 3:16
425 Revelation 8:12
426 Isaiah 25:2
427 Isaiah 25:5

ones shall be brought low,"[428] "and the fortress of the high fort of thy walls shall he bring down, lay low, and bring to the ground, even to the dust,"[429] it is written.

9. In the Revelation, John says, "I beheld, and lo a black horse,"[430] and also, "I beheld, and, lo, a great multitude"[431] "clothed in white robes, and palms in their hands,"[432] for these must relate to that which says, "I beheld when he had opened the sixth seal, and, lo, there was a great earthquake."[433] From the time an apostate church should seduce her State for political favor to seat her self above her State, to the end she may resurrect the spirit of her mother for supreme dominance, until heaven's doctrine and priesthood should shine from out of heaven's Building, it is fair to conclude that the great earthquake of the sixth seal will go on, and it will end when every faithful supporter and patriot of the LORD's Temple and City is gathered together by the voice of His Christ to remain in His Faith's presence for ever more. That great earthquake will begin at the true and final falling of spiritual Babylon, until she is taken away for ever by the speech of the Spirit's High Priest. At this time, it will be known that "the LORD is the true God, he is the living God, and an everlasting king: at his wrath the earth shall tremble, and the nations shall not be able to abide his indignation."[434]

10. The sixth seal contains the scenes of the expected appearing of the LORD's voice in unprotected fury, for, joined to that great and strong people, and to that tumultuous host of the Spirit's sanctified ones, the Spirit says, "The appearance of them is as the appearance of horses."[435] "Like the noise of chariots on the tops of mountains shall they leap,"[436] for the vision is one in likeness to that prophesied of old, saying, "I will bring upon Ty'rus Nebuchadrez'zar king of Babylon, a king of kings, from the north, with horses, and with chariots, and with

---

428   Isaiah 25:5
429   Isaiah 25:12
430   Revelation 6:5
431   Revelation 7:9
432   Revelation 7:9
433   Revelation 6:12
434   Jeremiah 10:10
435   Joel 2:5
436   Joel 2:5

horsemen, and companies, and much people. He shall slay with the sword thy daughters in the field: and he shall make a fort against thee, and cast a mount against thee, and lift up the buckler against thee. And he shall set engines of war against thy walls, and with his axes he shall break down thy towers. By reason of the abundance of his horses their dust shall cover thee: thy walls shall shake at the noise of the horsemen, and of the wheels, and of the chariots, when he shall enter into thy gates, as men enter into a city wherein is made a breach. With the hoofs of his horses shall he tread down all thy streets: he shall slay thy people by the sword, and thy strong garrisons shall go down to the ground."[437]

11. As Cyrus is that figurative servant of the living God who was anointed of Him to conquer Babylon, and as this LORD says of the king of Babylon, "Nebuchadnez'zar the king of Babylon, my servant,"[438] so these two men; Cyrus and Nebuchadnez'zar; are figurative illustration of how His Faith will conquer the confidence of "Egypt" and "Babylon" and "Ty'rus" in an instant. Thus, "in his times he shall shew, who is the blessed and only Potentate, the King of kings, and Lord of lords."[439] "The Lamb shall overcome them: for he is Lord of lords, and King of kings: and they that are with him are called, and chosen, and faithful."[440]

12. It cannot be forgotten that the seals follow an established pattern cycled through an established ecclesiastical history. The sixth seal should not break the mold of the previous seals, for the Spirit's voice is without re-establishment. The sixth seal should contain the continuation of the history and work of the same spirit and institution of the previous seals, yet as she has done, so too will it be fulfilled against her in full, for it says, "Reward her even as she rewarded you, and double unto her double according to her works: in the cup which she hath filled fill to her double."[441] The sixth seal must then begin with the healing of this institution; which healing is the joining of *Egypt* and *Babylon* with *Ty'rus*; until the day the vengeance of the LORD's Spirit should arrive against her.

---

437 Ezekiel 26:7-11
438 Jeremiah 27:6
439 1 Timothy 6:15
440 Revelation 17:14
441 Revelation 18:6

10

The Sects Of The Controversy

1. Says Scripture, "He shall come up like a lion from the swelling of Jordan against the habitation of the strong: but I will suddenly make him run away from her: and who is a chosen man, that I may appoint over her? for who is like me? and who will appoint me the time? and who is that shepherd that will stand before me?"[442] This counsel was given against E'dom, for He said, "E'dom shall be a desolation"[443] "as in the overthrow of Sodom and Gomor'rah and the neighbour cities thereof."[444]

2. Again, Scripture says, "He shall come up like a lion from the swelling of Jordan unto the habitation of the strong: but I will make them suddenly run away from her: and who is a chosen man, that I may appoint over her? for who is like me? and who will appoint me the time? and who is that shepherd that will stand before me?"[445] This counsel was given against Babylon, for it says, "The word that the LORD spake against Babylon,"[446] "The most proud shall stumble and fall, and none

---

442   Jeremiah 49:19
443   Jeremiah 49:17
444   Jeremiah 49:18
445   Jeremiah 50:44
446   Jeremiah 50:1

shall raise him up."[447] "It is the vengeance of the LORD."[448] "Babylon, the glory of kingdoms, the beauty of the Chaldees' excellency, shall be as when God overthrew Sodom and Gomorrah."[449]

3. The same references are observed for both E'dom and Babylon because the two represent the same power. The Spirit says, "Boz'rah shall become a desolation, a reproach, a waste,"[450] for it is known, "Who is this that cometh from E'dom, with dyed garments from Boz'rah?"[451] "The LORD hath a sacrifice in Boz'rah, and a great slaughter in the land of Idume'a."[452] E'dom and Babylon are one figurative entity, therefore the word that says, "The earth is moved at the noise of their fall,"[453] and, "I will raise and cause to come up against Babylon an assembly of great nations from the north country,"[454] is one word and vision against one people. The Spirit said, "I will raise up against Babylon"[455] "a destroying wind"[456] "that shall fan her."[457] "The LORD of hosts hath sworn by himself, saying, Surely I will fill thee with men, as with caterpillars."[458] "Set ye up a standard in the land, blow the trumpet among the nations, prepare the nations against her, call together against her the kingdoms of A'rarat, Min'ni, and Ash'chenaz; appoint a captain against her; cause the horses to come up as the rough caterpillars. Prepare against her the nations with the kings of the Medes, the captains thereof, and all the rulers thereof, and all the land of his dominion."[459]

4. It is by this vision that we may understand why it is said that, at the sight of this "great people and a strong,"[460] "the earth shall quake before them; the heavens shall tremble: the sun and the moon shall be

---

447   Jeremiah 50:32
448   Jeremiah 50:15
449   Isaiah 13:19
450   Jeremiah 49:13
451   Isaiah 63:1
452   Isaiah 34:6
453   Jeremiah 49:21
454   Jeremiah 50:9
455   Jeremiah 51:1
456   Jeremiah 51:1
457   Jeremiah 51:2
458   Jeremiah 51:14
459   Jeremiah 51:27,28
460   Joel 2:2

dark, and the stars shall withdraw their shining,"[461] for these are the same ones that "come from a far country, from the end of heaven, even the LORD, and the weapons of his indignation, to destroy the whole land."[462] At the sight of them, "the stars of heaven and the constellations thereof shall not give their light: the sun shall be darkened in his going forth, and the moon shall not cause her light to shine."[463] "I will shake the heavens, and the earth shall remove out of her place,"[464] says the Spirit, for it says, "He is strong that executeth his word,"[465] even as it says of Cyrus, "He is my shepherd, and shall perform all my pleasure,"[466] and of His Christ's face, "To execute judgment upon all."[467]

5. Therefore, as Egypt, Babylon, E'dom, and Ty'rus are one, and the *Medes* also representing one spiritual body, heaven's host will fulfill the saying against *Egypt*, "Egypt shall be a desolation, and E'dom shall be a desolate wilderness."[468] As Scripture says, "The most proud shall stumble and fall, and none shall raise him up,"[469] it is in fact the same saying as that found in Daniel, which says, "He shall come to his end, and none shall help him,"[470] which is in fact the saying, "I will remove far off from you the northern army, and will drive him into a land barren and desolate."[471] The four powers that bear the same condemnation and report are here for us simplified to one common name, that is, "The Northern Army." It is this northern army that is to be demolished, in spirit and in name, by "Cyrus" and by "the Medes," or by "Nebuchadnez'zar" and "his company" joined by a multitude and army that "hath not been ever the like."[472] Such a work will not be done by the craft of priests and ministers, but by that Spirit who "in righteous-

---

461 Joel 2:10
462 Isaiah 13:5
463 Isaiah 13:10
464 Isaiah 13:13
465 Joel 2:11
466 Isaiah 44:28
467 Jude 1:15
468 Joel 3:19
469 Jeremiah 50:32
470 Daniel 11:45
471 Joel 2:20
472 Joel 2:2

ness he doth judge and make war."[473] "He was clothed with a vesture dipped in blood: and his name is called The Word of God. And the armies which were in heaven followed him upon white horses, clothed in fine linen, white and clean."[474]

6. Scripture says again of this time, "The sun and the moon shall be darkened, and the stars shall withdraw their shining. The LORD also shall roar out of Zion...and the heavens and the earth shall shake,"[475] and this prophecy being a direct fulfillment of how it says, "A voice of noise from the city, a voice from the temple, a voice of the LORD that rendereth recompence to his enemies,"[476] which is why it says, "Blow ye the trumpet in Zion, and sound an alarm in my holy mountain,"[477] for "there came a great voice out of the temple of heaven, from the throne, saying, It is done."[478]

7. As John beheld an earthquake at the opening of the sixth seal, he observed events that were to be conveyed by great and terrible symbolic imagery, as the previous seals convey of their own essence. The events that he saw were of "the wrath of the Lamb,"[479] for he saw the fulfillment of the saying, "A great whirlwind shall be raised up,"[480] even as it says, "The LORD will come with fire, and with his chariots like a whirlwind, to render his anger with fury, and his rebuke with flames of fire,"[481] for it says, "A fire devoureth before them,"[482] and, "The noise of chariots...the noise of a flame of fire that devoureth the stubble,"[483] and it says, "The proud, yea, and all that do wickedly, shall be stubble: and the day that cometh shall burn them up, saith the LORD of hosts."[484] Scripture says, "He shall also blow upon them, and

---

473 Revelation 19:11
474 Revelation 19:13,14
475 Joel 3:15,16
476 Isaiah 66:6
477 Joel 2:1
478 Revelation 16:17
479 Revelation 6:16
480 Jeremiah 25:32
481 Isaiah 66:15
482 Joel 2:3
483 Joel 2:5
484 Malachi 4:1

they shall wither, and the whirlwind shall take them away as stubble,"[485] therefore "there was a great earthquake"[486] "and the heaven departed as a scroll"[487] during the sixth seal. What we see in the sixth seal is the overthrowing and changing of the heavens and the earth, for what is observed is how it says, "Thou hast taken to thee thy great power, and hast reigned."[488]

8. There is no question that the sixth seal contains the true revelation of the Spirit's Word to the earth's then spiritually negligent inhabitants, for Scripture blatantly confesses the fact. Yet the sixth seal is not, and should not be without the opposition and target of His wrath. The sixth seal cannot therefore open with any earthy natural movements, such as a literal earthquake, for then there should be a pause in the vision that does not exist in any of the other seals. It is not fair or right to break the established structure set up by the LORD's Spirit.

9. The vision of the sixth seal is one vision containing major events relating to the expected wrath of the Spirit and the formation of that northern force. Scripture says that this is "the year of recompenses for the controversy of Zion,"[489] and Zion cannot exist without first belonging to "mount Si'on,"[490] "the city of the living God, the heavenly Jerusalem,"[491] even that "Zion, the city of our solemnities,"[492] "the mother of us all,"[493] who houses "the general assembly and church of the firstborn, which are written in heaven."[494] The name of the LORD's Son will rescue them that keep the commandments of God and the Faith of His Spirit's doctrine from them that are in conflict with "his name, and his tabernacle, and them that dwell in heaven."[495] The power to be established will be one that strikes up a controversy with heaven's

---

485 Isaiah 40:24
486 Revelation 6:12
487 Revelation 6:14
488 Revelation 11:17
489 Isaiah 34:8
490 Hebrews 12:22
491 Hebrews 12:22
492 Isaiah 33:20
493 Galatians 4:26
494 Hebrews 12:23
495 Revelation 13:6

Faith, even the confidence and seal of the Spirit's House in heaven, and there is only one spirit who accomplishes this work, "and it was given unto him to make war with the saints, and to overcome them,"[496] even as it says, "Tidings out of the east and out of the north shall trouble him: therefore he shall go forth with great fury to destroy, and utterly to make away many."[497]

10. This is why Joel omits certain terms from his prophecy that Zephaniah does not. The fury of falsehood's ecclesiastical power must last until it is said, "After the glory hath he sent me unto the nations which spoiled you,"[498] wherefore it is said, "Proclaim ye this among the Gentiles; Prepare war, wake up the mighty men, let all the men of war draw near; let them come up,"[499] and, "The indignation of the LORD is upon all nations, and his fury upon all their armies."[500] These things must be considered because the "war" is against them that have chosen to place error's spirit and conversation above the Word and His will by establishing, and honoring, a universal creed for *legal* observance. "As many as would not worship the image of the beast";[501] this same established jurisdiction founded upon a pagan church and State government; and whosoever should disobey the religious laws of this State, "should be killed,"[502] therefore it will be fulfilled, "The dragon was wroth with the woman, an went to make war with the remnant of her seed, which keep the commandments of God, and have the testimony of Jesus Christ."[503]

11. The sixth seal cannot begin without the full healing of such a perverse economy, which kingdom will then be given what it deserves for the service it performs against souls and spirits, for it says, "Babylon the great came in remembrance before God, to give unto her the cup of the wine of the fierceness of his wrath."[504]

---

496 Revelation 13:7
497 Daniel 11:44
498 Zechariah 2:8
499 Joel 3:9
500 Isaiah 34:2
501 Revelation 13:15
502 Revelation 13:15
503 Revelation 12:17
504 Revelation 16:19

11

The Stage Of The Controversy

1. "And I beheld when he had opened the sixth seal, and, lo, there was a great earthquake; and the sun became black as sackcloth of hair, and the moon became as blood; and the stars of heaven fell unto the earth...And the heaven departed as a scroll when it is rolled together; and every mountain and island were moved out of their places."[505]

2. Such events cannot fail of falling in line with how it is said, "There was a great earthquake, such as was not since men were upon the earth, so mighty an earthquake, and so great. And the great city was divided into three parts, and the cities of the nations fell: and great Babylon came in remembrance before God, to give unto her the cup of the wine of the fierceness of his wrath. And every island fled away, and the mountains were not found."[506]

3. The language used in both of the visions here quoted foreshadows what occurred when "the seventh angel poured out his vial into the air."[507] It is at this time that the Spirit's Word will fulfill the saying, "He shall come up as clouds, and his chariots shall be as a whirlwind,"[508]

---

505   Revelation 6:12-14
506   Revelation 16:18-20
507   Revelation 16:17
508   Jeremiah 4:13

and, "I will send and take all the families of the north, saith the LORD, and Nebuchadrez'zar the king of Babylon, my servant, and will bring them against this land."[509] Therefore the saying will be fulfilled, "The Lord GOD shall blow the trumpet, and shall go with whirlwinds of the south. The LORD of hosts shall defend them."[510] "For I will gather all nations against Jerusalem to battle; and the city shall be taken, and the houses rifled, and the women ravished,"[511] says the Spirit. "And ye shall flee to the valley of the mountains; for the valley of the mountains shall reach unto A'zal: yea, ye shall flee, like as ye fled from before the earthquake in the days of Uzzi'ah king of Judah: and the LORD my God shall come, and all the saints with thee."[512]

4. Now, Scripture says that the LORD will go with the whirlwinds of the south, and Scripture says, "He caused an east wind to blow in the heaven: and by his power he brought in the south wind."[513] Now, "the east wind brought the locusts,"[514] therefore it is said, "He gave also their increase unto the caterpiller, and their labour unto the locust. He destroyed their vines with hail, and their sycomore trees with frost. He gave up their cattle also to the hail, and their flocks to hot thunderbolts. He cast upon them the fierceness of his anger, wrath, and indignation, and trouble, by sending evil angels among them."[515] The east wind, although it brought locusts, is, in reality, "angels," which "angels" are likened to hail, which "hail" is likened to His wrath and fury, therefore the Spirit says, "The treasures of the hail, which I have reserved against the time of trouble, against the day of battle and war,"[516] which is why John records, "There fell upon men a great hail out of heaven."[517]

---

509 Jeremiah 25:9
510 Zechariah 9:14,15
511 Zechariah 14:2
512 Zechariah 14:5
513 Psalm 78:26
514 Exodus 10:13
515 Psalm 78:46-49
516 Job 38:22,23
517 Revelation 16:21

5. The "day of trouble and distress,"[518] "of wasteness and desolation,"[519] precedes that "day of darkness and gloominess,"[520] for while indeed it is "a day of wrath,"[521] even the wrath of the dragon as heaven's wrath is pouring out upon the dragon and his host, after this short period of the dragon's fury, the vision will be fulfilled, "The land is as the garden of Eden before them, and behind them a desolate wilderness."[522] What is this garden like? It says, "Like the garden of the LORD; joy and gladness shall be found therein, thanksgiving, and the voice of melody,"[523] for which cause, at this time it will be fulfilled by *Nebuchadrez'zar*; who is a figurative illustration of the Word's host headed by His Spirit's chief Faith; "I will take from them the voice of mirth, and the voice of gladness, the voice of the bridegroom, and the voice of the bride, the sound of the millstones, and the light of the candle. And this whole land shall be a desolation."[524] Herein is the vision of the sixth seal concerning the sun, the moon, and the stars, for He says, "I will gather all nations against Jerusalem to battle; and the city shall be taken, and the houses rifled, and the women ravished."[525]

6. Now, Joseph once dreamed, "and he dreamed yet another dream, and told it his brethren, and said, Behold, I have dreamed a dream more; and, behold, the sun and the moon and the eleven stars made obeisance to me. And he told it to his father, and to his brethren: and his father rebuked him, and said unto him, What is this dream that thou hast dreamed? Shall I and thy mother and thy brethren indeed come to bow down ourselves to thee to the earth?"[526]

7. Joseph's mother is doubtless "a mother of nations,"[527] which is why it says of Babylon, "Your mother shall be sore confounded; she that bare you shall be ashamed: behold, the hindermost of the nations

---

518   Zephaniah 1:18
519   Zephaniah 1:18
520   Zephaniah 1:18
521   Zephaniah 1:18
522   Joel 2:3
523   Isaiah 51:3
524   Jeremiah 25:10,11
525   Zechariah 14:2
526   Genesis 37:9
527   Genesis 17:16

shall be a wilderness, a dry land, and a desert."[528] As for Joseph's father, he was Israel, and "he was head over a people, and of a chief house,"[529] for which cause it is reported of the voice of the LORD's High Priest during His day, "Thou woundedst the head out of the house of the wicked."[530] As this Christ "received from God the Father honour and glory,"[531] to the end His name's learning became for us "the Sun of righteousness,"[532] so too there should be a minister standing in the sun, "where the light is as darkness,"[533] even "the son of perdition"[534] in that counterfeit *light* of "the prince of this world,"[535] who is "the king of terrors."[536] Hence, this head of error's house bears sway over the mother of nations, and this premiere church has a seed or children, as it says, "The counsel of the wise counsellors of Pharaoh,"[537] and, "The astrologers, the stargazers, the monthly prognosticators."[538]

8. This is why Scripture says of Pharaoh and Egypt, "The Egyptians will I give over into the hand of a cruel lord; and a fierce king shall rule over them,"[539] for the LORD said, "I will give the land of Egypt unto Nebuchadrez'zar king of Babylon."[540] "I will strengthen the arms of the king of Babylon, and put my sword in his hand: but I will break Pharaoh's arms, and he shall groan before him with the groanings of a deadly wounded man."[541]

9. There is only one other power who suffers a deadly wound in Scripture, for it says, "I saw one of his heads as it were wounded to death,"[542] and this is Papal Rome. Again we see proof that Egypt and

---

528 Jeremiah 50:12
529 Numbers 25:15
530 Habakkuk 3:13
531 2 Peter 1:17
532 Malachi 4:2
533 Job 10:22
534 2 Thessalonians 2:3
535 John 12:31
536 Job 18:14
537 Isaiah 19:11
538 Isaiah 47:13
539 Isaiah 19:4
540 Ezekiel 29:19
541 Ezekiel 30:24
542 Revelation 3:3

Rome are spiritually synonymous, therefore in Pharaoh should "that man of sin be revealed, the son of perdition,"[543] because it says, "He shall have power over the treasures of gold and of silver, and over all the precious things of Egypt,"[544] for which cause, concerning Egypt, it is promised, "The LORD shall smite Egypt: he shall smite and heal it."[545] He will allow that force, whose foundations lead "to the idols, and to the charmers, and to them that have familiar spirits, and to the wizards,"[546] to find *health* and restoration, for it says, "His deadly wound was healed."[547] This He will do to make one last examination among them that "profess that they know God."[548]

10. "A sword is upon the Chalde'ans, saith the LORD, and upon the inhabitants of Babylon, and upon her princes, and upon her wise men. A sword is upon the liars; and they shall dote: a sword is upon her mighty men; and they shall be dismayed. A sword is upon their horses, and upon their chariots, and upon all the mingled people that are in the midst of her; and they shall become as women: a sword is upon her treasures; and they shall be robbed."[549] "In that day, saith the LORD, that I will cut off thy horses out of the midst of thee, and I will destroy thy chariots: and I will cut off the cities of thy land, and throw down all thy strong holds: and I will cut off witchcrafts out of thine hand; and thou shalt have no more soothsayers: thy graven images also will I cut off, and thy standing images out of the midst of thee; and thou shalt no more worship the work of thine hands. And I will pluck up thy groves out of the midst of thee: so will I destroy thy cities. And I will execute vengeance in anger and fury upon the heathen, such as they have not heard."[550]

11. As the sun of the sixth seal denotes the counterfeit bridegroom standing in the *light* and works of his father, so the moon represents

---

543 2 Thessalonians 2:3
544 Daniel 11:43
545 Isaiah 19:22
546 Isaiah 19:3
547 Revelation 3:3
548 Titus 3:16
549 Jeremiah 50:35-37
550 Micah 5:10-15

the woman or church that error's son is the head of, and their stars representing "her wise men, her captains, and her rulers, and her mighty men";[551] "the wise men, the astrologers, the magicians, the soothsayers,"[552] even "all the wise men of the nations, and in all their kingdoms."[553]

12. Concerning "stars," like as the Spirit revealed at the beginning of the Revelation, "The seven stars are the angels of the seven churches,"[554] so John "saw a star fall from heaven unto the earth."[555] As a "star" is an "angel," and as an "angel" is a "ministering spirit, sent forth to minister,"[556] so John beheld a minister fall to the earth with a doctrine that would produce a people that had "stings in their tails,"[557] for it says, "The prophet that teacheth lies, he is the tail."[558] John saw, in the sixth seal, stars falling to the earth, for he observes false spiritual leaders and their doctrines coming to an end, which prophets and creeds are of the combined institution of the sun and the moon. Therefore, at the appointed time, it will be fulfilled, "The terrible of the nations, have cut him off,"[559] even "Nebuchadrez'zar king of Babylon. He and his people with him, the terrible of the nations."[560]

13. Indeed it will be fulfilled, "The land of Judah shall be a terror unto Egypt, every one that maketh mention thereof shall be afraid in himself, because of the counsel of the LORD of hosts, which he hath determined against it. In that day shall five cities in the land of Egypt speak the language of Canaan, and swear to the LORD of hosts...In that day shall there be an altar to the LORD in the midst of the land of Egypt, and a pillar at the border thereof to the LORD,"[561] for "he shall

---

551   Jeremiah 51:57
552   Daniel 2:27
553   Jeremiah 10:7
554   Revelation 1:20
555   Revelation 9:1
556   Hebrews 1:14
557   Revelation 9:10
558   Isaiah 9:15
559   Ezekiel 31:12
560   Ezekiel 30:10,11
561   Isaiah 19:17-19

send them a saviour, and a great one, and he shall deliver them."⁵⁶² The "savior" here mentioned is no literal *Christ* from the clouds of the sky, for it is promised, "Saviours shall come up in mount Zion to judge the mount of Esau,"⁵⁶³ even them that will speak by the LORD's Spirit, as it says, "Testifiedst against them by thy spirit in thy prophets."⁵⁶⁴ These ministers fulfill the saying, "He that is left in Zion, and he that remaineth in Jerusalem,"⁵⁶⁵ "when the Lord shall have washed away the filth of the daughters of Zion."⁵⁶⁶ Again, these priests will fulfill the saying, "They that understand among the people shall instruct many,"⁵⁶⁷ for it says, "Tidings out of the east and out of the north shall trouble him."⁵⁶⁸

14. These are them "that turn many to righteousness,"⁵⁶⁹ and at the time "when the Assyrian shall come into our land."⁵⁷⁰ "Then shall we raise against him seven shepherds, and eight principal men,"⁵⁷¹ or the Word's complete and newly purified assembly with their then converts, for it will be fulfilled, "The sons of strangers shall build up thy walls,"⁵⁷² and, the Father says, "I will sow the house of Israel and the house of Judah with the seed of man."⁵⁷³ "The strangers shall be joined with them, and they shall cleave to the house of Jacob. And the people shall take them, and bring them to their place: and the house of Israel shall possess them in the land of the LORD for servants and handmaids: and they shall take them captives, whose captives they were; and they shall rule over their oppressors."⁵⁷⁴ Yet as this work is done by men during a time of wrath against them for their loyalty to the LORD's Faith and Ten Commandments, these will not, and cannot fulfill the

---

562 Isaiah 19:20
563 Obadiah 1:21
564 Nehemiah 9:30
565 Isaiah 4:3
566 Isaiah 4:4
567 Daniel 11:33
568 Daniel 11:44
569 Daniel 12:3
570 Micah 5:5
571 Micah 5:5
572 Isaiah 60:10
573 Jeremiah 31:27
574 Isaiah 14:1,2

vision of their own will or name, for the Spirit says, "My determination is to gather the nations, that I may assemble the kingdoms, to pour upon them mine indignation, even all my fierce anger."[575]

15. Israel, concerning that dream of Joseph, said to his son, "Should I and thy mother and thy brethren bow down ourselves to thee to the earth?"[576] for which cause the Spirit says, "Unto me every knee shall bow, every tongue shall swear."[577] As the people of the LORD at this time herald that report out of the east and the north, they properly explain the name of "one from the north"[578] and "from the rising of the sun."[579] Nebuchadrez'zar and Cyrus; who are figures of the LORD's chief will and confidence; will *appear* to the *earth* through His army from "the north, the city of the great King,"[580] and "from the east,"[581] for "the glory of the God of Israel came from the way of the east."[582] Scripture says, "The sun shall be turned into darkness, and the moon into blood, before the great and terrible day of the LORD."[583] The Spirit's Faith and Ten Commandments, and most emphatically His fourth commandment, will be warred against, but then the doctrine of falsehood will also be warred against, to where its sun of error became black, for to be black is to confess, "I hurt; I am black."[584]

16. During this period of time, the word should again be met and fulfilled, "The serpent cast out of his mouth water as a flood after the woman,"[585] and this will be accomplished because "her merchandise and her hire shall be holiness to the LORD,"[586] seeing as how "her merchandise shall be for them that dwell before the LORD."[587] After this space of time; in which the saying will be fulfilled, "I will sift the

---

575 Zephaniah 3:8
576 Genesis 37:10
577 Isaiah 45:23
578 Isaiah 41:25
579 Isaiah 41:25
580 Psalms 48:2
581 Revelation 7:2
582 Ezekiel 43:2
583 Joel 2:31
584 Jeremiah 8:21
585 Revelation 12:15
586 Isaiah 23:18
587 Isaiah 23:18

house of Israel among all nations";[588] the word will go out, "I rise up to the prey,"[589] because "at that time shall Mi'chael stand up,"[590] for "the LORD standeth up to plead, and standeth to judge the people."[591]

17. "He shall judge among the nations, and shall rebuke many people."[592] "Enter into the rock, and hide thee in the dust, for fear of the LORD, and for the glory of his majesty."[593] "For the day of the LORD of hosts shall be upon every one that is proud and lofty."[594] "Upon all the cedars of Leb'anon, that are high and lifted up, and upon all the oaks of Ba'shan, and upon all the high mountains, and upon all the hills that are lifted up, and upon every high tower, and upon every fenced wall, and upon all the ships of Tar'shish, and upon all pleasant pictures."[595] For, as it says of His name's host, "Before their face the people shall be much pained: all faces shall gather blackness";[596] at this time "shall all hands be faint, and every man's heart shall melt: and they shall be afraid: pangs and sorrows shall take hold of them; they shall be in pain as a woman that travaileth: they shall be amazed one at another; their faces shall be as flames."[597] At the revelation of the face of heaven's High Priest, "they shall lay hold every one on the hand of his neighbour, and his hand shall rise up against the hand of his neighbour."[598]

18. Such are the scenes put forth by the sixth seal. Although the vision is one vision, the symbolism fits the work that should be accomplished by the then ministers of modern Babylon, and by the name of the Spirit's Priest through the then sanctified assembly of the living God. "These shall make war with the Lamb,"[599] and that war is no literal or

---

588   Amos 9:9
589   Zephaniah 3:8
590   Daniel 12:1
591   Isaiah 3:13
592   Isaiah 2:4
593   Isaiah 2:10
594   Isaiah 2:12
595   Isaiah 2:13-16
596   Joel 2:6
597   Isaiah 13:7,8
598   Zechariah 14:13
599   Revelation 17:14

celestial battle with *God's Man* at the head of a literal "angelic" troop, but His name is with them that have "his Father's name written in their foreheads."[600] At this time, "the dragon was wroth with the woman, and went to make war with the remnant of her seed,"[601] but "they know not the thoughts of the LORD, neither understand they his counsel: for he shall gather them as the sheaves into the floor"[602] to fulfill the saying, "I will pour out my spirit unto you, I will make known my words unto you."[603]

---

600   Revelation 14:1
601   Revelation 12:17
602   Micah 4:12
603   Proverbs 1:23

12

The Year Of Commotion

1. John writes, "I beheld when he had opened the sixth seal, and, lo, there was a great earthquake; and the sun became black as sackcloth of hair, and the moon became as blood,"[604] and this vision is no different from how it is written, "The moon shall be confounded, and the sun ashamed, when the LORD of hosts shall reign in mount Zion, and in Jerusalem, and before his ancients gloriously."[605]

2. As it says, "When the LORD will reign in mount Zion,"[606] it is as said, "The Lord God omnipotent reigneth,"[607] and, "Thou hast taken to thee thy great power, and hast reigned."[608] And when it says, "He will reign before His ancients,"[609] this saying brings the attention to the time "when the Lord Jesus shall be revealed from heaven with his mighty angels, in flaming fire taking vengeance on them that know not God, and that obey not the gospel of our Lord Jesus Christ: who shall be punished with everlasting destruction from the presence of the

---

604 Revelation 6:12
605 Isaiah 24:23
606 Isaiah 24:33
607 Revelation 19:6
608 Revelation 11:17
609 Isaiah 24:23

Lord, and from the glory of his power; when he shall come to be glorified in his saints, and to be admired in all them that believe."[610] For, "the mean man shall be brought down, and the mighty man shall be humbled, and the eyes of the lofty shall be humbled: but the LORD of hosts shall be exalted in judgment, and God that is holy shall be sanctified in righteousness."[611]

3. Herein it is well to understand, in order to rightly grasp Paul's vision, that "the Lord Jesus Christ our Saviour"[612] is; in right context of language; "the commandment of God our Savior,"[613] which commandment is "the doctrine of God our Saviour."[614] In the previous chapter, we read how it says, "The land of Judah shall be a terror unto Egypt, every one that maketh mention thereof shall be afraid in himself, because of the counsel of the LORD of hosts, which he hath determined against it,"[615] for *Egypt* will suffer, at the time appointed, creation's commandment and counsel in great fury. It is the Spirit's intention to pour out His name upon *Egypt's* men in great anger, even as He says, "All the earth shall be devoured with the fire of my jealousy,"[616] and, "Then will I turn to the people a pure language.[617] Language is not physical, nor can any change in language by physically accomplished. Language is mental, and heaven's language must be understood through the "eyes," that is, "the eyes of your understanding."[618] This is why it says, "Every eye shall see him,"[619] for the Word's will and commandment, at the time appointed, will be revealed to the understanding of *Egypt's* host, and this mental and spiritual revelation will fulfill the saying, "The whole

---

610	2 Thessalonians 1:7-10
611	Isaiah 5:15,16
612	Titus 1:4
613	Titus 1:3
614	Titus 2:10
615	Isaiah 19:17
616	Zephaniah 3:8
617	Zephaniah 3:9
618	Ephesians 1:18
619	Revelation 1:7

earth was of one language and of one speech,"[620] "for the Lord God omnipotent reigneth."[621]

4. Such a day has caused the sun to say, "I hurt; I am black; astonishment hath taken hold on me,"[622] for "the gates thereof languish; they are black unto the ground; and the cry of Jerusalem is gone up."[623] And as this moon is seen as becoming blood, or confounded, astonished, or perplexed, it says of the LORD's Word, "That frustrateth the tokens of the liars, and maketh diviners mad."[624] Why should the sun and the moon be in this condition? It says, "Because they have transgressed the laws, changed the ordinance, broken the everlasting covenant."[625] It is at this time of transgression that the saying will be fulfilled, "In the city is left desolation, and the gate is smitten with destruction. When thus it shall be in the midst of the land among the people, there shall be as the shaking of an olive tree, and as the gleaning grapes when the vintage is done. They shall lift up their voice, they shall sing for the majesty of the LORD."[626] Such imagery leads the mind to remember how it is said, "Even as a fig tree casteth her untimely figs,"[627] for, concerning this time, "it is even the time of Jacob's trouble; but he shall be saved out of it."[628]

5. The LORD's Christ once said, "Watch ye therefore: for ye know not when the master of the house cometh, at even, or at midnight, or at the cockcrowing, or in the morning,"[629] therefore it is recorded for our observation, "At midnight Paul and Silas prayed, and sang praises unto God: and the prisoners heard them. And suddenly there was a great earthquake, so that the foundations of the prison were shaken: and immediately all the doors were opened, and every one's bands were

---

620	Genesis 11:1
621	Revelation 19:6
622	Jeremiah 8:21
623	Jeremiah 14:2
624	Isaiah 44:25
625	Isaiah 24:5
626	Isaiah 24:12-15
627	Revelation 6:13
628	Jeremiah 30:7
629	Mark 13:15

loosed."[630] For this cause it is written, "Wherefore do I see every man with his hands on his loins, as a woman in travail, and all faces are turned into paleness?"[631] "It is even the time of Jacob's trouble; but he shall be saved out of it. For it shall come to pass in that day, saith the LORD of hosts, that I will break his yoke from off thy neck, and will burst thy bonds, and strangers shall no more serve themselves of him: but they shall serve the LORD their God, and David their king, whom I will raise up unto them. Therefore fear thou not, O my servant Jacob, saith the LORD; neither be dismayed, O Israel: for, lo, I will save thee from afar, and thy seed from the land of their captivity."[632]

6. Thus, "before their face the people shall be much pained,"[633] for the Spirit says, "I will also gather all nations, and will bring them down into the valley of Jehosh'aphat, and will plead with them there for my people and for my heritage Israel, whom they have scattered among the nations, and parted my land."[634] "In that day, that the LORD shall punish the host of the high ones that are on high, and the kings of the earth upon the earth. And they shall be gathered together."[635] Thus, where it says, "A fire devoureth before them,"[636] truly it is that, "The name of the LORD cometh from far, burning with his anger, and the burden thereof is heavy: his lips are full of indignation, and his tongue as a devouring fire: and his breath, as an overflowing stream, shall reach to the midst of the neck, to sift the nations with the sieve of vanity."[637] "The LORD shall cause his glorious voice to be heard, and shall shew the lighting down of his arm, with the indignation of his anger, and with the flame of a devouring fire, with scattering, and tempest, and hailstones. For through the voice of the LORD shall the Assyrian be beaten down, which smote with a rod."[638]

---

630   Acts 16:25,26
631   Jeremiah 30:6
632   Jeremiah 30:7-10
633   Joel 2:6
634   Joel 3:2
635   Isaiah 24:21,22
636   Joel 2:3
637   Isaiah 30:27,28
638   Isaiah 30:30,31

7. The great earthquake involving both Paul and Silas happened at a time when a "multitude rose up together against them: and the magistrates rent off their clothes, and commanded to beat them. And when they had laid many stripes upon them, they cast them into prison."[639] This scene of Paul and Silas represents them who will be reprimanded abused for the commandments of the Word and of His Priest's knowledge, but they will not be left to perish. The doors of the chambers of spiritual mutilation will open, and the chains on their conversation's conscience will fall, for the Spirit promises, "Ga'za shall be forsaken, and Ash'kelon a desolation: they shall drive out Ash'dod at the noon day, and Ek'ron shall be rooted up. Woe unto the inhabitants of the sea coast, the nation of the Cher'ethites! the word of the LORD is against you; O Canaan, the land of the Philis'tines, I will even destroy thee, that there shall be no inhabitant."[640]

8. Who are the Philis'tines? Says the Spirit, "Thus saith the Lord GOD; Because the Philis'tines have dealt by revenge, and have taken vengeance with a despiteful heart, to destroy it for the old hatred; therefore thus saith the Lord GOD; Behold, I will stretch out mine hand upon the Philis'tines, and I will cut off the Cher'ethims, and destroy the remnant of the sea coast. And I will execute great vengeance upon them with furious rebukes; and they shall know that I am the LORD, when I shall lay my vengeance upon them."[641] These are them that fulfill the word, "He will stretch out his hand against the north, and destroy Assyria; and will make Nineveh a desolation, and dry like a wilderness."[642] "This is the rejoicing city that dwelt carelessly, that said in her heart, I am, and there is none beside me: how is she become a desolation, a place for beasts to lie down in! every one that passeth by her shall hiss, and wag his hand."[643] For, there is only one that remains careless, as it says, "Sit in the dust, O virgin daughter of Babylon,"[644]

---

639 Acts 16:22,23
640 Zephaniah 2:4,5
641 Ezekiel 25:15-17
642 Zephaniah 2:13
643 Zephaniah 2:15
644 Isaiah 47:1

and, "Hear now this, thou that art given to pleasures, that dwellest carelessly, that sayest in thine heart, I am, and none else beside me."[645]

9. Such an institution is called, "A rejoicing city,"[646] or rather, as it says, "As at the report concerning Egypt, so shall they be sorely pained at the report of Tyre."[647] "Who hath taken this counsel against Tyre, the crowning city, whose merchants are princes, whose traffickers are the honourable of the earth?"[648] "The LORD hath given a commandment against the merchant city, to destroy the strong holds thereof."[649]

10. Again, we are brought to conclude that Egypt, Babylon, and Tyre, or Ty'rus, are one spiritual entity, and added to their body is the Philis'tines. Therefore the saying is fulfilled against this army by the name of the LORD's Son, "Thus saith the LORD; Behold, waters rise up out of the north, and shall be an overflowing flood, and shall overflow the land, and all that is therein; the city, and them that dwell therein: then the men shall cry, and all the inhabitants of the land shall howl. At the noise of the stamping of the hoofs of his strong horses, at the rushing of his chariots, and at the rumbling of his wheels, the fathers shall not look back to their children for feebleness of hands; because of the day that cometh to spoil all the Philis'tines, and to cut off from Ty'rus and Zi'don every helper that remaineth: for the LORD will spoil the Philis'tines."[650] "Baldness is come upon Ga'za; Ash'kelon is cut off with the remnant of their valley."[651]

11. Earlier it was mentioned, concerning the sun's institution at this time, "The gates thereof languish; they are black unto the ground; and the cry of Jerusalem is gone up."[652] This "Jerusalem," in context, is not the living God's Building, but is rather that tabernacle fulfilling the saying, "O Canaan, the land of the Philis'tines, I will even destroy thee."[653] There is a woe pronounced against Canaan at this time, or

---

645 Isaiah 47:8
646 Zephaniah 2:15
647 Isaiah 23:5
648 Isaiah 23:8
649 Isaiah 23:11
650 Jeremiah 47:2-4
651 Jeremiah 47:5
652 Jeremiah 14:2
653 Zephaniah 2:5

rather, against "the glorious land,"[654] for it has allowed itself to become a servant of the spirit of the Philis'tines, as it says, "He shall have power over the treasures of gold and of silver, and over all the precious things of Egypt."[655] If this is indeed that counterfeit Jerusalem, then she must have a *David*, which is why, at this time, the word will be fulfilled, "David lifted up his eyes, and saw the angel of the LORD stand between the earth and the heaven, having a drawn sword in his hand stretched out over Jerusalem. Then David and the elders of Israel, who were clothed in sackcloth, fell upon their faces."[656] Without a doubt, by this saying we return to the vision of the sixth seal to observe how "the sun became black as sackcloth of hair, and the moon became as blood; and the stars of heaven fell unto the earth."[657]

12. Again, it was told David on one occasion, "Thou shalt go no more out with us to battle, that thou quench not the light of Israel."[658] As David was that light of Israel, so too will that counterfeit *David* be that *light* of the sun for the then *Philis'tines* of *Canaan*, for the then modern *Egypt* and *Babylon* of the Revelation.

13. John observes the events leading up to the fall of this power, and at first he sees an earthquake occurring. Such an earthquake cannot fail of fulfilling the saying, "The graves were opened; and many bodies of the saints which slept arose, and came out of the graves after his resurrection, and went into the holy city, and appeared unto many. Now when the centurion, and they that were with him, watching Jesus, saw the earthquake, and those things that were done, they feared greatly, saying, Truly this was the Son of God."[659]

14. These things happened at the crucifixion and resurrection of the Word's Man. It is at this time, when the body of His knowledge should again find itself openly crucified, that the word will be fulfilled, "I will open your graves, and cause you to come up out of your graves,

---

654   Daniel 11:41
655   Daniel 11:43
656   1 Chronicles 21:16
657   Revelation 6:12,13
658   2 Samuel 21:17
659   Matthew 27:52-54

and bring you into the land of Israel,"⁶⁶⁰ and, "I seek out my sheep, and will deliver them out of all places where they have been scattered in the cloudy and dark day. And I will bring them out from the people, and gather them from the countries, and will bring them to their own land."⁶⁶¹ Ezekiel begins this time of reformation at a similar point mentioned by Joel, within the second chapter of Joel, for the two are bringing to light the same events designed for the same hour. On that day of "darkness" and "gloominess," of "clouds" and "thick darkness," "I will destroy the fat and the strong; I will feed them with judgment,"⁶⁶² says the Spirit. For this cause, it should be remembered how that, concerning His Christ's passing, an earthquake then took place, but at His resurrection, a great earthquake, or a terrible commotion, appeared. He warned, "Ye shall hear of wars and commotions,"⁶⁶³ for John saw, in the sixth seal, a great commotion, a great spiritual or doctrinal war in action, which "war" is the result of a resurrected mind boasting a supremacy framed around the *God* of the first day, for it was on the first day of the week that this great earthquake anciently occurred.

15. That of the cloudy and dark day cannot take place until the first earthquake has commenced. The crucifixion and resurrection are separate events with days between them. The crucified body of heaven's knowledge is the fulfillment of the saying, "Whosoever transgresseth, and abideth not in the doctrine of Christ,"⁶⁶⁴ but that second great earthquake occurs for fulfilling the saying, "Fear took hold upon them there, and pain, as of a woman in travail."⁶⁶⁵ When that great earthquake occurred, the soldiers became as dead men within their mind when observing the revelation of the Spirit's messenger. So too when that great earthquake of the sixth seal commences, there will be a very great shaking within the land of the living. The force of the heavenly Sanctuary will descend from its Place because the law of His Christ's

---

660   Ezekiel 37:12
661   Ezekiel 34:12,13
662   Ezekiel 34:16
663   Luke 21:9
664   2 John 1:9
665   Psalms 48:6

name, and the throne of His LORD God, have been violated, as it says, "They have transgressed the laws, changed the ordinance, broken the everlasting covenant."[666] The ordinance here mentioned is of "the ordinances of justice,"[667] in "that we might be justified by the faith of Jesus."[668] So then, "of how much sorer punishment, suppose ye, shall he be thought worthy, who hath trodden under foot the Son of God, and hath counted the blood of the covenant, wherewith he was sanctified, an unholy thing, and hath done despite unto the Spirit of grace?"[669]

16. The doctrine of Christ will be trifled with before the name of its LORD is violated, for this is how it began of old. The report against the early church was, "Thou hast left thy first love,"[670] and such a fall from the Spirit's pure doctrine occurred because they "became vain in their imaginations,"[671] for they honored "the creature more than the Creator."[672] As Eve obeyed the voice of the serpent, so the elders of the Christian church began to hold their perception of *the doctrine of Christ* above the fact and understanding contained within it, for they had no "love in the Spirit."[673] Obedience to the wisdom and knowledge of heaven's mediation will unseal the blessing that says, "To them gave he power to become the sons of God,"[674] and "this spake he of the Spirit which they that believe on him should receive."[675] This is why it says, "We might receive the promise of the Spirit through faith,"[676] for "we might be justified by faith"[677] on His Son's full name, but the error within Christian elders moved them to confess, "You are justified by the law,"[678] and, "Righteousness come by the law."[679]

---

666   Isaiah 24:5
667   Isaiah 58:2
668   Galatians 2:16
669   Hebrews 10:29
670   Revelation 2:4
671   Romans 1:21
672   Romans 1:25
673   Colossians 1:8
674   John 1:13
675   John 7:39
676   Galatians 3:14
677   Galatians 3:24
678   Galatians 5:4
679   Galatians 2:21

17. Grosser apostasy must first occur within that church professing service to *the LORD and Christ of the Bible* before she may then awaken and resurrect her sleeping mother's spirit to initiation a terrible earthquake. As apostasy entered into the early church by a falling away from the doctrine of His Christ's voice, and from abandoning sanctification by an experimental faith on heaven's will to then stubbornly observe the saying, "Made perfect by the flesh,"[680] so again it will be fulfilled in like manner. An image to the leopard beast will be erected and enforced within the government of the then religious world to remove minds from the Spirit's will to capture the desire of coarse priests. After worship should commence to that resurrected leopard beast, a great commotion or tumult will begin to forward its waves of ascendency, for it says, "Thine enemies make a tumult: and they that hate thee have lifted up the head. They have taken crafty counsel against thy people, and consulted against thy hidden ones. They have said, Come, and let us cut them off from being a nation; that the name of Israel may be no more in remembrance. For they have consulted together with one consent: they are confederate against thee."[681] Herein it is fulfilled, "The dragon was wroth with the woman, and went to make war with the remnant of her seed."[682]

18. Thus, ancient history will repeat itself according to the saying, "The Philis'tines put themselves in array against Israel."[683] "When E'li heard the noise of the crying, he said, What meaneth the noise of this tumult? And the man came in hastily, and told E'li. Now E'li was ninety and eight years old; and his eyes were dim, that he could not see. And the man said unto E'li, I am he that came out of the army, and I fled to day out of the army. And he said, What is there done, my son? And the messenger answered and said, Israel is fled before the Philistines, and there hath been also a great slaughter among the people, and thy two sons also, Hoph'ni and Phin'ehas, are dead, and the ark of God is taken."[684]

---

680   Galatians 3:3
681   Psalms 83:2-5
682   Revelation 12:17
683   1 Samuel 4:2
684   1 Samuel 4:14-17

19. Therefore "with the noise of a great tumult he hath kindled fire upon it, and the branches of it are broken. For the LORD of hosts, that planted thee, hath pronounced evil against thee, for the evil of the house of Israel and of the house of Judah, which they have done against themselves to provoke me to anger."[685] "Therefore will I do unto this house, which is called by my name, wherein ye trust, and unto the place which I gave to you and to your fathers, as I have done to Shi'loh. And I will cast you out of my sight, as I have cast out all your brethren, even the whole seed of E'phraim."[686] "I make this house like Shi'loh, and will make this city a curse to all the nations of the earth,"[687] says the Spirit.

20. At some point after the already apostate *Christian* church furthers her apostasy, every *Jewish* institution will fulfill the saying, "In that day seven women shall take hold of one man, saying, We will eat our own bread, and wear our own apparel: only let us be called by thy name, to take away our reproach."[688] Thus, it is fair to conclude that the sixth seal contains the formation of the image of the beast; of the established *Roman* Republic of Pagan Apostate *Christian Jews*; with the healing of the deadly wound of that impure spirit to form the *Papal Jewish* Republic of the Pagan States. Herein marks the beginning of great and terrible tremors upon the earth of the spiritually negligent against heaven's LORD and High Priest. Such amalgamation of two impure religious institutions demands the rebuke, "Babylon the great is fallen, is fallen, and is become the habitation of devils, and the hold of every foul spirit, and a cage of every unclean and hateful bird,"[689] therefore it says, "Shall I not visit for these things? saith the LORD: shall not my soul be avenged on such a nation as this?"[690]

---

685 Jeremiah 11:16,17
686 Jeremiah 7:14,15
687 Jeremiah 26:6
688 Isaiah 4:1
689 Revelation 18:2
690 Jeremiah 5:29

13

An Unfolding Vengeance

1. Scripture states, "The sun shall be turned into darkness, and the moon into blood, before the great and the terrible day of the LORD come."[691]

2. Before that wrath of the Lamb should appear, the sun and the moon will suffer, which is why the Spirit says, "I will shew wonders in the heavens and in the earth."[692] The wonders in the heavens and in the earth, and not simply in one or the other, bring the mind to consider the saying, "I will shake the heavens, and the earth shall remove out of her place, in the wrath of the LORD of hosts, and in the day of his fierce anger."[693]

3. The LORD's wrath is one event divided into two phases: the first being the wrath of plagues by the living God's Spirit; the second being the day of His Spirit's unrestrained anger through the face of His Son's knowledge. Before the day of His hot anger, the sun and the moon will suffer, and doubtless before His face's day is come, these wonders will ruin error's glory, even as it was said of old, "I will stretch out my hand,

---

691 Joel 2:31
692 Joel 2:30
693 Isaiah 13:13

and smite Egypt with all my wonders."⁶⁹⁴ These wonders that the Spirit calls, "Great judgments,"⁶⁹⁵ were plagues, which is why John wrote, "I heard another out of the altar say, Even so, Lord God Almighty, true and righteous are thy judgments,"⁶⁹⁶ for it says, "I heard a great voice out of the temple saying to the seven angels, Go your ways, and pour out the vials of the wrath of God upon the earth."⁶⁹⁷

4. Before she is handled by the LORD's Spirit, the institution that should again "speak great words against the most High, and shall wear out the saints of the most High, and think to change times and laws,"⁶⁹⁸ will be doubly visited of the Word for her overflowing cup of violation against Him and His assembly. This is why it is written, "Thou shalt know that I am the LORD, and that I have heard all thy blasphemies which thou hast spoken against the mountains of Israel, saying, They are laid desolate, they are given us to consume. Thus with your mouth ye have boasted against me, and have multiplied your words against me: I have heard them."⁶⁹⁹

5. When it should be fulfilled, "The dragon was wroth with the woman, and went to make war,"⁷⁰⁰ then it will be said, "He that toucheth you toucheth the apple of his eye."⁷⁰¹ There is enough proof to show that while the seven plagues fall against them that would willingly find themselves contrary to the Word's Faith, hard secular and spiritual events should take place against the Spirit's faithful. One visitation of God's Spirit will lead to another more complete judgment, and this will frustrate error's Regime. For as it says, "I will take from them the voice of mirth, and the voice of gladness, the voice of the bridegroom, and the voice of the bride, the sound of the millstones, and the light of the candle,"⁷⁰² so will it be fulfilled against "the people of the prince,"⁷⁰³

---

694   Exodus 3:20
695   Exodus 7:4
696   Revelation 1:7
697   Revelation 16:1
698   Daniel 7:25
699   Ezekiel 35:12,13
700   Revelation 12:17
701   Zechariah 2:8
702   Jeremiah 25:10
703   Daniel 9:26

"The light of a candle shall shine no more at all in thee; and the voice of the bridegroom and of the bride shall be heard no more at all in thee."[704] "Strong is the Lord God who judgeth her,"[705] for it says, "Who is this King of glory? The LORD strong and mighty, the LORD mighty in battle."[706] Therefore "he is strong that executeth his word: for the day of the LORD is great and very terrible; and who can abide it?"[707]

6. Of old, "The waters returned, and covered the chariots, and the horsemen, and all the host of Pharaoh that came into the sea after them; there remained not so much as one of them."[708] For this cause Moses said, "The LORD is a man of war."[709] "In the greatness of thine excellency thou hast overthrown them that rose up against thee: thou sentest forth thy wrath, which consumed them as stubble."[710] "The dukes of Edom shall be amazed; the mighty men of Moab, trembling shall take hold upon them; all the inhabitants of Canaan shall melt away. Fear and dread shall fall upon them; by the greatness of thine arm they shall be as still as a stone."[711] "The LORD shall reign for ever and ever."[712] "He hath triumphed gloriously: the horse and his rider hath he thrown into the sea."[713]

7. Before the LORD God was moved to deliver His people, plagues fell on Egypt. Before He appeared to save His own inheritance by His own power and understanding, He said, "I will at this time send all my plagues upon thine heart, and upon thy servants, and upon thy people; that thou mayest know that there is none like me in all the earth."[714] "I will cause it to rain a very grievous hail, such as hath not been in Egypt since the foundation thereof even until now."[715] "The LORD

---

704 Revelation 18:23
705 Revelation 18:8
706 Psalms 24:8
707 Joel 2:11
708 Exodus 14:28
709 Exodus 15:3
710 Exodus 15:7
711 Exodus 15:15,16
712 Exodus 15:18
713 Exodus 15:21
714 Exodus 9:14
715 Exodus 9:18

sent thunder and hail, and the fire ran along upon the ground; and the LORD rained hail upon the land of Egypt. So there was hail, and fire mingled with the hail, very grievous, such as there was none like it in all the land of Egypt since it became a nation."[716] For this cause it is said, when "the seventh angel poured out his vial into the air,"[717] "There fell upon men a great hail out of heaven, every stone about the weight of a talent: and men blasphemed God because of the plague of the hail; for the plague thereof was exceeding great."[718]

8. Of old it was said, "He had wrought his signs in Egypt, and his wonders in the field of Zo'an: and had turned their rivers into blood; and their floods, that they could not drink. He sent divers sorts of flies among them, which devoured them; and frogs, which destroyed them. He gave also their increase unto the caterpillar, and their labour unto the locust. He destroyed their vines with hail, and their sycomore trees with frost. He gave up their cattle also to the hail, and their flocks to hot thunderbolts. He cast upon them the fierceness of his anger, wrath, and indignation, and trouble, by sending evil angels among them. He made a way to his anger; he spared not their soul from death, but gave their life over to the pestilence; and smote all the firstborn in Egypt; the chief of their strength in the tabernacles of Ham."[719] Such events that took place of old, and before Israel was delivered from Pharaoh, will be done in the like *manner* as against them that "worship the beast and his image, and receive his mark in his forehead, or in his hand."[720]

9. By the time we reach the seventh plague, we arrive at the unfolding of the controversy within the sixth seal, for, by this plague, "every island fled away, and the mountains were not found,"[721] even as it is said, "Every mountain and island were moved out of their places."[722] When it is that we hear of His "hail," truly this moment marks that which says, "At the brightness that was before him his thick

---

716 Exodus 9:23,24
717 Revelation 16:17
718 Revelation 16:21
719 Psalm 78:43-51
720 Revelation 14:9
721 Revelation 16:20
722 Revelation 6:14

clouds passed, hail stones and coals of fire,"[723] for which cause it says, "A day of clouds and of thick darkness, as the morning spread upon the mountains";[724] this day is as "the light of the morning, when the sun riseth,"[725] for "his going forth is prepared as the morning."[726] Thus, says the psalmist, "My soul waiteth for the Lord more than they that watch for the morning,"[727] for "the night cometh, when no man can work,"[728] and this time of "night" is understood by the saying, "He hath laid my vine waste, and barked my fig tree: he hath made it clean bare, and cast it away; the branches thereof are made white,"[729] for it says, "Say not ye, There are yet four months, and then cometh harvest? behold, I say unto you, Lift up your eyes, and look on the fields; for they are white already to harvest."[730] This is why John writes, "Another angel came out of the temple, crying with a loud voice to him that sat on the cloud, Thrust in thy sickle, and reap: for the time is come for thee to reap; for the harvest of the earth is ripe."[731]

10. Notice that it is the harvest of the *earth* that is reaped, even "them that dwell on the earth, and to every nation, and kindred, and tongue, and people."[732] These of the *earth* are not that Israel of the Word, for His Spirit's Israel, at this time, are "redeemed from among men";[733] are sectioned out and personally purified by His wisdom and knowledge beforehand; for it says, "These are they which were not defiled with women."[734] Herein the word is fulfilled, "They may possess the remnant of Edom, and of all the heathen, which are called by my name, saith the LORD."[735] After the time that the conversion of the then Gentiles should come, after all have heard and have had the

---

723 Psalms 18:12
724 Joel 2:2
725 2 Samuel 23:24
726 Hosea 6:3
727 Psalms 130:6
728 John 9:4
729 Joel 1:7
730 John 4:35
731 Revelation 14:15
732 Revelation 14:6
733 Revelation 14:4
734 Revelation 14:4
735 Amos 9:12

chance to either reject or accept the Spirit's full name and doctrine, after the perverse institution of the age should find fault with these men joined to the Spirit's heavenly House, and after that institution should move her State to erase them, all traditional reaping will cease, and it will be that "another angel came out of the temple which is in heaven, he also having a sharp sickle. And another angel came out from the altar, which had power over fire; and cried with a loud cry to him that had the sharp sickle, saying, Thrust in thy sharp sickle, and gather the clusters of the vine of the earth; for her grapes are fully ripe."[736]

11. The clusters of the vine of the earth are those ministers of Pharaoh's household that "drink of the wine of the wrath of her fornication,"[737] and that woman of wrath being that gross institution called, "Great Babylon."[738] The clusters of the vine of the earth; "the kings of the earth"[739] that "have committed fornication, and the inhabitants of the earth"[740] that "have been made drunk with the wine of her fornication";[741] and the earth herself, is eventually delivered "into the great winepress of the wrath of God,"[742] which wrath is synonymous with that noted by John, who writes, "He treadeth the winepress of the fierceness and wrath of Almighty God."[743] At this time, "great Babylon came in remembrance before God, to give unto her the cup of the wine of the fierceness of his wrath."[744] Thus far the instruction was, "Pour out the vials of the wrath of God upon the earth,"[745] yet now, in the seventh plague, the institution of error is singled out, even to where it is said, "Rejoice over her, thou heaven, and ye holy apostles and prophets; for God hath avenged you on her."[746]

---

736   Revelation 14:17,18
737   Revelation 14:8
738   Revelation 16:19
739   Revelation 17:2
740   Revelation 17:2
741   Revelation 17:2
742   Revelation 14:19
743   Revelation 19:15
744   Revelation 16:19
745   Revelation 16:1
746   Revelation 18:20

12. As it was accomplished of old, so it will be done again. Before the LORD God should, by His Spirit, actually *save* His host to plant all eyes within His mountain, seven final plagues will first fall, and at some point during those plagues, there will come a time of anxiety for heaven's assembly, a season of agitation where Pharaoh will rise up in anger for the spiritual shame that will come upon his operation, but he will not harm that family known and separated of the Word, for his estate will be overthrown by the words of the face of heaven's General. The saying will be fulfilled, "Jeremiah wrote in a book all the evil that should come upon Babylon."[747] "And Jeremiah said to Seraiah";[748] "this Seraiah was a quiet prince";[749] "When thou hast made an end of reading this book, thou shalt bind a stone to it, and cast it into the midst of Euphra'tes: and thou shalt say, Thus shall Babylon sink, and shall not rise from the evil that I will bring upon her."[750] For this cause it is said, "And a mighty angel took up a stone like a great millstone, and cast it into the sea, saying, Thus with violence shall that great city Babylon be thrown down, and shall be found no more at all."[751]

13. The events of the sixth seal cannot find place at any time before the spirit of the ecclesiastical history mentioned in the previous seals should be healed to continue its reign over the religious world. This healing cannot fail to begin at any time before it is fulfilled, "Babylon hath been a golden cup in the LORD'S hand, that made all the earth drunken: the nations have drunken of her wine; therefore the nations are mad,"[752] even as it is said, "The nations were angry."[753]

14. Before His conversion, Paul confessed of his actions towards heaven's servants, saying, "Being exceedingly mad against them, I persecuted them,"[754] for to be "mad" is to be wroth or drunken with a feverish religious violence, wherefore it says, "The dragon was wroth

---

747 Jeremiah 51:60
748 Jeremiah 51:61
749 Jeremiah 51:59
750 Jeremiah 51:63,64
751 Revelation 18:21
752 Jeremiah 51:7
753 Revelation 11:18
754 Acts 26:11

with the woman."⁷⁵⁵ Of old it says, "Ye provoked the LORD to wrath, so that the LORD was angry with you to have destroyed you,"⁷⁵⁶ for the "angry" nations are the "mad" and "drunk" denominations provoked to wrath against a specific congregation, and their anger cannot fully turn to wrath until they are made drunk, therefore the tremors of the great commotion of the sixth seal should last from the healing of the deadly wound until it should again be fulfilled, "Take the wine cup of this fury at my hand, and cause all the nations, to whom I send thee, to drink it. And they shall drink, and be moved, and be mad, because of the sword that I will send among them."⁷⁵⁷

15. The denominations will be enraged against them that are not damaged by the plagues, yet it says, "A noise shall come even to the ends of the earth; for the LORD hath a controversy with the nations, he will plead with all flesh; he will give them that are wicked to the sword, saith the LORD."⁷⁵⁸ For "the slain of the LORD shall be at that day from one end of the earth even unto the other end of the earth: they shall not be lamented, neither gathered, nor buried; they shall be dung upon the ground."⁷⁵⁹

16. "The day is near, even the day of the LORD is near, a cloudy day";⁷⁶⁰ "a day of darkness and of gloominess, a day of clouds and of thick darkness";⁷⁶¹ "it shall be the time of the heathen. And the sword shall come upon Egypt, and great pain shall be in Ethio'pia, when the slain shall fall in Egypt, and they shall take away her multitude, and her foundations shall be broken down."⁷⁶² "Thus saith the Lord GOD; I will also make the multitude of Egypt to cease by the hand of Nebuchadrez'zar king of Babylon. He and his people with him, the terrible of the nations, shall be brought to destroy the land: and they shall draw their swords against Egypt, and fill the land with the slain."⁷⁶³

---

755   Revelation 12:17
756   Deuteronomy 9:8
757   Jeremiah 25:15,16
758   Jeremiah 25:31
759   Jeremiah 25:33
760   Ezekiel 30:3
761   Joel 2:2
762   Ezekiel 30:3,4
763   Ezekiel 30:10,11

17. This king of Babylon is representative of that commanding Faith who "hath on his vesture and on his thigh a name written, KING OF KINGS, AND LORD OF LORDS,"[764] and with this chief understanding are "the armies which were in heaven."[765] The events of the sixth seal conceal the time of the angry nations through to the time of the wrath and reign of heaven's throne religion. Seeing as how drunkenness leads to fornication, and that intoxication will lead to persecution, which persecution will lead to the fury of the Spirit's plagues to further anger the nations; which denominations will fall by the Spirit's sword for good on His name's appointed day; the angering of the nations, and that wrath and victory mentioned by the elders of the nations,[766] cannot be any thing but the summation of the events of the sixth seal.

18. Pharaoh must again be made mad, and this anger upheld by his heart hardening from a message by heaven's representatives, as it says, "Tidings out of the east and out of the north shall trouble him: therefore he shall go forth with great fury to destroy, and utterly to make away many."[767] At some point after these messages are given, "there shall be a great cry throughout all the land of Egypt,"[768] and the plagues therein will further harden the heart of error's men to execute their anger in full, and no longer by warnings. Then will the shape of the Spirit's Priest rise up; "then shall the LORD go forth, and fight against those nations, as when he fought in the day of battle";[769] for it says, "The heaven departed as a scroll when it is rolled together; and every mountain and island were moved out of their places."[770]

---

764 Revelation 19:16
765 Revelation 19:14
766 Revelation 11:16-18
767 Daniel 11:44
768 Exodus 11:6
769 Zechariah 14:3
770 Revelation 6:14

14

A Quaking Line

1. John writes, "I beheld when he had opened the sixth seal, and, lo, there was a great earthquake; and the sun became black as sackcloth of hair, and the moon became as blood; and the stars of heaven fell unto the earth, even as a fig tree casteth her untimely figs, when she is shaken of a mighty wind. And the heaven departed as a scroll when it is rolled together; and every mountain and island were moved out of their places."[771]

2. As it is seen, for example, in the fifteenth division of the Revelation, that John saw seven angels holding the seven plagues of the Spirit's wrath, and was then shown them that did escape that wrath, and the ones for whom that wrath is ordained, to then fall back into his first sight of the scene of the outpouring of the Spirit's wrath, so too may the sixth seal be understood as a moving vision of one event. Before the day that the LORD God's name should come, the *light* of the sun and moon should find themselves in strange pain, for as John says of the Word's new dispensation, "I saw no temple therein,"[772] and, "The city had no

---

771 Revelation 6:12-14
772 Revelation 21:22

need of the sun, neither of the moon, to shine in it,"[773] it is evident that the sun and the moon comprise the established temple of error's then kingdom. We are made to observe a suffering temple within the sixth seal, yet that temple and its rule is not yet handled, for it is yet alive while changed. Upon the sixth seal's opening, John observes a great earthquake, and it appears that after he beholds a terrible commotion, he is then brought to a point where history pronounces the fall of this empire.

3. The beginning of the end of the institution of these later times cannot begin at any other time than at the seven last plagues. The first three plagues appear to set in motion a reaction from them suffering under the fourth plague, who "blasphemed the name of God, which hath power over these plagues."[774] It is the violation of the Spirit's name; which is the name and doctrine of the LORD and Father of heaven's throne; that ultimately demands His falling wrath. This is true because it says, "They repented not to give him glory,"[775] for John previously heard them that had overcome the times say, "Who shall not fear thee, O Lord, and glorify thy name? for thou only art holy."[776] There is a reason why these should say that the LORD God is the only holy name in existence, for they remember how He once said, "To whom will ye liken me, and make me equal, and compare me, that we may be like?"[777] for, there should exist *a name* in full civil and ecclesiastical power "who opposeth and exalteth himself above all that is called God, or that is worshipped."[778] This "son of perdition"[779] would not allow service to the true Word upon his perdition after his *healing,* for, under his national jurisdiction, the message was outlawed, "Fear God, and give glory to him...worship him that made heaven, and earth, and the sea, and the fountains of waters."[780]

---

773 Revelation 21:23
774 Revelation 16:9
775 Revelation 16:9
776 Revelation 15:4
777 Isaiah 46:5
778 2 Thessalonians 2:4
779 2 Thessalonians 2:3
780 Revelation 14:7

4. The name of the living God is concealed within this message, for it reveals the creative authority of His voice, even as it says, "In six days the LORD made heaven and earth, the sea, and all that in them is, and rested the seventh day: wherefore the LORD blessed the Sabbath day, and hallowed it."[781] The Word's creation will have "the seal of God in their foreheads,"[782] even as it says, "Having his Father's name written in their foreheads."[783] The name of the Spirit is His LORD's seal, and the controversy of the age will be over the Word's name, even as it will be against them that "worship the beast and his image, and receive his mark in his forehead, or in his hand."[784] The "marks" and the "seals" are not literal, but are those things written on the conscience of the conversation to establish service and security to a religious ideal. Because the Spirit's name is blasphemed, them that carry the seal of His LORD and Father aggravate priests and ministers that observe the name and day of the error, and who also honor his government, therefore it should, throughout the plagues, be fulfilled, "He opened his mouth in blasphemy against God, to blaspheme his name, and his tabernacle, and them that dwell in heaven. And it was given unto him to make war with the saints."[785]

5. Blasphemy against the Word's name is followed by persecution. Of the fourth angel within the fourth plague, it says, "Power was given unto him to scorch men with fire,"[786] even as the Spirit says of His two witnesses,[787] "If any man will hurt them, fire proceedeth out of their mouth."[788] It is the name of God that has power over these plagues, and the Spirit confesses of His witnesses, "These have power to shut heaven, that it rain not in the days of their prophecy: and have power over waters to turn them to blood, and to smite the earth with all plagues, as often as they will."[789]

---

781 Exodus 20:11
782 Revelation 9:4
783 Revelation 14:1
784 Revelation 14:9
785 Revelation 13:6,7
786 Revelation 16:8
787 Revelation 11:3
788 Revelation 11:5
789 Revelation 11:6

6. He who had power to shut up heaven fulfills the saying, "Eli'as was a man subject to like passions as we are, and he prayed earnestly that it might not rain: and it rained not on the earth."[790] And he who had power to smite with plagues and turn waters to blood was Moses, even as it says, "He lifted up the rod, and smote the waters that were in the river, in the sight of Pharaoh, and in the sight of his servants; and all the waters that were in the river were turned to blood."[791]

7. Scripture says, "The name of God, which hath power over these plagues,"[792] for that name is synonymous with that one of whom it is written, "There arose not a prophet since in Israel like unto Moses."[793] Moses is a figurative illustration of the LORD's immutable Word, even as he himself says of his office, "I stood between the LORD and you at that time, to shew you the word of the LORD."[794] It was this man that said, "Thou shalt fear the LORD thy God, and serve him, and shalt swear by his name,"[795] thus placing the first four commandments as a necessary and binding duty upon the LORD's assembly, which duty, if broken, would fulfill the promise, "I will even appoint over you terror, consumption, and the burning ague, that shall consume the eyes, and cause sorrow of heart."[796] "I will destroy your high places, and cut down your images, and cast your carcases upon the carcases of your idols, and my soul shall abhor you. And I will make your cities waste, and bring your sanctuaries unto desolation, and I will not smell the savour of your sweet odours. And I will bring the land into desolation: and your enemies which dwell therein shall be astonished at it."[797]

8. In order for the seven last plagues to fall, man-kind must fill up the cup of their allowed violation against the name and authority of the Word's heavenly ministry. The Spirit's name is indeed violated by the time the first of the final seven plagues fall, for herein the saying is

---

790 James 5:17
791 Exodus 7:20
792 Revelation 16:9
793 Deuteronomy 34:10
794 Deuteronomy 5:5
795 Deuteronomy 6:13
796 Leviticus 26:16
797 Leviticus 26:30-32

fulfilled, "Shall the throne of iniquity have fellowship with thee, which frameth mischief by a law?"[798] and, "It is time for thee, LORD, to work: for they have made void thy law."[799] At this point in history, the saying is fulfilled, "Therefore hath the curse devoured the earth, and they that dwell therein are desolate: therefore the inhabitants of the earth are burned, and few men left,"[800] "because they have transgressed the laws, changed the ordinance, broken the everlasting covenant,"[801] yet during this time is "the dragon wroth with the woman, and went to make war with the remnant of her seed, which keep the commandments of God, and have the testimony of Jesus."[802]

9. Eli'jah represents messengers that possess the Spirit's testimony during a time of great apostasy, being one called, "He that troubleth Israel."[803] Out of fear and distress Eli'jah said, "It is enough; now, O LORD, take away my life,"[804] for he had just heard of a great threat against his life. "Jez'ebel sent a messenger unto Eli'jah, saying, So let the gods do to me, and more also, if I make not thy life as the life of one of them by to morrow,"[805] for he had beforehand slain the false prophets of Israel. Such that are the Word's representatives, at the time of a worldwide pagan apostate *Christian* dominion, will hear from the Spirit's host, "Ye may know how that the LORD doth put a difference between the Egyptians and Israel,"[806] for the saying will be fulfilled, "He shall deliver thee from the snare of the fowler, and from the noisome pestilence,"[807] and, "A thousand shall fall at thy side, and ten thousand at thy right hand; but it shall not come nigh thee."[808] Therefore, "Come, my people, enter thou into thy chambers, and shut thy doors about

---

798 Psalms 94:20
799 Psalms 119:126
800 Isaiah 24:6
801 Isaiah 24:5
802 Revelation 12:17
803 1 Kings 18:17
804 1 Kings 19:4
805 1 Kings 19:2
806 Exodus 11:7
807 Psalm 91:3
808 Psalm 91:7

thee: hide thyself as it were for a little moment, until the indignation be overpast,"[809] heaven's host will announce.

10. The falling plagues will in fact devour them that do not have the Spirit's seal within the spirit of their mind, and this will enrage them against those who suffer no inward trauma by them, seeing as how they are already kept by the wisdom of the LORD's Spirit. This band of people will be known as them that have brought on these plagues because they do not reverence the mandated government religion, and for this reason "there shall be a time of trouble, such as never was since there was a nation even to that same time."[810] But it is not the seed of Eli'jah and of Abraham that execute the plagues; it is "the name of God, which hath power over these plagues."[811] It is here, at the fourth plague that, if they have not begun to already do so, the dragon should further engage his self against heaven's seed. The desecration of the LORD's name is followed by persecution, and seeing as how, at this plague, power is given to the sun to scorch ministers with fire, even as it was given to His witnesses to scorch with fire, the LORD's laws and testimony, at this time, should equally be united in suffering grosser hardship as His host goes forward conquering in His name.

11. At this time of the sixth seal, "the great city"[812] is known of the Word, for that "great Babylon came in remembrance before God."[813] Although this great earthquake of the sixth seal may be likened to that outpouring of the seventh vial of wrath, it appears John beholds the events that should contain both the resurrection and fall of a city within the sixth seal, and with her works that warrant the Spirit's plagues, which works provoke such a great earthquake. Although it may be fair to say that both great earthquakes mentioned in the sixth seal and seventh plague are synonymous, again, the established line of the previous seals should not be forgotten. An earthquake builds up in force until it quits, and the sixth seal should begin with a trembling of those powers on earth that seek to shake also the heavens, yet she who desires fame will

---

809   Isaiah 26:20
810   Daniel 12:1
811   Revelation 16:9
812   Revelation 16:19
813   Revelation 16:19

bring upon herself that force of the Spirit, which omnipotence shakes both the heavens and the earth. Thus, it appears that John beheld an earthquake in vision illustrating a line of events that should contain the elevation and wrathful dominion of the spirit of the church of the seals, only to end with the complete overthrow of this abomination for the reign of the heavenly Sanctuary's name and throne by His Son's vengeful voice.

12. That earthquake owning power such as was not since men were upon the earth is but the last event of the sixth seal's earthquake, for the seventh plague brings to view how it is said, "I saw the beast, and the kings of the earth, and their armies, gathered together to make war against him that sat on the horse, and against his army,"[814] where the result will be, "The heaven departed as a scroll when it is rolled together,"[815] and, "Every island fled away, and the mountains were not found."[816] This earthquake of the seventh plague appears to be the end of that earthquake mentioned within the sixth seal; this is the great earthquake of the sixth seal at its height; and that sixth seal beginning with the great commotion to bring back to life the spirit of that woman who suffered a terrible wound, only to see her suffer plagues, and a woe, for the unsanctified ambition enclosed within her heart. Each of the previous seals contain the history of the same spirit of the same church, and the sixth seal is no different. She will again "kill with sword, and with hunger, and with death, and with the beasts of the earth,"[817] yet, for her works, she will feel pain that will harden her heart, only to have the voice of heaven's Son, in the now unbearable light of His LORD and Father's name, deliver the final blow to her reign and influence.

13. If indeed the great earthquake of the sixth seal should be linked to that vision saying, "The same hour was a great earthquake, and the tenth part of the city fell, and in the earthquake were slain of men seven thousand: and the remnant were affrighted, and gave glory to the God of heaven,"[818] then the link should not be naturally or literally made,

---

814 Revelation 19:19
815 Revelation 6:14
816 Revelation 16:20
817 Revelation 6:8
818 Revelation 11:13

but formed in likeness of a figure, for it is a spiritual representation. How she fell of old, she will again fall, except her fall will be accomplished by the name of the Word's Faith in omnipotent force, and her true bridegroom to be "cast into the bottomless pit"[819] to inevitably fulfill the saying, "The devil that deceived them was cast into the lake of fire and brimstone, where the beast and the false prophet are."[820] The sixth seal brings to view the fully resurrected spirit of an apostate church; for it "shall ascend out of the bottomless pit, and go into perdition";[821] her counterfeit glory and dominion, the terrible persecution committed by her while the seven last plagues pour out on her, and also the supreme reign of the living God's science by the vengeance of His Word and Spirit. Therefore, this sixth seal cannot open at any time later, or earlier, than the full ascendancy of the mind and labor of the leopard beast from out of the place where it rests.

14. The angel tells John that this same beast that he saw should come up out her grave and go into perdition a second time. The first five seals make no mention of her complete fall, but only of her elevation. As there is no fall mentioned of her, it is almost as if it is not an important subject of the seals, for she continues as if never subdued, and indeed the complexion of the seals give off that notion until the sixth. As the previous seals open with the sound of thunder, which sound delineates some sort of overthrowing, so too the sixth seal includes the overthrowing and shaking of the *earth* by the institution of the seals, only to have her government completely overturned by the Spirit of heaven's throne. Again, it is observed that from the time the nations should be angry, and until the wrath of heaven's will is come, the sound and vibrations of an earthquake increasing in strength should shake the inhabitants of heaven and earth.

---

819 Revelation 20:3
820 Revelation 20:10
821 Revelation 17:8

15

Establishing Judgment's Line

1. There is enough evidence here presented to properly discern that the vision of the sixth seal is not a singular vision, but is rather a line of events exposing two major themes. The primary focus of the five previous seals was the ecclesiastical history of an apostate Christian institution and her labor to fraudulently establish her voice as king and queen of the LORD's earth, and the sixth seal should confess to matters that are no different. This vision of the sixth seal relays information that contains imagery not only of her rule and authority, but also of that relating to her decay and sentence of judgment. The vision most emphatically exposes her overthrow by the true Word of the earth; which Word is the law and commandment of the LORD's High Priest; while also advancing the vision of that counterfeit *David*, whose doctrine is framed by the spirit of the son of perdition.

2. John wrote, "I beheld when he had opened the sixth seal, and, lo, there was a great earthquake,"[822] and it is fair to say that John, by this vision, is present, in spirit, in the day when this should occur. As he sees what he sees transpiring, it is that he is become them that should afterwards behold that scene at the appointed time of its fulfillment. John observes a great earthquake at the opening of the sixth seal, and

---

822 Revelation 6:12

so the question is, "What is an earthquake?" We find the answer in the sayings, "The earth was divided,"[823] and, "There was a division among the people because of him."[824] The sudden and unscheduled movement of rock within the earth's crust causes an earthquake. Thus, at this point in church history, the word is fulfilled, "Of the Rock that begat thee thou art unmindful, and hast forgotten God that formed thee,"[825] and, "The fool hath said in his heart, There is no God. They are corrupt, they have done abominable work,"[826] for it says, "They have made void thy law,"[827] seeing as how such ministers "frameth mischief by a law"[828] to shake and divide the earth.

3. At this point in ecclesiastical history, "the earth also was corrupt before God, and the earth was filled with violence."[829] Says the psalmist, "I have seen violence and strife in the city. Day and night they go about it upon the walls thereof: mischief also and sorrow are in the midst of it. Wickedness is in the midst thereof: deceit and guile depart not from her streets,"[830] therefore it is said, "They shall run to and fro in the city; they shall run upon the wall, they shall climb up upon the houses; they shall enter in at the windows like a thief. The earth shall quake before them; the heavens shall tremble: the sun and the moon shall be dark, and the stars shall withdraw their shining."[831]

4. We see, by the vision of the sixth seal, the scene of the earth's corruption and the scene of her reform, for the sun became black because of the burning felt by them inhabiting the earth, as it says, "Black like an oven because of the terrible famine,"[832] for it is fulfilled, "Nebuchadnez'zar king of Babylon came, he, and all his host, against Jerusalem, and pitched against it."[833] "Famine prevailed in the city, and

---

823   1 Chronicles 1:19
824   John 7:43
825   Deuteronomy 32:18
826   Psalms 14:1
827   Psalms 119:126
828   Psalms 94:20
829   Genesis 6:11
830   Psalms 55:9-11
831   Joel 2:9,10
832   Lamentations 10:5
833   2 Kings 25:1

there was no bread for the people of the land."[834] The Spirit "brought upon them the king of the Chal'dees, who slew their young men with the sword in the house of their sanctuary, and had no compassion upon young man or maiden, old man, or him that stooped for age: he gave them all into his hand."[835] For this cause, we may understand that because of her violence against heaven's Faith, the institution of the sixth seal; that great Egyptian Babylon; and all that are within her, will fall by the hand of the appointed kingdom or family of the LORD's Spirit. For the Spirit said by the prophet, "What have Ye to do with me, O Tyre, and Zi'don, and all the coasts of Palestine?"[836] Who is Palestine? It says, "Sorrow shall take hold on the inhabitants of Palesti'na,"[837] and, "The inhabitants of Canaan shall melt away,"[838] for, "Palestine" and "Palesti'na" are one, meaning, in reality, "Philistine," which is why it says, "O Canaan, the land of the Philis'tines."[839]

5. A woe, at the sound of the sixth seal, is gone out against "Canaan," against "Jerusalem," that "glorious land," and the religious establishment they wholly uphold. A woe is gone out against "the nation of the Cher'ethites,"[840] but who are they? It says, "There went out after him Jo'ab's men, and the Cher'ethites, and the Pel'ethites, and all the mighty men: and they went out of Jerusalem,"[841] for these are mighty men of war descending from *Jerusalem*, even as one told David, "We made an invasion upon the south of the Cher'ethites, and upon the coast which belongeth to Judah."[842] A curse is therefore pronounced against that nation bearing the greatest army in the earth, which is why it is that the glorious land; who in vision is *Egypt*; should hand over "his power, and his seat, and great authority"[843] to her that should "ascend out of the

---

834   2 Kings 25:3
835   2 Chronicles 36:17
836   Joel 3:4
837   Exodus 15:14
838   Exodus 15:15
839   Zephaniah 2:5
840   Zephaniah 2:5
841   2 Samuel 20:7
842   1 Samuel 30:14
843   Revelation 13:2

bottomless pit,"[844] because it is with the denomination of this nation; in her grosser apostate form; that she does "go into perdition."[845] Against this nation trifling with the Rock of the LORD's earth to cause a terrible shaking in the earth; "and that Rock was Christ";[846] heaven's Spirit will arise to personally handle.

6. Herein is why the Spirit says, "The great city was divided into three parts, and the cities of the nations fell";[847] these three parts cannot be any thing else but the sun, the moon, and the stars. For this cause it will be fulfilled, "Thus saith the Lord GOD to Tyrus; Shall not the isles shake at the sound of thy fall, when the wounded cry, when the slaughter is made in the midst of thee? Then all the princes of the sea shall come down from their thrones, and lay away their robes, and put off their broidered garments: they shall clothe themselves with trembling; they shall sit upon the ground, and shall tremble at every moment, and be astonished at thee. And they shall take up a lamentation for thee, and say to thee, How art thou destroyed, that wast inhabited of seafaring men, the renowned city, which wast strong in the sea, she and her inhabitants, which cause their terror to be on all that haunt it!"[848]

7. Again, it will be fulfilled against the modern sect of the Philis'tines, "Thus saith the LORD; Behold, waters rise up out of the north, and shall be an overflowing flood, and shall overflow the land, and all that is therein; the city, and them that dwell therein: then the men shall cry, and all the inhabitants of the land shall howl. At the noise of the stamping of the hoofs of his strong horses, at the rushing of his chariots, and at the rumbling of his wheels, the fathers shall not look back to their children for feebleness of hands; because of the day that cometh to spoil all the Philis'tines, and to cut off from Ty'rus and Zi'don every helper that remaineth: for the LORD will spoil the Philis'tines, the remnant of the country of Caph'tor. Baldness is come upon Ga'za; Ash'kelon is cut off with the remnant of their valley: how long wilt thou cut thyself? O thou sword of the LORD, how long will it be ere thou be

---

844   Revelation 17:8
845   Revelation 17:8
846   1 Corinthians 10:4
847   Revelation 16:19
848   Ezekiel 26:15-17

quiet? put up thyself into thy scabbard, rest, and be still. How can it be quiet, seeing the LORD hath given it a charge against Ash'kelon, and against the sea shore? there hath he appointed it."[849]

8. What we have before us, in spirit, is the counterfeit king of the north versus the true king of the north. Egypt, Tyre, Ty'rus, the Philis'tines, and Edom, are all understood to be the same entity called, "The northern army."[850] Against this northern army will come the true king of the north and that right host, which assembly is that congregation bearing the name and will of heaven's Faith and Spirit; it will be the Faith and Spirit of heaven's host that personally devours the three divisions of great Babylon.

9. John saw that the moon became as blood, and this he saw because the vision is twofold. John said, "I saw the woman drunken with the blood of the saints, and with the blood of the martyrs of Jesus,"[851] for "in her was found the blood of prophets, and of saints, and of all that were slain upon the earth."[852] While the sun has been proven to be that false bridegroom; that counterfeit *David* of *Egypt*; the moon is the sun's bride; or his religious institution; and to the woman of this son of perdition belongs much blood and terror. It is for this reason that it says, "They have shed the blood of saints and prophets, and thou hast given them blood to drink; for they are worthy,"[853] and, "The angel thrust in his sickle into the earth, and gathered the vine of the earth, and cast it into the great winepress of the wrath of God. And the winepress was trodden without the city, and blood came out of the winepress."[854]

10. The vision of the sun and the moon is one vision explaining a line of events from start to finish. The institution that seeks to divide the earth; as it says, "He shall plant the tabernacles of his palace between the seas";[855] will forward a terrible famine that will result in many souls suffering her blood upon them, yet this same institution

---

849   Jeremiah 47:1-7
850   Joel 2:20
851   Revelation 17:6
852   Revelation 18:24
853   Revelation 16:6
854   Revelation 14:19,20
855   Daniel 11:44

will be filled with complete famine and complete sorrow for all that she has accomplished throughout her reign, and up until that time of her overthrow; this is true meaning of the fallen sun and moon.

11. Now, the stars also fell from heaven, even as John once said, "I saw a star fall from heaven,"[856] for we are told that "stars" are the "angels" or "messengers" of the churches.[857] Even though it should be fulfilled, "The dragon was wroth with the woman, and went to make war,"[858] and, "His tail drew the third part of the stars of heaven, and did cast them to the earth,"[859] truly this work will not go past the Spirit's eyes, for it will be fulfilled, "Howl, ye shepherds, and cry; and wallow yourselves in the ashes, ye principal of the flock: for the days of your slaughter and of your dispersions are accomplished; and ye shall fall like a pleasant vessel. And the shepherds shall have no way to flee, nor the principal of the flock to escape. A voice of the cry of the shepherds, and an howling of the principal of the flock, shall be heard: for the LORD hath spoiled their pasture. And the peaceable habitations are cut down because of the fierce anger of the LORD."[860]

12. These events fulfill that "lamentation for Ty'rus,"[861] which states, "Thy riches, and thy fairs, thy merchandise, thy mariners, and thy pilots, thy calkers, and the occupiers of thy merchandise, and all thy men of war, that are in thee, and in all thy company which is in the midst of thee, shall fall into the midst of the seas in the day of thy ruin."[862] "The merchandise of gold, and silver, and precious stones, and of pearls, and fine linen, and purple, and silk, and scarlet, and all thyine wood, and all manner vessels of ivory, and all manner vessels of most precious wood, and of brass, and iron, and marble, and cinnamon, and odours, and ointments, and frankincense, and wine, and oil, and fine flour, and wheat, and beasts, and sheep, and horses, and chariots, and slaves, and souls of men. And the fruits that thy soul lusted after are

---

856 Revelation 9:1
857 Revelation 1:20
858 Revelation 12:17
859 Revelation 12:4
860 Jeremiah 25:34-37
861 Ezekiel 27:2
862 Ezekiel 27:27

departed from thee, and all things which were dainty and goodly are departed from thee, and thou shalt find them no more at all."[863]

13. Notice how it says of the great city, "Thou shalt find them no more at all,"[864] and how that for Ty'rus it says, "Thou shalt be a terror, and never shalt be any more."[865] Again, all of the figures of old; Egypt, Tyre, Ty'rus, the Philis'tines, and E'dom; represent that spiritually gross age foreshadowed to appear under the sixth seal. The city will be divided into three by the seventh plague, and this is why the vision of the sixth seal cannot be randomly adjusted, for the institution of the sixth seal accomplishes the same work as heaven's Spirit, howbeit in ways contrary to His name. Therefore, as it says that the stars fell, so too at this time "the cities of the nations fell."[866] We read, concerning that "city," "The holy city,"[867] and, "The tabernacle of God,"[868] for the habitations of the denominations fell, along with their angels or messengers, or rather, the houses of "all the families of the kingdom of the north"[869] became no more through the impression of the Word's throne. "The clusters of the vine of the earth"[870] meet their end with the vine of the earth at this time, which is why the same great winepress of wrath for them is the same cup of the fierceness of His wrath, which wrath brings us to when His name's voice "treadeth the winepress of the fierceness and wrath of Almighty God."[871]

14. The vision of the sixth seal cannot begin at any other time than when all should be forced to have their heart and mind divided between heaven's course and the serpent's philosophy. When "they have done violence to the law,"[872] when "they gather themselves together against the soul of the righteous, and condemn the innocent blood,"[873] then

---

863 Revelation 18:12-14
864 Revelation 18:14
865 Ezekiel 27:36
866 Revelation 16:19
867 Revelation 21:2
868 Revelation 21:3
869 Jeremiah 1:15
870 Revelation 14:18
871 Revelation 19:15
872 Zephaniah 3:4
873 Psalms 94:21

will "they have said, Come, and let us cut them off from being a nation; that the name of Israel may be no more in remembrance."[874] The name of *Israel* is contained within the name of their LORD and God. These are them that say, "The desire of our soul is to thy name, and to the remembrance of thee."[875] It is not just that there is war against a certain people for no reason, but there is war for the sake of a name, and there is controversy over absolute civil and religious authority over the soul and conscience of mankind. When the *earth* should be greatly divided because of a mark of authority, then should that great commotion in the earth begin, and as its waves of terror rise in height, another division will occur, and them that are divided in this division will see their confidence come to an end, and will be no more of that former mind.

15. "The LORD trieth the righteous: but the wicked and him that loveth violence his soul hateth. Upon the wicked he shall rain snares, fire and brimstone, and an horrible tempest: this shall be the portion of their cup."[876]

---

874 Psalms 83:4
875 Isaiah 26:8
876 Psalms 11:5,6

16

The Philis'tines, Saul, And Jonathan

1. An investigation of the scenes within the first book of Samuel, chapters thirteen and fourteen, reveal the very nature of the events that are to take place against that perverse institution at the end of the religious age. From closely examining the characters of this ancient history, and from correctly placing their position within the scene of action, the endeavors of the institution of the sixth seal will be clearly discerned, along with her complete demise.

2. The information to be expounded upon cannot be looked at from a natural standpoint, that is, from a surface reading or understanding. Saul's figure is discerned from the fact that "Saul built an altar unto the LORD,"[877] that is, "the first altar that he built"[878] was "to his house to Gib'eah of Saul."[879] Upon a controversy within the camp, Saul said, "Bring me hither every man his ox,"[880] signifying that, in this act, "he transgressed against the LORD his God, and went into the temple of

---
877   1 Samuel 14:35
878   1 Samuel 14:35
879   1 Samuel 15:34
880   1 Samuel 14:34

the LORD to burn incense upon the altar of incense."[881] To any king, "it appertaineth not"[882] "to burn incense unto the LORD, but to the priests the sons of Aaron."[883] It was said of Saul at that moment, "Thou hast trespassed; neither shall it be for thine honour from the LORD God,"[884] for "Saul said, Bring hither a burnt offering to me, and peace offerings. And he offered the burnt offering."[885]

3. Saul portrays the image and doctrine of his *God*, which *God* is according to the saying, "Thou hast said in thine heart, I will ascend into heaven, I will exalt my throne above the stars of God: I will sit also upon the mount of the congregation, in the sides of the north: I will ascend above the heights of the clouds; I will be like the most High."[886] Such a heart bears a likeness to that of the prince of Ty'rus, and it says of him, "Thou hast said, I am a God, I sit in the seat of God, in the midst of the seas,"[887] and also to that of No; a capital of Egypt "that was situate among the rivers, that had the waters round about it, whose rampart was the sea, and her wall was from the sea";[888] which bears a resemblance to "the son of perdition; who opposeth and exalteth himself above all that is called God, or that is worshipped; so that he as God sitteth in the temple of God, shewing himself that he is God."[889] Saul is he who should fulfill the vision, "In that day seven women shall take hold of one man,"[890] and is that spirit mirroring how it says, "A woman...upon a scarlet coloured beast, full of names of blasphemy, having seven heads and ten horns."[891]

4. Now, Jonathan is the son of Saul, and as the son of Saul, he is the image and the minister of Saul. Being the minister of Saul, Saul is, in figure, that dragon which should give "him his power, and his seat, and

---

881   2 Chronicles 26:16
882   2 Chronicles 26:18
883   2 Chronicles 26:18
884   2 Chronicles 26:18
885   1 Samuel 13:9
886   Isaiah 14:13,14
887   Ezekiel 28:2
888   Nahum 3:8
889   2 Thessalonians 2:3,4
890   Isaiah 4:1
891   Revelation 17:3

great authority."[892] The "dragon" is a symbol of State or government authority, and it is the order or mission of the dragon to persecute the Spirit's woman; the Word's church; that aggravates his reign, as it says, "He persecuted the woman,"[893] and, "His tail drew the third part of the stars of heaven, and did cast them to the earth."[894] As the institution of perdition rests in the midst of the seas, it is that this is "where the whore sitteth"[895] while on top of her dragon, and for this dragon it is further said, "Pharaoh king of Egypt, the great dragon that lieth in the midst of his rivers,"[896] and, "Who is this that cometh up as a flood, whose waters are moved as the rivers? Egypt riseth up like a flood, and his waters are moved like the rivers; and he saith, I will go up, and will cover the earth; I will destroy the city and the inhabitants thereof."[897]

5. Jonathan is an illustration of Egypt; for Egypt is symbolized by the dragon; and as the dragon represents the civil authority of a pagan State, when it is viewed by itself in the twelfth division of the Revelation, it is a figure representing, in reality, pagan Rome; for the twelfth division of the Revelation begins in Rome; of which was based upon a pagan church and State government. Jonathan being the son of Saul represents an environment or nation constructed after the image of his father. Thus, Scripture says, "They should make an image to the beast,"[898] for Jonathan represents the earth beast that should take on the image of the first beast before him, a nation upheld by the principles of the Papal Roman Empire, a dominion functioning after the policies of a government under the union of law and religion. Therefore that armourbearer of Jonathan; within the fourteenth division of the first book of Samuel; represents the unionized force employed by the nation under the image of the beast, for the armourbearer said to Jonathan at one time, "I am with thee according to thy heart,"[899]

---

892   Revelation 13:2
893   Revelation 12:13
894   Revelation 12:4
895   Revelation 17:15
896   Ezekiel 29:3
897   Jeremiah 46:7,8
898   Revelation 13:14
899   1 Samuel 14:7

bearing witness to the word concerning the ten horns or kings of the dragon, which states, "God hath put in their hearts to fulfil his will, and to agree, and give their kingdom unto the beast, until the words of God shall be fulfilled."[900]

6. With our characters in place, it is now right to analyze the meaning of the chapters under investigation in relation to the Revelation's vision. Says Scripture, "Now it came to pass upon a day, that Jonathan the son of Saul said unto the young man that bare his armour, Come, and let us go over to the Philis'tines' garrison, that is on the other side. But he told not his father."[901]

7. Herein it should be observed that those contrary to Israel at this time are later called, in addition to being acknowledged as "Philis'tines," "The garrison of these uncircumcised."[902] As the time we have entered is not the literal time of these events, but rather a revelation of spiritual facts, the ones "uncircumcised" should not be understood as them existing "in the flesh made by hands,"[903] but are them of that "circumcision made without hands";[904] roles and distinctions are reversed in error's official age. The Philis'tines, in this sense, are not the enemy, but are rather the ones "made as the filth of the world, and are the offscouring of all things."[905] These Philis'tines are recognized as that enemy to error's Republic.

8. As Jonathan and his armourbearer represent one full power; even the two-horned earth beast regulated by an openly apostate *Bible* keeping State; it is that, at some point, this nation should fulfill the saying, "He spake as a dragon,"[906] even as it says, "They fell before Jonathan; and his armourbearer slew after him."[907] This was "that first slaughter, which Jonathan and his armourbearer made,"[908] for which cause it says of the earth beast, "He had power to give life unto the

---

900 Revelation 17:17
901 1 Samuel 14:1
902 1 Samuel 14:6
903 Ephesians 2:11
904 Colossians 2:11
905 1 Corinthians 4:13
906 Revelation 13:11
907 1 Samuel 14:14
908 1 Samuel 14:14

image of the beast, that the image of the beast should both speak, and cause that as many as would not worship the image of the beast should be killed."[909] Scripture tells us that this was the first slaughter by Jonathan and his servant, letting us know that there is another, and indeed there was another accomplished by "the Israelites that were with Saul and Jonathan."[910]

9. There are two slaughters headed by two different entities, and upon the second slaughter, the first entity of the first slaughter now takes a secondary role, yet it was known, "Jonathan smote the garrison of the Philis'tines,"[911] and, "Jonathan...wrought this great salvation in Israel,"[912] yet "all Israel heard say that Saul had smitten the garrison."[913] As the dragon once worked alone, the second slaughter tells of the fact that the image is joined to his father, and that the one upholding the image accomplishes the work for his father. In that first slaughter "there was trembling in the host, in the field, and among all the people: the garrison, and the spoilers, they also trembled, and the earth quaked: so it was a very great trembling,"[914] and this great earthquake fulfilling the word, "In the city is left desolation, and the gate is smitten with destruction. When thus it shall be in the midst of the land among the people, there shall be as the shaking of an olive tree, and as the gleaning grapes when the vintage is done."[915]

10. We have entered in to the time when it should be fulfilled, "The dragon was wroth with the woman, and went to make war with the remnant of her seed, which keep the commandments of God, and have the testimony of Jesus Christ."[916] The two slaughters represent two separate times of religious trouble and distress, and these times of trouble cannot fall before it is said, "The ark of God was at that time with the children of Israel,"[917] that is, since by this illustration our

---

909 Revelation 13:15
910 1 Samuel 14:21
911 1 Samuel 14:15
912 1 Samuel 14:45
913 1 Samuel 13:14
914 1 Samuel 14:15
915 Isaiah 24:12,13
916 Revelation 12:17
917 1 Samuel 14:18

character assignments are reversed, the Spirit's Faith is under bondage to the children or priesthood of the established Egyptian Babylon. In the second slaughter, Scripture says, "Saul and all the people that were with him assembled themselves, and they came to the battle: and, behold, every man's sword was against his fellow, and there was a very great discomfiture,"[918] for "the LORD saved Israel that day,"[919] when in reality it was Saul who gathered his forces together while taking courage on the LORD's voice. Herein we understand that the second slaughter will be accomplished by that dreadful State institution backed by the full power of her *God*, even as it says, "Ye are of your father the devil, and the lusts of your father ye will do."[920]

11. It cannot be ignored how that the events thus mentioned are synonymous with how it is said, "There was a great earthquake; and the sun became black as sackcloth of hair, and the moon became as blood; and the stars of heaven fell unto the earth, even as a fig tree casteth her untimely figs, when she is shaken of a mighty wind."[921] There will be "a time of trouble, such as never was since there was a nation,"[922] but this quaking of the earth will not be without that "great earthquake, such as was not since men were upon the earth."[923] Thus the saying will be fulfilled, "And the Philis'tines gathered themselves together to fight with Israel, thirty thousand chariots, and six thousand horsemen, and people as the sand which is on the sea shore in multitude: and they came up, and pitched in Mich'mash, eastward from Beth-a'ven. When the men of Israel saw that they were in a strait, (for the people were distressed,) then the people did hide themselves in caves, and in thickets, and in rocks, and in high places, and in pits."[924]

12. Now, the people did hide themselves in caves, and in thickets, and in rocks, and in high places, and in pits, and this scene cannot fail to have place as a fulfillment of how it is written, "And the heaven

---

918 1 Samuel 14:20
919 1 Samuel 14:23
920 John 8:44
921 Revelation 6:12,13
922 Daniel 12:1
923 Revelation 16:18
924 1 Samuel 13:5,6

departed as a scroll when it is rolled together; and every mountain and island were moved out of their places. And the kings of the earth, and the great men, and the rich men, and the chief captains, and the mighty men, and every bondman, and every free man, hid themselves in the dens and in the rocks of the mountains."[925] This is why it says, "Enter into the rock, and hide thee in the dust, for fear of the LORD, and for the glory of his majesty,"[926] and, "They shall go into the holes of the rocks, and into the caves of the earth, for fear of the LORD, and for the glory of his majesty, when he ariseth to shake terribly the earth."[927] Herein it is fulfilled, "Great Babylon came in remembrance before God, to give unto her the cup of the wine of the fierceness of his wrath. And every island fled away, and the mountains were not found."[928]

13. As the Philis'tines; in this context; represent the LORD's house; which house is the uncircumcised according to that age's standard; who fulfill the word, "I will bring forth a seed out of Jacob, and out of Judah an inheritor of my mountains";[929] so when the Word of the Philis'tines receives confirmation to execute vengeance for His company, He will say aloud, "The year of my redeemed is come,"[930] and, "I will burn her chariots in the smoke, and the sword shall devour thy young lions: and I will cut off thy prey from the earth, and the voice of thy messengers shall no more be heard."[931] Again, the word will be fulfilled, "The stars of heaven fell unto the earth, even as a fig tree casteth her untimely figs, when she is shaken of a mighty wind. And the heaven departed as a scroll,"[932] for it says, "All thy strong holds shall be like fig trees with the firstripe figs: if they be shaken, they shall even fall into the mouth of the eater. Behold, thy people in the midst of thee are women: the gates of thy land shall be set wide open unto thine enemies: the fire shall devour thy bars."[933]

---

925 Revelation 6:14,15
926 Isaiah 2:10
927 Isaiah 2:19
928 Revelation 16:19,20
929 Isaiah 65:9
930 Isaiah 63:4
931 Nahum 2:13
932 Revelation 6:13,14
933 Nahum 3:12,13

14. Therefore, before heaven's Philis'tines, "the earth shall quake before them; the heavens shall tremble: the sun and the moon shall be dark, and the stars shall withdraw their shining."[934] "There shall the fire devour thee; the sword shall cut thee off, it shall eat thee up like the cankerworm: make thyself many as the cankerworm, make thyself many as the locusts. Thou hast multiplied thy merchants above the stars of heaven: the cankerworm spoileth, and flieth away. Thy crowned are as the locusts, and thy captains as the great grasshoppers, which camp in the hedges in the cold day, but when the sun ariseth they flee away, and their place is not known where they are. Thy shepherds slumber, O king of Assyria: thy nobles shall dwell in the dust: thy people is scattered upon the mountains, and no man gathereth them. There is no healing of thy bruise; thy wound is grievous: all that hear the bruit of thee shall clap the hands over thee: for upon whom hath not thy wickedness passed continually?"[935]

15. Thus, it is evident that the events of the sixth seal enclose the final scenes of the ecclesiastical history of that church whose faith is cast as a cloud over the earth, and this seal cannot be unsealed until that spirit of the previous seals should be healed or resurrected. As an earthquake advances in height, so that great earthquake of the sixth seal should advance in power until a slaughter should find place among those deemed uncircumcised, only to have another time of trouble commence fairly soon afterwards, the likes of which the ministers of the religious world has never seen, for a great period of wrath will find itself unleashed upon them that call their conversation "Circumcised," and this vengeance by the Father's voice, and also upon the Father's host by these same ungodly ministers of *Egypt*. Yet the times will find order, for the Spirit of the perceived "uncircumcised"; who are those priests "having his Father's name written in their foreheads";[936] will "descend from heaven with a shout, with the voice of the archangel, and with the trump of God"[937] "in flaming fire taking vengeance on

---

934   Joel 2:10
935   Nahum 3:15-19
936   Revelation 14:1
937   1 Thessalonians 4:16

them that know not God, and that obey not the gospel of our Lord Jesus Christ."[938]

16. It is evident that the nations being angry, and the wrath that should come by them, is when the dragon should be wroth with heaven's seed, only to have the brilliance of the name of heaven's Captain administer judgment against their course. Contained within the sixth seal are these events which should begin with the saying, "Babylon the great is fallen, is fallen";[939] for, by this time, "his deadly wound was healed";[940] "yet he shall come to his end, and nine shall help him."[941]

---

938 2 Thessalonians 1:8
939 Revelation 18:2
940 Revelation 13:3
941 Daniel 11:45

17

E'dom's Appointed End

1. Says Scripture, "And the stars of heaven fell unto the earth, even as a fig tree casteth her untimely figs, when she is shaken of a mighty wind. And the heaven departed as a scroll when it is rolled together."[942]

2. Again, "And all the host of heaven shall be dissolved, and the heavens shall be rolled together as a scroll: and all their host shall fall down, as the leaf falleth off from the vine, and as a falling fig from the fig tree. For my sword shall be bathed in heaven: behold, it shall come down upon Idume'a, and upon the people of my curse, to judgment."[943]

3. Such are the scenes of the true execution of judgment upon the disobedient by the Father through His "sword of the Spirit, which is the word of God."[944] Herein the saying is fulfilled, "They shall run like mighty men; they shall climb the wall like men of war...They shall run to and fro in the city...like the noise of chariots on the tops of mountains shall they leap, like the noise of a flame of fire that devoureth the stubble, as a strong people set in battle array."[945] This vision is indeed the fulfillment of how it is written, "At the noise of the tumult the people fled; at the lifting up of thyself the nations were scattered. And

---

942   Revelation 6:13,14
943   Isaiah 34:4,5
944   Ephesians 6:17
945   Joel 2:5-9

your spoil shall be gathered like the gathering of the caterpiller: as the running to and fro of locusts shall he run upon them."[946]

4. Such warfare is waged against Idume'a, but who is Idume'a? Says Scripture, "O mount Seir, and all Idume'a."[947] Idume'a belongs to the people of Seir, and who are these people? It is written, "Seir in the land of E'dom,"[948] and, "The land of Seir, the country of E'dom."[949] Now, concerning E'dom, the Spirit says, "Thou exalt thyself as the eagle,"[950] and, "Thy terribleness hath deceived thee, and the pride of thine heart, O thou that dwellest in the clefts of the rock, that holdest the height of the hill: though thou shouldest make thy nest as high as the eagle, I will bring thee down from thence, saith the LORD. Also E'dom shall be a desolation: every one that goeth by it shall be astonished, and shall hiss at all the plagues thereof. As in the overthrow of Sodom and Gomor'rah and the neighbour cities thereof, saith the LORD, no man shall abide there, neither shall a son of man dwell in it."[951]

5. The "sword" of the LORD is against Idume'a, who represents the country of E'dom, therefore the heaven that is to be rolled together is not a literal heaven, but is rather the fulfillment of the saying, "The kingdom is departed from thee."[952] It is the kingdom of E'dom that is to fail at the appearing of the LORD's Word, even as it says, "Egypt shall be a desolation, and E'dom shall be a desolate wilderness, for the violence against the children of Judah,"[953] and in this sense, the counsel is also fulfilled, "I make mount Seir most desolate, and cut off from it him that passeth out and him that returneth. And I will fill his mountains with his slain men: in thy hills, and in thy valleys, and in all thy rivers, shall they fall that are slain with the sword. I will make thee perpetual desolations, and thy cities shall not return."[954] "As thou didst rejoice at the inheritance of the house of Israel, because it was deso-

---

946 Isaiah 33:3,4
947 Ezekiel 35:15
948 Genesis 36:21
949 Genesis 32:3
950 Obadiah 1:4
951 Jeremiah 49:16-18
952 Daniel 4:31
953 Joel 3:19
954 Ezekiel 35:7-9

late, so will I do unto thee: thou shalt be desolate, O mount Seir, and all Idume'a, even all of it,"[955] says the Spirit.

6. Such a scene as depicted by Ezekiel constrains the mind to remember how it is said, "The indignation of the LORD is upon all nations, and his fury upon all their armies."[956] "Their slain also shall be cast out, and their stink shall come up out of their carcases, and the mountains shall be melted with their blood,"[957] for it is written, "He shall give a shout, as they that tread the grapes, against all the inhabitants of the earth. A noise shall come even to the ends of the earth; for the LORD hath a controversy with the nations, he will plead with all flesh; he will give them that are wicked to the sword, saith the LORD. Thus saith the LORD of hosts, Behold, evil shall go forth from nation to nation, and a great whirlwind shall be raised up from the coasts of the earth. And the slain of the LORD shall be at that day from one end of the earth even unto the other end of the earth: they shall not be lamented, neither gathered, nor buried; they shall be dung upon the ground."[958]

7. This is the day of our LORD and Father, and "he will not spare in the day of vengeance,"[959] that is, "the day of the LORD'S vengeance, and the year of recompences for the controversy of Zion."[960] It is during this hour that the name and country of E'dom will become no more, as it says, "Edom shall be a desolation: every one that goeth by it shall be astonished, and shall hiss at all the plagues thereof,"[961] even as the promise was made for Babylon according to the saying, "Because of the wrath of the LORD it shall not be inhabited, but it shall be wholly desolate: every one that goeth by Babylon shall be astonished, and hiss at all her plagues."[962] The condemnation is the same for the two parties; Edom and Babylon; because both represent the same figure. Against E'dom it was said, "He shall come up and fly as the eagle, and

---

955 Ezekiel 35:15
956 Isaiah 34:2
957 Isaiah 34:3
958 Jeremiah 25:30-33
959 Proverbs 6:34
960 Isaiah 34:8
961 Jeremiah 49:17
962 Jeremiah 50:13

spread his wings over Boz'rah: and at that day shall the heart of the mighty men of E'dom be as the heart of a woman in her pangs,"[963] for it was fulfilled, "The king of Babylon hath heard the report of them, and his hands waxed feeble: anguish took hold of him, and pangs as of a woman in travail."[964]

8. The word went out against these two nations, "He shall come up like a lion from the swelling of Jordan unto the habitation of the strong: but I will make them suddenly run away from her: and who is a chosen man, that I may appoint over her? for who is like me? and who will appoint me the time? and who is that shepherd that will stand before me?"[965] for the two were to suffer a similar fate, even as it is said, "Babylon...shall be as when God overthrew Sodom and Gomor'rah."[966] "I will stir up the Medes against them."[967] As before it was said, "At the noise of the tumult the people fled,"[968] so it will be fulfilled, "The noise of a multitude in the mountains, like as of a great people; a tumultuous noise of the kingdoms of nations gathered together: the LORD of hosts mustereth the host of the battle."[969] For, "the LORD hath raised up the spirit of the kings of the Medes: for his device is against Babylon, to destroy it; because it is the vengeance of the LORD, the vengeance of his temple."[970] Therefore when "the Lord cometh with ten thousands of his saints,"[971] then will the Spirit's *Medes* lift up the "day of the trumpet and alarm against the fenced cities, and against the high towers."[972]

9. Herein we come to understand who and what the country of E'dom; that heaven that must depart at the sight of the Father's unmerciful revelation; is and should consist of, for it says, "Moab shall be as Sodom, and the children of Ammon as Gomor'rah, even the breeding

---

963 Jeremiah 49:22
964 Jeremiah 50:43
965 Jeremiah 50:44
966 Jeremiah 49:19
967 Isaiah 13:17
968 Isaiah 33:3
969 Isaiah 13:4
970 Jeremiah 51:11
971 Jude 1:14
972 Zephaniah 1:16

of nettles, and saltpits, and a perpetual desolation."[973] "He will stretch out his hand against the north, and destroy Assyria; and will make Nineveh a desolation, and dry like a wilderness."[974]

10. "Saith the Lord GOD concerning the Ammonites,"[975] "I will pour out mine indignation upon thee, I will blow against thee in the fire of my wrath, and deliver thee into the hand of brutish men, and skilful to destroy. Thou shalt be for fuel to the fire; thy blood shall be in the midst of the land; thou shalt be no more remembered."[976] Such a fate will fall on them because it is said of them by the Spirit, "Thou saidst, Aha, against my sanctuary, when it was profaned,"[977] even as it is reported of E'dom, "Neither shouldest thou have rejoiced over the children of Judah in the day of their destruction; neither shouldest thou have spoken proudly in the day of distress."[978] "I have heard all thy blasphemies which thou hast spoken against the mountains of Israel, saying, They are laid desolate, they are given us to consume."[979] "As thou didst rejoice at the inheritance of the house of Israel, because it was desolate, so will I do unto thee: thou shalt be desolate, O mount Seir, and all Idume'a."[980]

11. Therefore "behold, the LORD cometh forth out of his place, and will come down, and tread upon the high places of the earth. And the mountains shall be molten under him, and the valleys shall be cleft, as wax before the fire, and as the waters that are poured down a steep place."[981] "I will send a fire upon Te'man, which shall devour the palaces of Boz'rah,"[982] says the Spirit, for it is written, "Nebuchadrez'zar king of Babylon hath taken counsel against you, and hath conceived a purpose against you,"[983] and, "Call together the archers against Babylon."[984]

---

973 Zephaniah 2:9
974 Zephaniah 2:13
975 Ezekiel 21:28
976 Ezekiel 21:31,32
977 Ezekiel 25:3
978 Obadiah 1:12
979 Ezekiel 35:12
980 Ezekiel 35:15
981 Micah 1:3,4
982 Amos 1:12
983 Jeremiah 49:39
984 Jeremiah 50:29

12. "A people shall come from the north, and a great nation, and many kings shall be raised up from the coasts of the earth. They shall hold the bow and the lance: they are cruel, and will not shew mercy: their voice shall roar like the sea, and they shall ride upon horses, every one put in array, like a man to the battle, against thee, O daughter of Babylon."[985] "I will raise up against Babylon, and against them that dwell in the midst of them that rise up against me, a destroying wind; and will send unto Babylon fanners, that shall fan her, and shall empty her land: for in the day of trouble they shall be against her round about,"[986] says the Spirit. "Set ye up a standard in the land, blow the trumpet among the nations, prepare the nations against her, call together against her the kingdoms";[987] "cause the horses to come up as the rough caterpillers. Prepare against her the nations with the kings of the Medes, the captains thereof, and all the rulers thereof, and all the land of his dominion. And the land shall tremble and sorrow."[988]

13. Herein the word is fulfilled, "Blow ye the trumpet in Zion, and sound an alarm in my holy mountain."[989] "The LORD will roar from Zion, and utter his voice from Jerusalem; and the habitations of the shepherds shall mourn, and the top of Carmel shall wither."[990]

14. Against E'dom, Egypt, Ammon, Moab, Babylon, and Assyria, against this country and its armies or host of the north; who are understood to be, in the Revelation, one power that the Spirit calls Babylon the great; the "sword" of heaven's LORD and Father will fall. This is why it says, "Moab shall be trodden down under him, even as straw is trodden down for the dunghill."[991] "And the fortress of the high fort of thy walls shall he bring down, lay low, and bring to the ground, even to the dust."[992] The LORD God's name will prevail against the armies of Egypt; the living God will, and by His Spirit's Word, devour the country

---

985 Jeremiah 50:41,42
986 Jeremiah 51:1,2
987 Jeremiah 51:27
988 Jeremiah 51:27-29
989 Joel 2:1
990 Amos 1:2
991 Isaiah 25:10
992 Isaiah 25:12

of E'dom with her cities. It is for this reason that there is enough proof to conclude that the heaven of the vision of the sixth seal is not literal, but is rather "the sun, and the moon, and the stars, even all the host of heaven,"[993] of religious error. This heaven is that spiritual economy of the kingdom or dominion of the Lamb's enemy understanding, and it will be this realm that fails during the day when creation's Faith vengefully appears, for as error's heaven departs, the saying will again find itself fulfilled against the then king of Babylon, "The kingdom is departed from thee."[994]

15. This is the day of the wrath of the Lamb against them that are found contrary to the character of His wisdom when the first phase of the Spirit's wrath is finished, when the seven last plagues are finished. For, says the Spirit concerning "Pharaoh king of Egypt,"[995] "Thou art like a young lion of the nations, and thou art as a whale in the seas: and thou camest forth with thy rivers, and troubledst the waters with thy feet, and fouledst their rivers. Thus saith the Lord GOD; I will therefore spread out my net over thee with a company of many people; and they shall bring thee up in my net. Then will I leave thee upon the land, I will cast thee forth upon the open field, and will cause all the fowls of the heaven to remain upon thee, and I will fill the beasts of the whole earth with thee. And I will lay thy flesh upon the mountains, and fill the valleys with thy height. I will also water with thy blood the land wherein thou swimmest, even to the mountains; and the rivers shall be full of thee. And when I shall put thee out, I will cover the heaven, and make the stars thereof dark; I will cover the sun with a cloud, and the moon shall not give her light. All the bright lights of heaven will I make dark over thee, and set darkness upon thy land, saith the Lord GOD.[996]

16. "I will also vex the hearts of many people, when I shall bring thy destruction among the nations, into the countries which thou hast not known. Yea, I will make many people amazed at thee, and their kings shall be horribly afraid for thee, when I shall brandish my sword before them; and they shall tremble at every moment, every man for his own

---

993 Deuteronomy 4:19
994 Daniel 4:31
995 Ezekiel 32:2
996 Ezekiel 32:2-8

life, in the day of thy fall. For thus saith the Lord GOD; The sword of the king of Babylon shall come upon thee. By the swords of the mighty will I cause thy multitude to fall, the terrible of the nations, all of them: and they shall spoil the pomp of Egypt, and all the multitude thereof shall be destroyed."[997]

17. It may now be understood why "every mountain and island were moved out of their places,"[998] for the mountains and the islands comprise Egypt's religious earth, and at this time, Egypt's known heaven will be no more in existence. The vision of the times under the imagery of the sixth seal reveals power no longer by fleshly horse and rider over the conscience of the conversation, but rather by heaven's right will and commandment through faith's higher learning, for the power of the institution of the five previous seals has reached its height in the sixth. It is then a fact that the sixth seal contains the history of the resurrection and annihilation of the spirit of the church of the seals, and it is not possible that any other such events should be held to this vision, seeing as how it is a figurative illustration of what should take place against them that desire to exalt their name and spirit of error above the LORD's name, and above the Spirit of His throne's will and doctrine.

---

997   Ezekiel 32:9-12
998   Revelation 6:14

18

A Time Of Change

1. Says Scripture, "And the heaven departed as a scroll when it is rolled together; and every mountain and island were moved out of their places. And the kings of the earth, and the great men, and the rich men, and the chief captains, and the mighty men, and every bondman, and every free man, hid themselves in the dens and in the rocks of the mountains; and said to the mountains and rocks, Fall on us, and hide us."[999]

2. The rocks and the mountains are not literal. Scripture says of old, "David abode in the wilderness in strong holds, and remained in a mountain in the wilderness of Ziph. And Saul sought him every day, but God delivered him not into his hand. And David saw that Saul was come out to seek his life: and David was in the wilderness of Ziph in a wood."[1000] A mountain is a "strong hold," and a strong hold is a "wood," for it says, concerning a "wood," "As the fire burneth a wood, and as the flame setteth the mountains on fire."[1001] Herein it is understood that a "wood" is a "mountain."

3. Again, it was said of old, "If thou be a great people, then get thee up to the wood country, and cut down for thyself there in the land of

---

999   Revelation 16:14-17
1000   1 Samuel 23:14,15
1001   Psalms 83:14

the Per'izzites and of the giants. The mountain shall be thine; for it is a wood, and thou shalt cut it down."[1002] A "mountain" is a "wood," but now it is observed that a "wood" is a "country of giants," a city or place for "giants in the earth,"[1003] for "mighty men,"[1004] "men of renown,"[1005] even for "princes of the assembly, famous in the congregation, men of renown."[1006] For this cause we read, "I will cut off the cities of thy land, and throw down all thy strong holds,"[1007] and, "O tower of the flock, the strong hold of the daughter of Zion,"[1008] for a "strong hold," being a "city," is also is a "tower." Therefore, concerning these "mountains" of the sixth seal, we read, "My fortress; my high tower, and my deliverer; my shield, and he in whom I trust,"[1009] and, "He is my refuge and my fortress,"[1010] for a tower is a place of defense and deliverance, a fortress, and a fortress is a refuge. The mountains and the rocks are herein understood to be places of spiritual refuge believed to possess spiritual deliverance and inward security.

4. The scene of the kings of the earth running in to the "dens" fulfills the saying, "Ye shall appoint you cities to be cities of refuge for you; that the slayer may flee thither, which killeth any person at unawares. And they shall be unto you cities for refuge from the avenger; that the manslayer die not, until he stand before the congregation in judgment."[1011]

5. "The congregation shall deliver the slayer out of the hand of the revenger of blood, and the congregation shall restore him to the city of his refuge, whither he was fled: and he shall abide in it unto the death of the high priest, which was anointed with the holy oil. But if the slayer shall at any time come without the border of the city of his refuge, whither he was fled; and the revenger of blood find him without

---

1002 Joshua 17:15,16
1003 Genesis 6:4
1004 Genesis 6:4
1005 Genesis 6:4
1006 Numbers 16:2
1007 Micah 5:11
1008 Micah 4:8
1009 Psalms 144:2
1010 Psalms 91:2
1011 Numbers 35:11,12

the borders of the city of his refuge, and the revenger of blood kill the slayer; he shall not be guilty of blood: because he should have remained in the city of his refuge until the death of the high priest: but after the death of the high priest the slayer shall return into the land of his possession. So these things shall be for a statute of judgment unto you throughout your generations in all your dwellings."[1012]

6. It appears, according to the vision of the sixth seal, that chief priests and elders, after discerning wrong committed by them, are fleeing to fortresses of refuge. These cities of old were for them that killed without understanding, which is why it appears that those who beg for death at the revelation of the Spirit's vengeful Word are them that do not have full knowledge of their errors against that Word. Nevertheless, realizing their fate, and the result of their decision for choosing to reject the living God and His throne's doctrine, they are fleeing to the mountains and rocks, to locations of refuge wherein is spiritual comfort. Seeing as how they are fleeing, it is that they are outside of the main place of their refuge and are become open to the Avenging Word, to the Revenger of the blood of His people, to that Spirit who has "put on the garments of vengeance for clothing"[1013] and who "will take vengeance on his adversaries."[1014] Of old, the ones who had their guilt made known to their conscience ran to specific cities for experiencing right repentance. These individuals in vision appear to abandon their then high priest for their heart's amendment, refusing to remain by his side when they finally see that his establishment is built upon sand.

7. Herein is the fulfillment of the saying: "I saw the beast, and the kings of the earth, and their armies, gathered together to make war against him that sat on the horse, and against his army. And the beast was taken, and with him the false prophet that wrought miracles before him, with which he deceived them that had received the mark of the beast, and them that worshipped his image. These both were cast alive

---
1012 Numbers 35:25-29
1013 Isaiah 59:17
1014 Nahum 1:2

into a lake of fire burning with brimstone. And the remnant were slain with the sword of him that sat upon the horse."[1015]

8. Babylon the great is handled by the voice of the Word's High Priest through the testimony of the Spirit's then assembly. It says "the beast"; that is, the spirit of the leopard beast that was wounded and then healed; and the false prophet; the two-horned earth beast after a pagan apostate church and State economy, who is that deceiving earth beast; are taken alive, but the kings of the institution of the then religious world are excluded and not mentioned, therefore these running ministers appear to be that remnant of the beast and the false prophet. The spirit mentioned with the kings of the earth is the same spirit of the seventeenth division of the Revelation that goes into perdition, but rather its modern version, that is, the spirit of Papal Rome upheld by the new Pagan Religious Republic, which is the leopard beast supported by the two-horned earth beast. These two must first be taken alive and perpetually silenced at the revelation of the Word's name and glory, and the remnant of this institution, being convinced, convicted, and devoured by the knowledge of their error, are them that seek to hide self from the face of the Spirit's name.

9. Says Scripture, "I saw three unclean spirits like frogs come out of the mouth of the dragon, and out of the mouth of the beast, and out of the mouth of the false prophet. For they are the spirits of devils, working miracles, which go forth unto the kings of the earth and of the whole world, to gather them to the battle."[1016]

10. The kings of the earth are deceived by that which comes out of the heart of great Egyptian Babylon, therefore they are, in a sense, here exposed as being separate from her. Again, Scripture says, "The great whore that sitteth upon many waters: with whom the kings of the earth have committed fornication, and the inhabitants of the earth have been made drunk with the wine of her fornication."[1017] The kings of the earth, or rather, the priests[1018] of the earth of the religious world, are made drunk by this mind and institution of religious error. For

---
1015 Revelation 19:19-21
1016 Revelation 16:13,14
1017 Revelation 17:1,2
1018 Revelation 5:10; Revelation 1:6

this cause the angel says, "The woman which thou sawest is that great city, which reigneth over the kings of the earth,"[1019] for the great city is the great whore, that impure church of spiritual negligence against the name of the LORD's Spirit and High Priest, and she holds a royal office above the kings or priests of the earth.

11. So then Babylon the great will indeed first suffer; the beast and the false prophet, which institution is the spirit of Papal Catholicism joined to the civil power of a pagan apostate religious State; which is why John observed how it is said, "The kings of the earth, who have committed fornication and lived deliciously with her, shall bewail her, and lament for her, when they shall see the smoke of her burning, standing afar off for the fear of her torment, saying, Alas, alas, that great city Babylon, that mighty city! for in one hour is thy judgment come."[1020] "The merchants of the earth shall weep and mourn over her; for no man buyeth their merchandise any more."[1021] The kings of the earth; who are those religious ministers joined to her endeavor; are them that "were made rich by her,"[1022] and it appears that before they are slain by the Spirit's voice, they have the privilege of beholding the fate of the empire that they have entrusted with their entire being.

12. "How is the city of praise not left, the city of my joy!"[1023] they will say. "What city is like Ty'rus, like the destroyed in the midst of the sea?"[1024] they will sing. For which cause it is written, "Who hath taken this counsel against Tyre, the crowning city, whose merchants are princes, whose traffickers are the honourable of the earth? The LORD of hosts hath purposed it, to stain the pride of all glory, and to bring into contempt all the honourable of the earth. Pass through thy land as a river, O daughter of Tar'shish: there is no more strength. He stretched out his hand over the sea, he shook the kingdoms: the LORD

1019   Revelation 17:18
1020   Revelation 18:9,10
1021   Revelation 18:11
1022   Revelation 18:15
1023   Jeremiah 49:25
1024   Ezekiel 27:32

hath given a commandment against the merchant city, to destroy the strong holds thereof."[1025]

13. "Prepare against her the nations with the kings of the Medes, the captains thereof, and all the rulers thereof, and all the land of his dominion. And the land shall tremble and sorrow: for every purpose of the LORD shall be performed against Babylon, to make the land of Babylon a desolation without an inhabitant. The mighty men of Babylon have forborn to fight, they have remained in their holds: their might hath failed; they became as women: they have burned her dwellingplaces; her bars are broken. One post shall run to meet another, and one messenger to meet another, to shew the king of Babylon that his city is taken at one end, and that the passages are stopped, and the reeds they have burned with fire, and the men of war are affrighted."[1026] "How is She'shach taken! and how is the praise of the whole earth surprised! how is Babylon become an astonishment among the nations!"[1027] "Her cities are a desolation, a dry land, and a wilderness, a land wherein no man dwelleth, neither doth any son of man pass thereby."[1028]

14. When the sword and doctrine of the Word's High Priest comes, it will strike the kingdom of the beast first, which at this time is the city and fortress of the whole earth's praise. Therefore, after this work is accomplished against the then *Egypt* and *Jerusalem*, the Word's voice will fulfill the saying, "He burnt the house of the LORD, and the king's house, and all the houses of Jerusalem, and every great man's house burnt he with fire. And all the army of the Chal'dees, that were with the captain of the guard, brake down the walls of Jerusalem round about. Now the rest of the people that were left in the city, and the fugitives that fell away to the king of Babylon, with the remnant of the multitude, did Neb'uzar-a'dan the captain of the guard carry away."[1029]

15. Again, "He brought upon them the king of the Chal'dees, who slew their young men with the sword in the house of their sanctuary, and had no compassion upon young man or maiden, old man, or him

---

1025 Isaiah 23:8-11
1026 Jeremiah 51:28-32
1027 Jeremiah 51:41
1028 Jeremiah 51:43
1029 2 Kings 25:9-11

that stooped for age: he gave them all into his hand. And all the vessels of the house of God, great and small, and the treasures of the house of the LORD, and the treasures of the king, and of his princes; all these he brought to Babylon. And they burnt the house of God, and brake down the wall of Jerusalem, and burnt all the palaces thereof with fire, and destroyed all the goodly vessels thereof."[1030] Herein is brought to view that great and final destruction of E'dom; who is Egypt, who is that great Babylon; and it is no literal revelation, but a spiritual illustration of the relentless fury of the LORD's Spirit within the spirit and conscience of "men which had the mark of the beast, and upon them which worshipped his image."[1031]

16. The focus of His vengeance is against the king's house of *Jerusalem*, which house, being his sanctuary, is representative of his religious doctrine. The remnant that are slain after the beast and the false prophet are handled are those fugitives of Tar'shish, even a people escaped from a scene of wrath who are now hiding in strong holds and towers of refuge. The Word does not seem to execute His wrath instantly on every thing found contrary to His LORD, but there rather appears to be an order of execution, even as it was fulfilled of old. After heaven's Spirit should consume the main tabernacle of contrary palaces, heaven's fire then appears to handle the kings of the earth who are turned to cities of deliverance, and herein appears to be the fulfillment of the saying, "The cities of the nations fell."[1032] At this time "a man shall cast his idols of silver, and his idols of gold, which they made each one for himself to worship, to the moles and to the bats; to go into the clefts of the rocks, and into the tops of the ragged rocks, for fear of the LORD, and for the glory of his majesty, when he ariseth to shake terribly the earth."[1033]

17. The "dens," the "mountains," and the "rocks," do not find relevance in a literal plane of existence, but rather appear to serve as a vehicle for proper spiritual perspective. It is written, "They couch

---

1030 2 Chronicles 36:17-19
1031 Revelation 16:1
1032 Revelation 16:19
1033 Isaiah 2:20,21

in their dens, and abide in the covert,"[1034] and, "A tabernacle for a shadow in the daytime from the heat, and for a place of refuge, and for a covert,"[1035] for the "dens" and "mountains" are tabernacles of safety supervised by them that are *alive* during the earth's terrible consumption. At this time, concerning the earth's ministers, "their flesh shall consume away while they stand upon their feet, and their eyes shall consume away in their holes, and their tongue shall consume away in their mouth. And it shall come to pass in that day, that a great tumult from the LORD shall be among them; and they shall lay hold every one on the hand of his neighbour, and his hand shall rise up against the hand of his neighbour."[1036]

1034   Job 38:40
1035   Isaiah 4:6
1036   Zechariah 14:12,13

19

A Running Fever

1. Scripture reports of this great time of the LORD's Word, "Nothing shall escape them";[1037] them that devour and spoil in His name; therefore the word is met and fulfilled, "Call together the archers against Babylon: all ye that bend the bow, camp against it round about; let none thereof escape: recompense her according to her work; according to all that she hath done, do unto her: for she hath been proud against the LORD, against the Holy One of Israel. Therefore shall her young men fall in the streets, and all her men of war shall be cut off in that day, saith the LORD."[1038]

2. Thus, the saying will be fulfilled against the entire kingdom and institution of the then earth, "The high places of Isaac shall be desolate, and the sanctuaries of Israel shall be laid waste; and I will rise against the house of Jerobo'am with the sword."[1039] "The Lord GOD called to contend by fire,"[1040] for, "I will set fire in Egypt,"[1041] says the

---

1037   Joel 2:3
1038   Jeremiah 50:29,30
1039   Amos 6:9
1040   Amos 7:4
1041   Ezekiel 30:16

Spirit, and, "It shall be the time of the heathen."[1042] For this cause, it will be accomplished by His voice: "I will destroy your high places, and cut down your images, and cast your carcases upon the carcases of your idols, and my soul shall abhor you. And I will make your cities waste, and bring your sanctuaries unto desolation, and I will not smell the savour of your sweet odours. And I will bring the land into desolation: and your enemies which dwell therein shall be astonished at it."[1043]

3. "I will give the land of Egypt unto Nebuchadrez'zar king of Babylon,"[1044] says the Spirit. "He and his people with him, the terrible of the nations, shall be brought to destroy the land: and they shall draw their swords against Egypt, and fill the land with the slain."[1045] For, "thus saith the Lord GOD; I will also destroy the idols, and I will cause their images to cease out of Noph; and there shall be no more a prince of the land of Egypt: and I will put a fear in the land of Egypt."[1046] "The day shall be darkened, when I shall break there the yokes of Egypt: and the pomp of her strength shall cease in her: as for her, a cloud shall cover her, and her daughters shall go into captivity. Thus will I execute judgments in Egypt."[1047]

4. "Thou shalt take up this proverb against the king of Babylon, and say, How hath the oppressor ceased! the golden city ceased! The LORD hath broken the staff of the wicked, and the sceptre of the rulers. He who smote the people in wrath with a continual stroke, he that ruled the nations in anger, is persecuted, and none hindereth. The whole earth is at rest, and is quiet: they break forth into singing."[1048]

5. Therefore concerning the definition of "the dens," "the rocks," and "the mountains," Scripture says, "Hear ye, O mountains...and ye strong foundations of the earth."[1049] Again Scripture says, "The mountain of the house of the LORD shall be established in the top of the

---

1042   Ezekiel 30:3
1043   Leviticus 26:30-32
1044   Ezekiel 29:19
1045   Ezekiel 30:11
1046   Ezekiel 30:13
1047   Ezekiel 30:18,19
1048   Isaiah 14:4-7
1049   Micah 6:2

mountains,"[1050] for the mountain of the LORD God is "the house of the God of Jacob."[1051] For this cause the Spirit says, "I will cut off the cities of thy land, and throw down all thy strong holds,"[1052] for it is written, "Ye shall flee to the valley of the mountains; for the valley of the mountains shall reach unto A'zal: yea, ye shall flee, like as ye fled from before the earthquake in the days of Uzzi'ah king of Judah: and the LORD my God shall come, and all the saints with thee."[1053] The "mountains" are places or churches of strong holds; they are the cities and sanctuaries of honor for the doctrine of their estate, and if they are being sought, then their estate is not of the earth's form, even as it says, "There came of all people to hear the wisdom of Solomon, from all kings of the earth, which had heard of his wisdom."[1054] Herein the saying is fulfilled, "The residue of my people shall spoil them, and the remnant of my people shall possess them."[1055]

6. Herein we are made to understand that the saying will be fulfilled, "I will raise and cause to come up against Babylon an assembly of great nations from the north country: and they shall set themselves in array against her; from thence she shall be taken: their arrows shall be as of a mighty expert man; none shall return in vain. And Chalde'a shall be a spoil: all that spoil her shall be satisfied, saith the LORD. Because ye were glad, because ye rejoiced, O ye destroyers of mine heritage, because ye are grown fat as the heifer at grass, and bellow as bulls; your mother shall be sore confounded; she that bare you shall be ashamed: behold, the hindermost of the nations shall be a wilderness, a dry land, and a desert.[1056]

7. "Because of the wrath of the LORD it shall not be inhabited, but it shall be wholly desolate: every one that goeth by Babylon shall be astonished, and hiss at all her plagues. Put yourselves in array against Babylon round about: all ye that bend the bow, shoot at her,

---

1050 Micah 4:1
1051 Micah 4:2
1052 Micah 5:11
1053 Zechariah 14:5
1054 1 Kings 4:34
1055 Zephaniah 2:9
1056 Jeremiah 50:9-12

spare no arrows: for she hath sinned against the LORD. Shout against her round about: she hath given her hand: her foundations are fallen, her walls are thrown down: for it is the vengeance of the LORD: take vengeance upon her; as she hath done, do unto her. Cut off the sower from Babylon, and him that handleth the sickle in the time of harvest: for fear of the oppressing sword they shall turn every one to his people, and they shall flee every one to his own land."[1057]

8. Them that should come against Babylon are an assembly of great nations converted to heaven's throne religion and working for one purpose by one mind, even "a multitude in the mountains, like as of a great people; a tumultuous noise of the kingdoms of nations gathered together,"[1058] for they are "a great people and a strong,"[1059] and by their appearance, the word is gone out, "Howl ye; for the day of the LORD is at hand."[1060] The Medes are them that fulfill this ancient vision against Babylon, and the true fulfillment of this saying is accomplished by the voice of the Spirit's Christ through "the general assembly and church of the firstborn, which are written in heaven,"[1061] "and with the trump of God,"[1062] as it says, "I will send a fire upon Moab, and it shall devour the palaces of Ker'ioth: and Moab shall die with tumult, with shouting, and with the sound of the trumpet: and I will cut off the judge from the midst thereof, and will slay all the princes thereof with him, saith the LORD."[1063] Herein it is well to understand who are within these "rocks" and "mountains," "for it was so, when Jez'ebel cut off the prophets of the LORD, that Obadi'ah took an hundred prophets, and hid them by fifty in a cave, and fed them with bread and water."[1064]

9. The priests and ministers of the sanctuaries and cities of the then earth will run into the Spirit's strong holds for fear of what they see taking place within "the land of Assyria with the sword, and the land of

---

1057 Jeremiah 50:13-16
1058 Isaiah 13:4
1059 Joel 2:2
1060 Isaiah 13:6
1061 Hebrews 12:23
1062 1 Thessalonians 3:16
1063 Amos 2:2,3
1064 1 Kings 18:4

Nimrod."[1065] Again, the mountains and the rocks are not literal representations, but it rather appears that the remnant of the earth's vine escape to the places where there is good nourishment after realizing that they have not only been lied to by error's spirit, but that they have also deceived by the same spirit. Thus it will be fulfilled, "The children of Ammon and Moab stood up against the inhabitants of mount Se'ir, utterly to slay and destroy them: and when they had made an end of the inhabitants of Se'ir, every one helped to destroy another."[1066] Amen.

1065 Micah 5:6
1066 2 Chronicles 20:22-24

20

The Impact Of His Revelation

1. Says Scripture, "Every priest of the earth, and every one joined to them, hid themselves in dens and in the rocks of the mountains."[1067]

2. Says Scripture, "Strong is thy dwellingplace, and thou puttest thy nest in a rock,"[1068] for the kings or judges of the earth; as it says, "O ye kings: be instructed, ye judges of the earth,"[1069] for these kings are judges or ministers of their religion; flee to nests, to temples, to dwellingplaces, even as it says concerning "nests" and "strong holds," "Doth the eagle mount up at thy command, and make her nest on high? She dwelleth and abideth on the rock, upon the crag of the rock, and the strong place."[1070] In the dens and in the rocks of the mountains, or in the "strong rock,"[1071] in a particular "house of defence,"[1072] the ones "who have committed fornication and lived deliciously with her"[1073] will say

---

1067   Revelation 6:15
1068   Numbers 24:21
1069   Psalms 2:10
1070   Job 39:27,28
1071   Psalm 31:2
1072   Psalm 31:2
1073   Revelation 18:9

to them that have administered her end, "Fall on us,"[1074] when the error that they have committed has been made known to their conscience.

3. Who are these kings of the earth that are the judges of the earth? Scripture says, "Judges and officers shalt thou make thee in all thy gates, which the LORD thy God giveth thee, throughout thy tribes: and they shall judge the people with just judgment,"[1075] and, "And hast made us unto our God kings and priests."[1076]

4. This is why Moses counseled, "If there arise a matter too hard for thee in judgment, between blood and blood, between plea and plea, and between stroke and stroke, being matters of controversy within thy gates: then shalt thou arise, and get thee up into the place which the LORD thy God shall choose; and thou shalt come unto the priests the Levites, and unto the judge that shall be in those days, and enquire; and they shall shew thee the sentence of judgment: and thou shalt do according to the sentence, which they of that place which the LORD shall choose shall shew thee; and thou shalt observe to do according to all that they inform thee: according to the sentence of the law which they shall teach thee, and according to the judgment which they shall tell thee, thou shalt do: thou shalt not decline from the sentence which they shall shew thee, to the right hand, nor to the left. And the man that will do presumptuously, and will not hearken unto the priest that standeth to minister there before the LORD thy God, or unto the judge, even that man shall die: and thou shalt put away the evil from Israel."[1077]

5. And again, "If there be a controversy between men, and they come unto judgment, that the judges may judge them; then they shall justify the righteous, and condemn the wicked."[1078]

6. The kings and judges of the *earth* are "of the seed royal, and the princes of the king,"[1079] or are rather that kin of the king belonging to "his priests and his princes."[1080] Of the religious institution that will

---

1074   Revelation 6:16
1075   Deuteronomy 16:18
1076   Revelation 5:10
1077   Deuteronomy 17:8-12
1078   Deuteronomy 25:1
1079   Jeremiah 41:1
1080   Jeremiah 49:3

govern the then earth, "her princes, and her wise men, her captains, and her rulers, and her mighty men"[1081] are them that will see her demise and beg to be hidden from the face of the LORD's throne. "All the presidents of the kingdom, the governors, and the princes, the counsellors, and the captains"[1082] make up that category known as "the kings of the earth," and are like as "the princes of the tribes, and the captains of the companies that ministered to the king by course, and the captains over the thousands, and captains over the hundreds, and the stewards over all the substance and possession of the king, and of his sons."[1083] For this cause, the hierarchy of Error's institution should follow the pattern of how it says, "Jehoi'achin the king of Judah went out to the king of Babylon, he, and his mother, and his servants, and his princes, and his officers,"[1084] for the kings of the earth are the servants, the priests, the ministers, or the angels, of the earth's then king or kingdom.

7. The type of "kings" that flee at the time of the Lamb's hour are "the great men, and the rich men, and the chief captains, and the mighty men, and every bondman, and every free man,"[1085] so the analysis of such characters thus far does not reach outside of the vision of the sixth seal, for these are the particular priests and merchants of falsehood's religious denomination. As for free or bond men, it is written, "He that is called in the Lord, being a servant, is the Lord's freeman: likewise also he that is called, being free, is Christ's servant,"[1086] for the same free and bond man is the same king and prince and chief captain, and they are servants to the king, to his wife, and to her mother. It is then conclusive that "the princes, the governors, and the captains, the judges, the treasurers, the counsellors, the sheriffs, and all the rulers of the provinces,"[1087] comprise the third part of heaven in the vision of the sixth seal, even the stars, as the king is the sun, and his mother; which is also his wife of perdition; is the moon.

1081   Jeremiah 51:57
1082   Daniel 6:7
1083   1 Chronicles 28:1
1084   2 Kings 24:12
1085   Revelation 6:15
1086   1 Corinthians 7:22
1087   Daniel 3:2

8. In the sixth seal, the stars fall from heaven to the earth, for indeed the remnant clusters of the vine of the earth, after they now fully know their error, will confess to the priests and ministers that they have spoken against, "Fall on us, and hide us,"[1088] for the word is gone out against them, and is quickly fulfilling, that says, "I will set my throne in E'lam, and will destroy from thence the king and the princes, saith the LORD."[1089] "The voice of harpers, and musicians, and of pipers, and trumpeters, shall be heard no more at all in thee; and no craftsman, of whatsoever craft he be, shall be found any more in thee; and the sound of a millstone shall be heard no more at all in thee,"[1090] says the Spirit.

9. Scripture says, "The people did hide themselves in caves, and in thickets, and in rocks, and in high places, and in pits,"[1091] for, again, the rocks are synonymous with high places, and it says, "He sacrificed and burnt incense in high places,"[1092] and, "The houses of the high places."[1093] High places were pagan churches of worship, as it says, "He ordained him priests for the high places, and for the devils, and for the calves which he had made."[1094] The Revelation says that the earth's kings and judges, or the "merchants of the earth,"[1095] hid themselves in houses and nests of worship and learning, and it should be considered how it is said, "He beheld, and drove asunder the nations; and the everlasting mountains were scattered,"[1096] for these "mountains" are actually "nations," that is, are religious denominations. These priests of error, after their eyes discern the full and right name of the LORD and of His Word, will flee to that assembly contrary to the earth's empire, at which point it will be fulfilled, "The cities of the nations fell."[1097]

10. Again, the rocks of the mountains are churches and congregations of refuge modeled after the Faith of the heavenly Sanctuary for

---

1088 Revelation 6:16
1089 Jeremiah 49:38
1090 Revelation 18:22
1091 1 Samuel 13:6
1092 1 Kings 3:3
1093 2 Kings 17:29
1094 2 Chronicles 11:15
1095 Revelation 18:11
1096 Habakkuk 3:6
1097 Revelation 16:19

the earth's despised citizen, even as it says, "Whom hast thou here, that thou hast hewed thee out a sepulchre here, as he that heweth him out a sepulchre on high, and that graveth an habitation for himself in a rock?"[1098] The ministers in these places had to embrace such quarters due to the hate given to them by the earth's ministers, even as it was when "Obadi'ah took an hundred prophets, and hid them by fifty in a cave."[1099]

11. The rocks are the habitations of the denominations that make up the Spirit's "cities with their villages,"[1100] that is, "fenced cities, and of country villages."[1101] The apostles of old, for example, "preached the gospel in many villages of the Samaritans,"[1102] and "Jesus went about all the cities and villages, teaching in their synagogues, and preaching the gospel of the kingdom."[1103] Within the "village" or "city" is a "synagogue," and it is to the synagogues of refuge that the guilty will run in to for consolation during the day of the Word's fury. They will turn to "the lurking places of the villages: in the secret places"[1104] they will go. For as it says, "His secret place,"[1105] it means, "His pavilion,"[1106] therefore we read, "He shall hide me in his pavilion: in the secret of his tabernacle shall he hide me."[1107] The kings of the earth will hide their heart in synagogues unharmed by the Spirit's wrath, for, before this time, "because of the Mid'ianites the children of Israel made them dens which are in the mountains, and caves, and strong holds."[1108]

12. The beast "that wrought miracles,"[1109] who "deceived them that had received the mark of the beast, and them that worshipped his image,"[1110] will cast a shadow over the reality of his aim so that his voice

---

1098 Isaiah 22:16
1099 1 Kings 18:4
1100 Joshua 15:44
1101 1 Samuel 6:18
1102 Acts 8:25
1103 Matthew 9:35
1104 Psalms 10:8
1105 Psalms 18:11
1106 Psalms 18:11
1107 Psalms 27:5
1108 Judges 6:2
1109 Revelation 19:20
1110 Revelation 19:20

may work to gather "the kings of the earth and of the whole world"[1111] under one banner. At last, when these men behold the end of their substance, they "which were made rich by her, shall stand afar off for fear of her torment, weeping and wailing, and saying Alas, alas that great city,"[1112] only to say "to the mountains and rocks, Fall on us."[1113] Notice that when inside of the rocks, the rocks and the mountains are now able to comprehend speech, for as it says, "Their gods, their rock in whom they trusted,"[1114] so these will run to places of spiritual confidence and approach unto the god of the rocks, and we may clearly understand these "gods" by how it says, "He called them gods, unto whom the word of God came."[1115] These leaders of the former and now fallen Error, who now understand their lie, will say to these apostles of heaven's will, "Stand, I pray thee, upon me, and slay me: for anguish is come upon me, because my life is yet whole in me,"[1116] and, "Rise thou, and fall upon us."[1117]

13. Herein is why it says, "The earth shall reel to and fro like a drunkard, and shall be removed like a cottage; and the transgression thereof shall be heavy upon it; and it shall fall, and not rise again. And it shall come to pass in that day, that the LORD shall punish the host of the high ones that are on high, and the kings of the earth upon the earth."[1118] "For the day of the LORD of hosts shall be upon every one that is proud and lofty,"[1119] "and upon all the high mountains, and upon all the hills that are lifted up, and upon every high tower, and upon every fenced wall, and upon all the ships of Tar'shish, and upon all pleasant pictures."[1120] For this cause it is written, "I will strengthen the arms of the king of Babylon, and the

---

1111 Revelation 16:14
1112 Revelation 18:15,16
1113 Revelation 6:16
1114 Deuteronomy 32:37
1115 John 10:35
1116 1 Samuel 1:9
1117 Judges 8:21
1118 Isaiah 24:20,21
1119 Isaiah 2:12
1120 Isaiah 2:14-16

arm of Pharaoh shall fall down."[1121] "Lo, I will call all the families of the kingdoms of the north, saith the LORD";[1122] that is, of "mount Zion, on the sides of the north, the city of the great King";[1123] and "every eye shall see him, and they also which pierced him: and all kindreds of the earth shall wail because of him."[1124]

1121   Ezekiel 30:25
1122   Jeremiah 1:15
1123   Psalms 48:2
1124   Revelation 1:7

21

An Appointed Meeting

1. When hearing that "the kings of the earth, and the great men, and the rich men, and the chief captains, and the mighty men, and every bondman, and every free man, hid themselves in the dens and in the rocks of the mountains,"[1125] we are witnessing the fulfillment of the vision that says, "The sons also of them that afflicted thee shall come bending unto thee; and all they that despised thee shall bow themselves down at the soles of thy feet; and they shall call thee, The city of the LORD, The Zion of the Holy One of Israel. Whereas thou hast been forsaken and hated, so that no man went through thee, I will make thee an eternal excellency, a joy of many generations."[1126] To hear of the rocks in the mountains, it is that we are hearing of how it is said, "The conies are but a feeble folk, yet make they their houses in the rocks."[1127] These "rocks" that the earth's priests are running in to for fear are "houses," and a "house" is figurative language denoting a church, even as it says, "The house of God, which is the church of the living God,"[1128] and, "The tabernacle of the house of God."[1129] These rocks of the mountains are dens of prayer wherein exists right knowl-

---
1125 Revelation 6:15
1126 Isaiah 60:14,15
1127 Psalm 30:26
1128 1 Timothy 3:15
1129 1 Chronicles 6:48

edge of the living God, even as it says concerning a "rock," "Be thou my strong rock, for an house of defence to save me,"[1130] and, "In the secret of his tabernacle shall he hide me; he shall set me up upon a rock."[1131]

2. Whatever is transpiring within the religious world, it is causing the ministers of error's doctrine to turn to them that fulfill the saying, "Thou hast a little strength, and hast kept my word, and hast not denied my name,"[1132] which is, in turn, fulfilling the promise, "Behold, I will make them of the synagogue of Satan, which say they are Jews, and are not, but do lie; behold, I will make them to come and worship before thy feet, and to know that I have loved thee."[1133] These ministers and priests of the earth's then confidence are the messengers of Satan's philosophy. This religious tradition encourages "sin" against the living God's name, "and the strength of sin is the law."[1134] The "law" mentioned by Paul is the legal religious law and ordinance handwritten by priests and elders; it is a persuasion "holding the tradition of the elders"[1135] through "the handwriting of ordinances."[1136] When we hear, "Behold the Lamb of God, which taketh away the sin of the world,"[1137] we are hearing of the Word's Christ preaching a doctrine removing "sin" out of His LORD's Faith. This "sin" and "transgression" is understood from how it says, "In transgressing and lying against the LORD, and departing away from our God, speaking oppression and revolt, conceiving and uttering from the heart words of falsehood,"[1138] allowing us to understand that where the Lamb is preached, the saying is fulfilled, "Having abolished in his flesh the enmity, even the law of commandments contained in ordinances."[1139]

3. The world that we have entered into, through the sixth seal, is one after the image of the beast before it, which image is understood

---

1130 Psalm 32:2
1131 Psalm 27:5
1132 Revelation 3:8
1133 Revelation 3:9
1134 1 Corinthians 15:56
1135 Mark 7:3
1136 Colossians 2:14
1137 John 1:29
1138 Isaiah 59:13
1139 Ephesians 2:15

by how it says, "I saw a woman sit upon a scarlet coloured beast."[1140] A "woman" is figurative language denoting a church; a "beast" is a figurative illustration of a State. This red beast with seven heads and ten horns is that same great red dragon fulfilling the saying, "The dragon gave him his power, and his seat, and great authority."[1141] The dragon is a symbol of a pagan State or government, and to see a church seated upon a State is to observe the definition of confusion, as it says, "Neither shall any woman stand before a beast to lie down thereto: it is confusion."[1142] To hear that the two-horned beast "exerciseth all the power of the first beast before him"[1143] is to hear of a church and State government forwarded by "sin" against the Word's will and Faith, for this two-horned religious republic maintains its authority by "the law of commandments contained in ordinances,"[1144] "and the strength of sin is the law."[1145] The handwritten tradition and doctrine of priests and elders is "sin" because it halts faith's right course; since "whatsoever is not of faith is sin,"[1146] it is become a fact that "the law is not of faith."[1147] By subscribing to the religious bill, the mind is restrained from rightly understanding the Spirit's will, keeping the heart within a fearful box. The then Babylon rules her subjects by such a spirit, but when the Lamb is revealed to her men, and in vengeful glory, all they can do is humble themselves before the rocks.

4. These priests of the earth's vine have no right understanding that they are sinners against heaven's LORD and High Priest, for they refuse to acknowledge their wrong. But when the Lamb's impression is made, and quite forcefully upon their conscience, "their flesh shall consume away while they stand upon their feet, and their eyes shall consume away in their holes, and their tongue shall consume away in their mouth."[1148] This language is not literal, but reveals the spiritual

---

1140 Revelation 17:3
1141 Revelation 13:2
1142 Leviticus 18:23
1143 Revelation 13:12
1144 Ephesians 2:15
1145 1 Corinthians 15:56
1146 Romans 14:23
1147 Galatians 3:12
1148 Zechariah 14:12

revival and reform occurring against them that uttered "blasphemy against God, to blaspheme his name, and his tabernacle, and them that dwell in heaven."[1149] We are told that "the heavens shall pass away with a great noise,"[1150] even as it says, "With the noise of a great tumult he hath kindled fire upon it, and the branches of it are broken,"[1151] and, "A noise of chariots, and a noise of horses, even the noise of a great host."[1152] Scripture's language reveals the fall of modern Egyptian Babylon by the Word's doctrine through the speech of His host, allowing us to understand that the Word's Christ will in fact appear in clouds before every eye, and concerning "clouds," we read, "Who maketh the clouds his chariot,"[1153] and of "eyes," we read, "The eyes of your understanding."[1154] The "clouds" are but an illustration of that host who "have washed their robes, and made them white in the blood of the Lamb."[1155] These are individuals who have done the Spirit's will to confess, "The law of the Spirit of life in Christ Jesus hath made me free from the law of sin and death,"[1156] becoming "the armies which were in heaven."[1157]

5. The rule of the then royal religious world will come to an end by an omnipotent doctrine, and that consumption will fulfill the saying, "Not by might, nor by power, but by my spirit, saith the LORD of hosts."[1158] The vision of the LORD's Son from the clouds is no literal physical foreshadowing or premonition, but is a figurative illustration of how the Spirit will conquer among the hardhearted. We cannot forget that the Word appears "to execute judgment upon all, and to convince all that are ungodly."[1159] Who are the ungodly? We read: "The wrath of God is revealed from heaven against all ungodliness and unrighteous-

---

1149 Revelation 13:6
1150 2 Peter 3:10
1151 Jeremiah 11:16
1152 2 Kings 7:6
1153 Psalm 104:3
1154 Ephesians 1:18
1155 Revelation 7:14
1156 Romans 8:2
1157 Revelation 19:14
1158 Zechariah 4:6
1159 Jude 1:15

ness of men, who hold the truth in unrighteousness."[1160] The ungodly are them that uphold *the LORD's Faith* by "unrighteousness," and since "all unrighteousness is sin,"[1161] we cannot escape the fact that "the strength of sin is the law."[1162] "Sinners" are individuals forwarding service to *the Word* by the legal religious ordinance, and the Word's wrath will fall upon them that support such a course. Now, if the Word is convicting the ungodly of their wrong against His will, can a physical or natural act of celestial or supernatural anger suffice? If we say that it does, then we possess that same intoxicated spirit of them that once said, "Wilt thou that we command fire to come down from heaven, and consume them, even as Eli'as did?"[1163]

6. Such an act from the sky is nonrealistic, "for the Son of man is not come to destroy men's lives, but to save them."[1164] This allows us to understand that the wrath to appear is higher than what the carnal or sensual imagination of flesh may presume, and it is. Concerning this wrath, we read, "If any man worship the beast and his image, and receive his mark in his forehead, or in his hand, the same shall drink of the wine of the wrath of God."[1165] This "wrath" is "wine"; there is no more or less than this. "God" is the Word. In the beginning, "the Word was God,"[1166] and today, and for ever more, the Word is still, and will always be, God. "Wine" is a term connoting doctrine, and to hear of "God's wrath," it is to hear of the Word's vengeance through doctrine. Because "God is a Spirit,"[1167] and because "a spirit hath not flesh and bones,"[1168] this wrath must find itself executed against no physical frame, but against the body and organs of the spirit of the mind. "There is a natural body, and there is a spiritual body,"[1169] and because "that

---

1160 Romans 1:18
1161 1 John 5:17
1162 1 Corinthians 15:56
1163 Luke 9:54
1164 Luke 9:56
1165 Revelation 14:9,10
1166 John 1:1
1167 John 4:24
1168 Luke 24:39
1169 1 Corinthians 15:44

which is born of the Spirit is spirit,"[1170] it is that "the Spirit of life";[1171] who is "the Word of life";[1172] must labor within the inward parts of the heart, even as it says, "Strengthened with might by his Spirit in the inner man."[1173] This strengthening of His Spirit is understood by how it says, "I am full of power by the spirit of the LORD, and of judgment, and of might,"[1174] and, "I have filled him with the spirit of God, in wisdom, and in understanding, and in knowledge."[1175]

7. When filled with the Word's Spirit, it is that the mind is edified "with the washing of water by the word."[1176] The Spirit devours the inward parts of the heart by His judgment, which judgment is that wisdom of His name and will, which wisdom, "when he is come, he will reprove the world of sin, and of righteousness, and of judgment."[1177] The earth's priests, in the sixth seal of the Revelation, are turned to heaven's ministers because they have just witnessed the religious world's correction, and by that rebuke have come to discern their sin against heaven's throne, moving them to confess to heaven's host, "I have borne chastisement, I will not offend any more: that which I see not teach thou me: if I have done iniquity, I will do no more."[1178] Thus, they say "to the mountains and rocks, Fall on us, and hide us from the face of him that sitteth on the throne, and from the wrath of the Lamb."[1179] These men are asking to be slain, and not literally, for they now care to learn of and do "the circumcision made without hands, in putting off the body of the sins of the flesh by the circumcision of Christ."[1180] These seek a conversation hidden from the fury of the face of the LORD's High Priest. The Lamb has come up before their eyes,

---

1170   John 3:6
1171   Revelation 11:11
1172   1 John 1:1
1173   Ephesians 3:16
1174   Micah 3:8
1175   Exodus 31:3
1176   Ephesians 5:26
1177   John 16:8
1178   Job 34:31,32
1179   Revelation 6:16
1180   Colossians 2:11

and they are ready to remove from "sin" against His LORD's name and throne.

8. They will accept and keep the Word's baptism, and we know that they will because John, at the end of this shaking, "heard as it were the voice of a great multitude, and as the voice of many waters, and as the voice of mighty thunderings, saying, Allelu'ia: for the Lord God omnipotent reigneth."[1181] When we hear of "water," it is well to remember how it says, "The waters...are peoples, and multitudes, and nations, and tongues."[1182] What we are made to observe in vision is the then Gentile host of the religious world converted to heaven's throne religion, and in company with heaven's priests and apostles, for the saying is fulfilled, "All nations shall come and worship before thee; for thy judgments are made manifest."[1183] When the name of the LORD's Son appears in vengeful glory, a great revival and reform will occur within the *earth*, accomplishing the earth's full and open reconciliation "to the general assembly and church of the firstborn, which are written in heaven, and to God the Judge of all, and to the spirits of just men made perfect, and to Jesus the mediator of the new covenant."[1184] Heaven's host, after the Word's speech fully devours earth's religious institution, will then place that spirit of "sin" "into the bottomless pit, and shut him up, and set a seal upon him, that he should deceive the nations no more, till the thousand years should be fulfilled."[1185]

9. When hearing that priests are running to the rocks, and are begging to be hid by them, we are hearing of a very great reform occurring. The religion of the serpent is being understood for what it is; his host is, along with all joined to them, understanding that they have been stoutly adhering to plain religious error. These individuals will burn before the Word and His host, and this burning is not literal or physical, but will occur within the heart of the conscience, even as it says, "I am poured out like water, and all my bones are out of joint: my

---

1181 Revelation 19:6
1182 Revelation 17:15
1183 Revelation 15:4
1184 Hebrews 12:23,24
1185 Revelation 20:3

heart is like wax; it is melted in the midst of my bowels,"[1186] and, "My bowels, my bowels! I am pained at my very heart; my heart maketh a noise in me."[1187] Therefore "by the spirit of judgment, and by the spirit of burning,"[1188] "the earth shall be filled with the knowledge of the glory of the LORD, as the waters cover the sea,"[1189] for it will then be said, "Blessed are they which are called unto the marriage supper of the Lamb."[1190]

10. Who are these that are called? We read, concerning the "called," "I called for you, to see you, and to speak with you."[1191] All who have communed with the Word's Spirit, all who have allowed the thoughts of their heart to embrace the thoughts of the living God's heart, all how have allowed the eyes of their faith to capture the revelation of His Son's name and form, and have allowed their face to be seen of His face, will find their place, in the age of the Lamb's marriage supper, at His table. Confusion will only last for a time, but then after that, it will be said, "Behold, how good and how pleasant it is for brethren to dwell together in unity!"[1192]

1186 Psalm 22:14
1187 Jeremiah 4:19
1188 Isaiah 4:4
1189 Habakkuk 2:14
1190 Revelation 19:9
1191 Acts 28:20
1192 Psalm 133:1

22

A Blessed Movement

1. A new time of praise and judgment commences when the earth's converted priests; who say, "The great day of his wrath is come; and who shall be able to stand";[1193] put "sin" away. For, who shall be able to stand what? Concerning what these men care to "stand" before, we read, "In controversy they shall stand in judgment,"[1194] and, "Then said Paul, I stand at Caesar's judgment seat, where I ought to be judged."[1195] This people of Egypt's institution did not know that the Lamb's wrath, and that the face of His LORD's throne, was against them, until the Lamb's force consumed their inwards. They did not know that the day of the Spirit's vengeance was pronounced against the judgment of their conversation, but now they know that "the ungodly shall not stand in the judgment, nor sinners in the congregation of the righteous."[1196] For this cause, the Spirit revealed to John a period of consolation. He writes, concerning the events after the Lamb's judgment: "After these things I saw four angels standing on the four corners of the earth, holding the four winds of the earth, that the wind should not blow on

---

1193 Revelation 6:17
1194 Ezekiel 44:24
1195 Acts 25:10
1196 Psalm 1:5

the earth, nor on the sea, nor on any tree. And I saw another angel ascending from the east, having the seal of the living God: and he cried with a loud voice to the four angels, to whom it was given to hurt the earth and the sea, saying, Hurt not the earth, neither the sea, nor the trees, till we have sealed the servants of our God in their foreheads."[1197]

2. The Revelation may not appear to be an orderly vision, but closer examination of the Spirit's thoughts will reveal the Revelation to be full of order. From the scenes of utter terror within the sixth seal, John records that after these things; after "the sun became black as sackcloth of hair, and the moon became as blood; and the stars of heaven fell unto the earth";[1198] and the ministers of that heaven "said to the mountains and rocks, Fall on us";[1199] after these things, John is made to observe a period of rest for sealing them that would reverence the Word.

3. The great appearing of the Word in omnipotent glory does not mean the end of the physical world, but rather a new age of learning for lawfully executing the Spirit's judgment. Now that error's institution is for ever blotted out, and now that the spirit of error is removed from the heart of the earth's men, it is become time that, since the religious world is enlightened on the living God's science, the religious world pass through their judgment. The appearing of heaven's Faith by the clouds signifies a specific movement occurring within the heavenly Sanctuary. When the LORD's High Priest was resurrected and taken in to the heavenly Sanctuary, His name commenced its office within the first Room of that Sanctuary. He would then, at the time appointed, move in to the second Room of that Temple to begin a new phase of His ministry, which movement of old was called, "The Day of Atonement." When this specific season was "thus ordained, the priests went always into the first tabernacle, accomplishing the service of God. But into the second went the high priest alone once every year, not without blood, which he offered for himself, and for the errors of the people: the Holy

---

1197 Revelation 7:1-3
1198 Revelation 6:12,13
1199 Revelation 6:16

Ghost this signifying, that the way into the holiest of all was not yet made manifest, while as the first tabernacle was yet standing."[1200]

4. When we hear John saying, "And the temple of God was opened in heaven, and there was seen in his temple the ark of his testament,"[1201] John, as a participant in this scene, represents them that should be alive to see, and live under, the season when the LORD's Christ passes in to the second Room of the heavenly Sanctuary, beginning heaven's day of atonement. This LORD's Christ did pass in to the second Room of the heavenly Sanctuary, and has long since been in that Room. We understand when He did pass in to this Room by how it says, "Unto two thousand and three hundred days; then shall the sanctuary be cleansed."[1202] The cleansing of the Sanctuary only occurred, under the ancient priesthood, once a year, and began within the most holy place of the tabernacle, or within the second apartment of the temple. We discern the beginning of the 2300 day or year[1203] prophecy within Daniel chapter nine, for the angel returns in that chapter to help explain to Daniel key events within that vision from the previous chapter. The seventy weeks (weeks of years) given to Daniel mark the beginning of the 2300-year vision, which beginning is understood by the commandment to restore Jerusalem, which commandment was given in 457BC to Ezra.

5. If we subtract 457 from the 2300 years, we arrive at the expected date when the LORD's High Priest entered in to the second Room of the heavenly Sanctuary, which date, because we are running numbers from BC to AD, is 1844AD. At this time the saying was fulfilled, "The temple of God was opened in heaven, and there was seen in his temple the ark of his testament."[1204]

6. There are only two rooms within the tabernacle, and Moses fashioned them after the likeness of what he saw within the LORD's heavenly City when in communion with His Spirit on the mount. This

---

1200   Hebrews 9:6-8
1201   Revelation 11:19
1202   Daniel 8:14
1203   A "day," in prophetic language, is a "year," even as it says, "I have appointed thee each day for a year," Ezekiel 4:6, and, "Forty days, each day for a year," Numbers 14:34.
1204   Revelation 11:19

Moses saw "a tabernacle made; the first, wherein was the candlestick, and the table, and the shewbread; which is called the sanctuary. And after the second veil, the tabernacle which is called the Holiest of all; which had the golden censer, and the ark of the covenant...and the tables of the covenant; and over it the cher'ubims of glory shadowing the mercyseat."[1205] When we hear from John that the temple containing the ark is now open, we may understand that the LORD's High Priest has left heaven's first Room and is entered in to the second, which Room the Spirit warned Moses of, saying, "Speak unto Aaron thy brother, that he come not at all times into the holy place within the vail before the mercy seat, which is upon the ark; that he die not."[1206] For "the priests went always into the first tabernacle, accomplishing the service of God. But into the second went the high priest alone once every year."[1207]

7. The ministry of the high priest on the Day of Atonement is for "reconciling the holy place, and the tabernacle of the congregation, and the altar,"[1208] to the Word's heavenly Sanctuary. The Day of Atonement begins within the second Room, and we alive today exist under this day of our reconciliation to the heavenly Sanctuary's Word and Spirit. When this day ends, our High Priest's face will then pass in to the first Room, to begin cleansing the host of that Room. The day of our High Priest's heavenly atonement is, in reality, an investigative judgment for the host within the Room of His operation. Therefore since 1844AD, and until the live goat is fully handled, the counsel is, "Fear God, and give glory to him; for the hour of his judgment is come: and worship him that made heaven, and earth, and the sea, and the fountains of waters."[1209] This is the year of our conversation's atonement to the living God's throne, and this reconciliation cannot commence without our willingness to do His name's judgment. Atonement only occurs by His judgment, and this judgment is a commandment that must be examined and executed by us, as He says, "A law shall proceed from me,

---

1205 Hebrews 9:2-5
1206 Leviticus 16:2
1207 Hebrews 9:6,7
1208 Leviticus 16:20
1209 Revelation 14:7

and I will make my judgment to rest for a light of the people."[1210] By the passing, regenerating, and priestly consecration of the LORD's Christ, "we have received a commandment from the Father"[1211] to learn of and do, and this judgment is "the law of the Spirit of life."[1212]

8. It is today our responsibility to learn of and do this law that we may find harmony with the Spirit, Word, and Ten Commandments, within the Room of our High Priest's current mediation. Every thing within this second Room is become crucial to our conversation's growth and development, but to have any regard for this Room, and the duty it relays to the one whose heart is within it, it is that the inwards must first be filled with the Spirit's Word. Them joined to this Room and High Priest are being examined on whether or not they will personally engage self with His voice, and this is done according to the saying, "To humble thee, and to prove thee, to know what was in thine heart, whether thou wouldest keep his commandments, or no."[1213] So then, seeing as how our conversation is examined, it is not that we fold our arms and devour our own self-cultivated and inherited flesh, but we are counseled, "Be ye transformed by the renewing of your mind, that ye may prove what is that good, and acceptable, and perfect, will of God."[1214] The cleansing of heaven's Sanctuary is a perfecting of its host, and we are to be "perfect, as pertaining to the conscience."[1215] Because the conscience of the conversation is the Spirit's concern, because it is the Word's intention to "purge your conscience from dead works to serve the living God,"[1216] it is that the mind of our conversation must experience the living God's blessing, which blessing He states by saying, "I will pour my spirit upon thy seed, and my blessing upon thine offspring,"[1217] and, "I will pour out my spirit unto you, I will make known my words unto you."[1218]

1210 Isaiah 51:4
1211 2 John 1:4
1212 Romans 8:2
1213 Deuteronomy 8:2
1214 Romans 12:2
1215 Hebrews 9:9
1216 Hebrews 9:14
1217 Isaiah 44:3
1218 Proverbs 1:23

9. Mental and spiritual discernment is that blessing to appear by examining and doing the Spirit's will and learning. This year of atonement is for cultivating a conversation in likeness to that of the LORD's High Priest, and because "that which is born of the Spirit is spirit,"[1219] the counsel is, "Be renewed in the spirit of your mind."[1220] Because "the ungodly shall not stand in the judgment, nor sinners in the congregation of the righteous,"[1221] it is that, in order to stand in the right congregation, "sin" against heaven's Word and LORD must cease. "Having abolished in his flesh the enmity, even the law of commandments contained in ordinances,"[1222] the passing flesh of the Spirit's Christ on the tree perpetually means that "the strength of sin is the law."[1223] This Christ on the tree is an illustration of what is erroneous to the Spirit's will and judgment, which is why it says, "He that is hanged is accursed of God."[1224] "Blotting out the handwriting of ordinances"[1225] and "nailing it to his cross,"[1226] this Christ has for ever condemned that body of knowledge forwarding service to *the Word* by the use of handcrafted religious laws and traditions. Such a course is accursed of the Word, becoming "sin" to heaven's higher learning. This Christ, therefore, although passing on the tree to illustrate the fact that the ghost is taken from the body of that religious error by the pen of priests and elders, being regenerated and brought in to the heavenly Sanctuary, preaches a doctrine of resurrection in heart and mind from "philosophy and vain deceit, after the tradition of men,"[1227] to the Word's will and learning within the heavenly Sanctuary.

10. Them that are joined to this Christ's heavenly assembly are become members of a judged host for sanctification. This judgment passes upon the Spirit's creation first, and then it moves to them that uphold devotion to *His LORD* and *Father* by "sin," that is, by a

---

1219 John 3:6
1220 Ephesians 4:23
1221 Psalm 1:5
1222 Ephesians 2:15
1223 1 Corinthians 15:56
1224 Deuteronomy 21:23
1225 Colossians 2:14
1226 Colossians 2:14
1227 Colossians 2:8

conversation *blessing* self through handwritten religious laws and doctrines. When this Christ moves from out of the second Room in to the first Room, atonement's season is not over, but is continuing; it is His Word's task, during this day of our atonement, to "make an atonement for the holy sanctuary, and he shall make an atonement for the tabernacle of the congregation, and for the altar, and he shall make an atonement for the priests, and for all the people of the congregation."[1228] When our Priest exits the holy temple, or "the temple of the tabernacle of the testimony in heaven,"[1229] He is moving in to the first Room of heaven's Building, which entrance begins a new judgment for a new host, as it says, "So shall he do for the tabernacle of the congregation, that remaineth among them in the midst of their uncleanness."[1230] This congregation is not that former congregation of the second Room, for the judgment of this people within the first Room is "upon the men which had the mark of the beast, and upon them which worshipped his image."[1231] We understand that our High Priest has moved in to the first Room from the second because, during the falling plagues, John notes, "I heard another out of the altar say, Even so, Lord God Almighty, true and righteous are thy judgments."[1232]

11. There is only one figure standing before the altar of incense at this time, and that is the high priest of the temple. We may therefore understand the time and mission of the plagues by what formerly took place when the Spirit's name found Himself in the first Room of the Temple upon its resurrection, for it says, "And the angel took the censer, and filled it with fire of the altar, and cast it into the earth: and there were voices, and thunderings, and lightnings, and an earthquake."[1233] When this Spirit's Faith was anointed as His High Priest within heaven's Temple, on earth, and among His host, "they were all filled with

---

1228 Leviticus 16:33
1229 Revelation 15:5
1230 Leviticus 16:16
1231 Revelation 16:2
1232 Revelation 16:7
1233 Revelation 8:5

the Holy Ghost";[1234] "it sat upon each of them."[1235] We understand that this event coincides with what took place within the heavenly Sanctuary by Peter, who says, "Therefore being by the right hand of God exalted, and having received of the Father the promise of the Holy Ghost, he hath shed forth this, which ye now see and hear."[1236] A great outpouring of blessing fell upon them that were gathered together after His Christ ascended in to heaven's first Room, and the same will occur again when the Word of His mediation, for the second and final time, arrives within the first Room of the heavenly Sanctuary. Concerning this "outpouring," it is defined for us by the Spirit, who says, "My doctrine shall drop as the rain."[1237] When our High Priest quits the second Room and re-appears within the first, a very great reformatory movement will commence by them that have been judged and approved from the formed examination.

12. The judgment of modern Egyptian Babylon will cause "a great earthquake, such as was not since men were upon the earth, so mighty an earthquake, and so great."[1238] For, by those ministers "having the seven plagues, clothed in pure and white linen, and having their breasts girded with golden girdles,"[1239] "the great city was divided into three parts, and the cities of the nations fell: and great Babylon came in remembrance before God, to give unto her the cup of the wine of the fierceness of his wrath."[1240] Hereafter "the heaven departed as a scroll when it is rolled together; and every mountain and island were moved out of their places. And the kings of the earth, and the great men, and the rich men, and the chief captains, and the mighty men, and every bondman, and every free man, hid themselves in the dens and in the rocks of the mountains; and said to the mountains and rocks, Fall on us, and hide us from the face of him that sitteth on the throne, and

---

1234 Acts 2:4
1235 Acts 2:3
1236 Acts 2:33
1237 Deuteronomy 32:2
1238 Revelation 16:18
1239 Revelation 15:7
1240 Revelation 16:19

from the wrath of the Lamb."[1241] "The beast was taken, and with him the false prophet that wrought miracles before him, with which he deceived them that had received the mark of the beast, and them that worshipped his image. These both were cast alive into a lake of fire burning with brimstone. And the remnant were slain with the sword of him that sat upon the horse."[1242]

13. This "sword" should not be thought of as a literal sword, nor should this slaying be understood as a natural event; this is "the sword of the Spirit, which is the word of God."[1243] Herein it is well to remember that "the word of God is quick, and powerful, and sharper than any twoedged sword, piercing even to the dividing asunder of soul and spirit, and of the joints and marrow, and is a discerner of the thoughts and intents of the heart,"[1244] for what the Revelation relates to us is the brutal slaying of consciences, as it says, "Being convicted by their own conscience."[1245] Such a conviction is not fully born of the plagues, for blasphemy against the Word is still alive during the plagues. But when the Spirit's will and law "treadeth the winepress of the fierceness and wrath of Almighty God,"[1246] then it will be said, "The kingdoms of this world are become the kingdoms of our Lord, and of his Christ; and he shall reign for ever and ever."[1247] This is that Spirit who "in righteousness he doth judge and make war,"[1248] and "righteousness" is no physical or natural act. The righteousness of the Word is summed up in the saying, "If the Spirit of him that raised up Jesus from the dead dwell in you, he that raised up Christ from the dead shall also quicken your mortal bodies by his Spirit,"[1249] and, "The law of the Spirit of life in Christ Jesus hath made me free from the law of sin and death."[1250]

1241 Revelation 6:14-16
1242 Revelation 19:20,21
1243 Ephesians 6:17
1244 Hebrews 4:12
1245 John 8:9
1246 Revelation 19:15
1247 Revelation 11:15
1248 Revelation 19:11
1249 Revelation 8:11
1250 Romans 8:2

Herein we understand that this war is in "word and doctrine"[1251] "both to exhort and to convince the gainsayers."[1252]

14. Therefore, when the war is ended, the Word's record will read: "Thou hast done well in executing that which is right in mine eyes, and hast done unto the house of Ahab according to all that was in mine heart,"[1253] and, "He put down the idolatrous priests, whom the kings of Judah had ordained to burn incense in the high places in the cities of Judah, and in the places round about Jerusalem; them also that burned incense unto Ba'al, to the sun, and to the moon, and to the planets, and to all the host of heaven. And he brought out the grove from the house of the LORD, without Jerusalem, unto the brook Kid'ron, and burned it at the brook Kid'ron, and stamped it small to powder, and cast the powder thereof upon the graves of the children of the people. And he brake down the houses of the sodomites, that were by the house of the LORD, where the women wove hangings for the grove. And he brought all the priests out of the cities of Judah, and defiled the high places where the priests had burned incense, from Ge'ba to Be'er-she'ba, and brake down the high places of the gates that were in the entering in of the gate of Joshua the governor of the city, which were on a man's left hand at the gate of the city."[1254]

15. It is after all of this is accomplished that John writes, "After these things I saw four angels standing on the four corners of the earth, holding the four winds of the earth."[1255]

16. After such a great reformatory movement, after the places of men are become the temples of the LORD God's throne, and of His Son's name, John then hears a message, saying, "Hurt not the earth, neither the sea, nor the trees, till we have sealed the servants of our God in their foreheads."[1256] Now that error's ministers comprehend their wrong, and are also informed of atonement's season, inquiring of

---

1251   1 Timothy 5:17
1252   Titus 1:9
1253   2 Kings 10:30
1254   2 Kings 23:5-8
1255   Revelation 7:1
1256   Revelation 7:3

heaven's apostles, "Sirs, what must I do to be saved?"[1257] John observes a period of judgment given to them that beg the rocks to slay them, and at the end of this judgment writes, "I heard the number of them which were sealed: and there were sealed an hundred and forty and four thousand of all the tribes of the children of Israel."[1258] Why such a little number? The earth's first, second, and third converted generation confidently dwelt by that testimony of their conscience impressed by the Lamb's wrath, but "there arose another generation after them, which knew not the LORD, nor yet the works which he had done for Israel. And the children of Israel did evil in the sight of the LORD, and served Ba'alim,"[1259] for "when the thousand years are expired, Satan shall be loosed out of his prison, and shall go out to deceive."[1260]

17. After a thousand years of right light and knowledge without the spirit of error, controversy against heaven's Word and LORD will again find itself reinstated for a second judgment and resurrection.

1257 Acts 16:30
1258 Revelation 7:4
1259 Judges 2:10,11
1260 Revelation 20:7,8

23

A Pot Of Flesh

1. When hearing that "the kings of the earth, and the great men, and the rich men, and the chief captains, and the mighty men, and every bondman, and every free man, hid themselves in the dens and in the rocks of the mountains,"[1261] we cannot forget that the prophet Isaiah also foresaw this scene, writing, "They shall go into the holes of the rocks, and into the caves of the earth, for fear of the LORD, and for the glory of his majesty, when he ariseth to shake terribly the earth. In that day a man shall cast his idols of silver, and his idols of gold, which they made each one for himself to worship, to the moles and to the bats."[1262] When Egypt's then priests and ministers observe the wisdom of the Word's revelation in wrathful tones, they will turn to the then "bats" and "moles" of the earth, whose dwelling is within the earth's "dens" and "rocks."

2. Falsehood's priests are, after witnessing their confidence meet her end; for "they cast dust on their heads, and cried, weeping and wailing, saying, Alas, alas";[1263] are running to them that are "a reproach

---

1261 Revelation 6:15
1262 Isaiah 2:19,20
1263 Revelation 18:19

of men, and despised of the people,"[1264] to learn how to stand during their judgment. Bats[1265] and moles[1266] are categorized in Scripture as unclean creatures, therefore when hearing that Egypt's men will cast their idols and ideologies to the bats and moles of the rocks, it is that we are hearing of individuals perceived to be unclean in understanding devouring the flesh of them that spoke against them.

3. A "bat" is, in the eleventh chapter of Leviticus, verse thirteen, categorized as a fowl, and in the same book and chapter, in verse twenty-nine, a "mole" is categorized as a thing creeping upon the earth. To hear of ministers becoming the meal of the bat and the mole is to observe the saying, "I saw an angel standing in the sun; and he cried with a loud voice, saying to all the fowls that fly in the midst of heaven, Come and gather yourselves together unto the supper of the great God,"[1267] and, "I will even give them into the hand of their enemies, and into the hand of them that seek their life: and their dead bodies shall be for meat unto the fowls of the heaven, and to the beasts of the earth."[1268] This language is not literal; the controversy at hand is not over the physical flesh of the human being; but it says, "In that day a man shall cast his idols of silver, and his idols of gold, which they made each one for himself to worship, to the moles and to the bats."[1269] The Spirit's wrath is "against the rulers of the darkness of this world, against spiritual wickedness in high places,"[1270] and by the unclean creatures of heaven, a great slaughter will be made against the "body" of every minister contrary to heaven's will and science. These "bodies" are not literal bodies, but are the personal and individual body of faith, for it is the Spirit's intention that we go forward "putting off the body of the sins of the flesh by the circumcision of Christ."[1271]

1264 Psalm 22:6
1265 Leviticus 11:19
1266 Leviticus 11:30
1267 Revelation 19:17
1268 Jeremiah 34:20
1269 Isaiah 2:20
1270 Ephesians 6:12
1271 Colossians 2:11

4. As unclean creatures, to hear that the bat and the mole are on the LORD God's side is to hear of converts to the LORD's Word working on behalf of His name among their own tribes and denominations. Isn't this already written to occur? Doesn't it say, "The strangers shall be joined with them, and they shall cleave to the house of Jacob,"[1272] and, "The house of Israel shall possess them in the land of the LORD for servants and handmaids: and they shall take them captives, whose captives they were; and they shall rule over their oppressors"?[1273] Again, isn't it written, concerning the then Egyptian host, "Her merchandise and her hire shall be holiness to the LORD,"[1274] and, "The residue of my people shall spoil them, and the remnant of my people shall possess them"?[1275]

5. The seven last plagues; which prepare the way for the seventh trumpet to sound the third woe; are designed to put the spirit and institution of the serpent to sleep, even as it says, "Egypt shall be a desolation, and E'dom shall be a desolate wilderness, for the violence against the children of Judah, because they have shed innocent blood in their land."[1276] With the third woe utterly destroying that institution of religious error holding the LORD's name in unrighteousness, converts from Egypt's philosophy will be won to the Word's will and doctrine, and those priests and churches will turn to the defense of salvation's right science, becoming an instrument of heaven's stewards against their own kind.

6. These bats and moles, although unclean to Egypt and Pharaoh, are become clean to the living God. These bats and moles are, through the vengeful impression of the Word, members of "the general assembly and church of the firstborn, which are written in heaven,"[1277] and at the time appointed, these ministers will fulfill their role, even according to how it says, "Speak unto every feathered fowl, and to every beast of the field, Assemble yourselves, and come; gather yourselves on every side

---

1272 Isaiah 14:1
1273 Isaiah 14:2
1274 Isaiah 23:18
1275 Zephaniah 2:9
1276 Joel 3:19
1277 Hebrews 12:23

to my sacrifice that I do sacrifice for you, even a great sacrifice upon the mountains of Israel, that ye may eat flesh, and drink blood. Ye shall eat the flesh of the mighty, and drink the blood of the princes of the earth, of rams, of lambs, and of goats, of bullocks, all of them fatlings of Ba'shan. And ye shall eat fat till ye be full, and drink blood till ye be drunken, of my sacrifice which I have sacrificed for you."[1278]

7. Again, this language is not literal. The same characters that Ezekiel notes are the same characters that John recognizes within the sixth seal. Ministers will accomplish this act, even as it says, "They shall lay hold every one on the hand of his neighbour, and his hand shall rise up against the hand of his neighbour."[1279] These scenes spoken of by John and Ezekiel are illustrations of religious ideologies, perceptions, doctrines, and conversations being swallowed up by the wisdom of the LORD's Faith, for, remember, concerning the one pronouncing this slaughter, John writes, "I saw an angel standing in the sun; and he cried with a loud voice, saying to all the fowls that fly in the midst of heaven, Come and gather yourselves together unto the supper of the great God."[1280]

8. This slaughter is over the conscience of the religious conversation, seeing as how, according to the Spirit's Faith, it is His Word's intention to "purge your conscience from dead works to serve the living God."[1281] No physical warfare can devour the conscience, which is why the voice of that angel in the sun spoke the charge for heaven's host. This "angel" and "sun" is an illustration of "the day star,"[1282] which is also "the bright and morning star."[1283] The Spirit defines an "angel" for us by saying, "The seven stars are the angels of the seven churches."[1284] A "star" is an "angel," and this "angel" is a message. The "sun" is a term denoting the "day" or the "morning," which terms denote "light," and "all things that are reproved are made manifest by the light: for

---

1278   Ezekiel 39:17-19
1279   Zechariah 14:13
1280   Revelation 19:17
1281   Hebrews 9:14
1282   2 Peter 1:19
1283   Revelation 22:16
1284   Revelation 1:20

whatsoever doth make manifest is light."[1285] This angel standing in the sun is a message of heaven's LORD standing in "the light of the knowledge of the glory of God in the face of Jesus Christ."[1286] This message is that revelation of "the power and coming of our Lord Jesus Christ,"[1287] which "coming" is according to the saying, "Until the day dawn, and the day star arise in your hearts."[1288] This allows us to understand that Scripture speaks of no physical or literal "coming" of "Jesus Christ," for "the Lord Jesus Christ our Saviour"[1289] is, in right context of language, "the commandment of God our Saviour."[1290]

9. The star or message standing in the light of the day is "the Lord Jesus Christ our Saviour,"[1291] which "Lord" and "Savior" is "the commandment of God our Saviour."[1292] The "day star" is the light of the Spirit's message, and seeing as how "the commandment is a lamp; and the law is light";[1293] the morning star to arise upon the heart is heaven's commandment of "the law of the Spirit of life."[1294] The inspiration behind the movement of heaven's mole and bat, or fowl and beast, is the law of redemption's right science. For, the "beast" mentioned is no literal animal, but is according to the saying, "I have fought with beasts at Eph'esus."[1295] Who is Paul talking about? We find our answer by how it says of Paul, "He sent to Eph'esus, and called the elders of the church."[1296] The fowls of the heaven and the beasts of the earth, they are priests and elders of religious error now assisting the Spirit's host, even as it says, "The sons of strangers shall build up thy walls, and their kings shall minister unto thee."[1297] Thus, at the time appointed, the Spirit's Word, through the third woe of the final trumpet, will utterly

---

1285 Ephesians 5:13
1286 2 Corinthians 5:6
1287 2 Peter 1:16
1288 2 Peter 1:19
1289 Titus 1:4
1290 Titus 1:3
1291 Titus 1:4
1292 Titus 1:3
1293 Proverbs 6:23
1294 Romans 8:2
1295 1 Corinthians 15:32
1296 Acts 20:17
1297 Isaiah 60:10

silence the institution of religious error, leaving Egypt's chief men without a home and running for terror from the LORD's face. And this "running" is not literal, but is according to the saying, "Write the vision, and make it plain upon tables, that he may run that readeth it."[1298]

10. Through the Word's omnipotent impression, the religious world will embrace the greatest revival and reform ever known among ministers professing *the LORD* and *Word* of *the Bible*; "many shall run to and fro, and knowledge shall be increased."[1299] This "running"; as it says, "The kings of the earth...hid themselves in the dens and in the rocks of the mountains";[1300] is a running of the fingers through Scripture to mentally and spiritually discern heaven's will and law, even as it says, "They shall run to and fro to seek the word of the LORD."[1301] These "dens" and "rocks" are figurative illustrations of assemblies and ministers condemned by Egypt's men and their institution. The bats and moles of these houses are unclean to the men of Egyptian Babylon, for they do reject Pharaoh's sovereignty and speak against the scepter of his throne. It is for this reason that they must take up a residence in the rocks of Egypt, for Egypt's men have forced them in to such a place, but, at the time appointed, the saying will be fulfilled, "They brought those men which had accused Daniel, and they cast them into the den of lions, them, their children, and their wives; and the lions had the mastery of them, and brake all their bones in pieces or ever they came at the bottom of the den."[1302]

11. This is but an illustration of what will take place under the sixth seal and to the earth's priests, for they, and their families, will have their bodies torn in pieces, and not one of them will gather up that body to themselves ever again. Again, these bodies are not literal or physical bodies, but are "bodies" according to the saying, "If ye through the Spirit do mortify the deeds of the body, ye shall live."[1303] The "body" under judgment is that body *blessed* by religious deeds, acts, doctrines,

---

1298 Habakkuk 2:2
1299 Daniel 12:4
1300 Revelation 6:15
1301 Amos 8:12
1302 Daniel 6:24
1303 Romans 8:13

and traditions, even as it says, "By the deeds of the law there shall no flesh be justified in his sight."[1304]

12. The "law" here mentioned by Paul is the legal religious law of priests and elders, and Egypt's creed is based upon service to religious laws and doctrines for *righteousness*; "Righteousness come by the law,"[1305] they preach. This *righteousness* is for the body of the faith, for the flesh of one's spiritual confidence, and it is given; according to the mind of ministers; only through obeying the pen of priests and elders; meanwhile the Spirit's Word preaches that our conversation is to be "written not with ink, but with the Spirit of the living God."[1306] By the LORD's Word, we are taught that His "Christ hath redeemed us from the curse of the law, being made a curse for us: for it is written, Cursed is every one that hangeth on a tree";[1307] to hear of a *Christ* preaching obedience to religious laws; to doctrines, ceremonies, traditions, and *sabbaths* concocted by men; is to observe a blatant liar speaking "blasphemy against God, to blaspheme his name, and his tabernacle, and them that dwell in heaven."[1308] As opposed to beautifying the outward appearance of the conversation, the living God's intention is the creation of a perfect conversation, and "perfect, as pertaining to the conscience."[1309]

13. When the serpent's army has revealed to them, and in wrathful tones, the Lamb's face, the body of their confidence will drop; "the slain of the LORD shall be at that day from one end of the earth even unto the other end of the earth: they shall not be lamented, neither gathered, nor buried; they shall be dung upon the ground."[1310] The "Lamb" is no literal creature, but is that law and commandment of the living God's heavenly Sanctuary. Where the Lamb is preached, there is no sin occurring against the LORD and Word of this Sanctuary's High Priest, and it is well to know that "the strength of sin is the

---

1304 Romans 3:20
1305 Galatians 2:21
1306 2 Corinthians 3:3
1307 Galatians 3:13
1308 Revelation 13:6
1309 Hebrews 9:9
1310 Jeremiah 25:33

law."[1311] Whosoever has the Lamb correctly preached to them, their conversation's conscience will fall in to the light of the living God's face, and by the law of that face, they will quit the pen of the religious age to "seek those things which are above, where Christ sitteth on the right hand of God."[1312] Understanding that their Regime enforced religious laws upon the conscience, and did order death upon any one not willing to take on that Regime's name and oath, and that it did so while professing *the Christ* of *the Bible*, "their flesh shall consume away while they stand upon their feet,"[1313] and, says the Spirit, "Their carcases will I give to be meat for the fowls of the heaven, and for the beasts of the earth."[1314]

14. When the third woe has accomplished its mission, Egypt will for ever be blotted out from the earth, and the conversation attached to it will undergo an earth-shaking reform.

1311 1 Corinthians 15:56
1312 Colossians 3:1
1313 Zechariah 14:12
1314 Jeremiah 19:7

24

Places Of Wonder

1. When the Word "treadeth the winepress of the fierceness and wrath of Almighty God,"[1315] this slaughter will be no physical or fleshly destruction or massacre; we understand this by how it says, "The Lord at thy right hand shall strike through kings in the day of his wrath. He shall judge among the heathen, he shall fill the places with the dead bodies; he shall wound the heads over many countries."[1316] This annihilation will leave "places" filled with dead bodies, and it is well to understand just what "places" the Spirit references to understand what "bodies" are desired at this time.

2. When Moses organized the tabernacle in the wilderness, he built this building with two "places"; the Spirit told him, "The vail shall divide unto you between the holy place and the most holy. And thou shalt put the mercy seat upon the ark of the testimony in the most holy place."[1317] The tabernacle is a building with two "places" or "rooms," which "places" the LORD calls, "My sanctuaries."[1318] What separated one room from the other room was a veil, for, in order to enter in to

---

1315 Revelation 19:15
1316 Psalm 110:5,6
1317 Exodus 26:33,34
1318 Leviticus 21:23

the second room; or the most holy place; the priest had to enter in to it from passing through the veil dividing it from the first room; which first room was the holy place, or "the tabernacle of the congregation without the vail, which is before the testimony."[1319] "For there was a tabernacle made; the first, wherein was the candlestick, and the table, and the shewbread; which is called the sanctuary. And after the second veil, the tabernacle which is called the Holiest of all; which had the golden censer, and the ark of the covenant overlaid round about with gold, wherein was the golden pot that had manna, and Aaron's rod that budded, and the tables of the covenant; and over it the cher'ubims of glory shadowing the mercyseat."[1320]

3. When the LORD's Christ was brought up to the LORD's throne, He was consecrated to begin a ministry for creation within the Rooms of the heavenly Sanctuary, which is why it says, "Christ is not entered into the holy places made with hands, which are the figures of the true; but into heaven itself, now to appear in the presence of God for us,"[1321] and, "He raised him from the dead, and set him at his own right hand in the heavenly places."[1322] The LORD's throne is within His heavenly Temple, and when His Spirit brought up His Christ to His throne; for it was "God the Father, who raised him from the dead";[1323] this LORD anointed His name, and His name's office, to be that Head Minister over His Spirit's science of salvation, which is why His Christ says, "I will declare the decree: the LORD hath said unto me, Thou art my Son; this day have I begotten thee."[1324] Moses structured the earthly tabernacle after the heavenly, for what Aaron accomplished on earth, at the time appointed, the LORD's Christ would accomplish in full. When therefore hearing that "places" will be filled with dead "bodies," the illustration is not of any literal killing, but of a consumption of priests and ministers of "places," even as it says concerning these "places," "LORD, I have loved the habitation of thy house, and the place where

---

1319 Exodus 27:21
1320 Hebrews 9:2-5
1321 Hebrews 9:24
1322 Ephesians 1:20
1323 Galatians 1:1
1324 Psalm 2:7

thine honour dwelleth,"[1325] and, "I have built an house of habitation for thee, and a place for thy dwelling for ever."[1326]

4. A "place" is a "habitation" or "house," and a "house" figuratively illustrates a church, as it says, "The house of God, which is the church of the living God."[1327] The great appearing of "Jesus Christ" is ordained to slaughter priests and preachers of churches, allowing us to further understand that this appearing is no literal event. "The Lord Jesus Christ our Saviour"[1328] is, in right context, "the commandment of God our Saviour."[1329] If this battle is "against the rulers of the darkness of this world, against spiritual wickedness in high places";[1330] and it is; then only spiritual means can suffice to accomplish the Spirit's will, wherefore it is well to "know that the law is spiritual."[1331] The phrase, "Jesus Christ," is, in reality, a term or moniker denoting the law or commandment of the LORD God's Spirit. This commandment is the Spirit's "truth," and concerning this "truth," we read how it says, "Thy word is truth,"[1332] and, "Thy law is the truth."[1333] What is called, "Jesus Christ," is, in Scripture, a phrase representing "the law of truth,"[1334] which "truth" is "the law of the Spirit of life."[1335] Now, "the Spirit is truth"[1336] because of "the law of the Spirit of life,"[1337] for this law is that doctrine of liberty for the conversation's conscience, which is why we are told, "The Son therefore shall make you free."[1338] What makes "free" is according to the saying, "The law of the Spirit of life in Christ Jesus hath made me free,"[1339] allowing us to understand

---

1325 Psalm 26:8
1326 2 Chronicles 6:2
1327 1 Timothy 3:15
1328 Titus 1:4
1329 Titus 1:3
1330 Ephesians 6:12
1331 Romans 7:14
1332 John 17:17
1333 Psalm 119:142
1334 Malachi 2:6
1335 Romans 8:2
1336 1 John 5:6
1337 Romans 8:2
1338 John 8:36
1339 Romans 8:2

that any appearing of the "Son" is an appearing of "truth," which is an appearing of creation's law upon the mind.

5. Doesn't it say, "The truth shall make you free"?[1340] Again, if it says, "Thy word is truth,"[1341] and, "Thy law is the truth,"[1342] then the Word of the Spirit's law establishes personal mental and spiritual liberty; every doer of creation's law will know that it is the Spirit's will to "purge your conscience from dead works to serve the living God."[1343] Thus, it is for this reason that every spirit doing the Word's will and law reports, "The law of the Spirit of life in Christ Jesus hath made me free from the law of sin and death."[1344] The entire point of heaven's Faith is resurrection and reformation of spiritual understanding, allowing the person to rightly possess self for the good of the conversation, which is why, when speaking on this Faith, Paul says, "If the Spirit of him that raised up Jesus from the dead dwell in you, he that raised up Christ from the dead shall also quicken your mortal bodies by his Spirit that dwelleth in you."[1345] Through the Spirit's law, all lame bodies will pass away, and we may understand that these "bodies" are not natural or fleshy bodies by what it means for the Spirit to dwell within the heart, and it says, "I am full of power by the spirit of the LORD, and of judgment, and of might,"[1346] and, "I have filled him with the spirit of God, in wisdom, and in understanding, and in knowledge."[1347] If the Spirit dwells within us, then knowledge of His name's wisdom rests within the spirit of our mind, which is why it says, "Be renewed in the spirit of your mind."[1348]

6. Herein we may understand what Paul means when saying, "If Christ be in you, the body is dead because of sin."[1349] The issue at had is the condition of the conversation's conscience, for, by doing the Spirit's

---

1340 John 8:32
1341 John 17:17
1342 Psalm 119:142
1343 Hebrews 9:14
1344 Romans 8:2
1345 Romans 8:11
1346 Micah 3:8
1347 Exodus 31:3
1348 Ephesians 4:23
1349 Romans 8:10

law, we are to claim a perfect conversation, and "perfect, as pertaining to the conscience."[1350] This allows us to understand that if "Christ" is within our conscience, that "sin" against His LORD and Word is removed from our conversation. It is this removing from "sin" that equates to a sober understanding conquering our faith's organs and body, and it should, seeing as how "the strength of sin is the law."[1351] The "law" spoken of is the legal religious law, and with this LORD's Christ "blotting out the handwriting of ordinances,"[1352] it is become an eternal fact that "Christ hath redeemed us from the curse of the law, being made a curse for us: for it is written, Cursed is every one that hangeth on a tree."[1353] The Spirit's law is blessed to liberate the conscience from the pen of flesh to know the benevolence decreed for the inward parts of the heart, which is why the doer of this law says, "The law of the Spirit of life in Christ Jesus hath made me free from the law of sin and death."[1354] Therefore, to observe a priest preaching, "Righteousness come by the law,"[1355] it is to observe a priest speaking against the fact that, concerning the LORD's Christ, His name is blessed "to redeem them that were under the law."[1356]

7. The wrath of this LORD's Spirit is sent to priests and elders mishandling His name, even as it says, "The wrath of God is revealed from heaven against all ungodliness and unrighteousness of men, who hold the truth in unrighteousness."[1357] Egypt's then host rules by "unrighteousness," and "all unrighteousness is sin,"[1358] "and the strength of sin is the law."[1359] These ministers preach that *the LORD's Christ* says, "You are justified by the law,"[1360] and by such a rule, possesses "merchandise of gold, and silver, and precious stones, and of

---

1350 Hebrews 9:9
1351 1 Corinthians 15:56
1352 Colossians 2:14
1353 Galatians 3:13
1354 Romans 8:2
1355 Galatians 2:21
1356 Galatians 4:5
1357 Romans 1:18
1358 1 John 5:17
1359 1 Corinthians 15:56
1360 Galatians 5:4

pearls, and fine linen, and purple, and silk, and scarlet, and all thyine wood, and all manner vessels of ivory, and all manner vessels of most precious wood, and of brass, and iron, and marble, and cinnamon, and odours, and ointments, and frankincense, and wine, and oil, and fine flour, and wheat, and beasts, and sheep, and horses, and chariots, and slaves, and souls of men."[1361] A most perverse government through a most grotesque *God* is preached by Egyptian Babylon, and it is forwarded under a pretended devotion to *the name* of *the living God*. It is because of this falsehood that the Word resting at the right hand of the LORD God is called upon, which Word is born for "piercing even to the dividing asunder of soul and spirit, and of the joints and marrow, and is a discerner of the thoughts and intents of the heart."[1362]

8. When "the Lord Jesus Christ our Saviour";[1363] which "Lord" and "Savior" is "the commandment of God our Saviour";[1364] is revealed in the omnipotent glory of His Father's throne, a great revelation of "the imagination of the thoughts of the heart"[1365] will commence. A great burning will then register within the conscience of error's then ministers, moving them to say, "Did not our heart burn within us, while he talked with us by the way, and while he opened to us the scriptures?"[1366] Then will "all hands be faint, and every man's heart shall melt: and they shall be afraid: pangs and sorrows shall take hold of them."[1367] Discerning their wrong against the heavenly ministry of the LORD's High Priest, they will mourn for their stubborn ignorance, for the Spirit's Priest says, "They shall look upon me whom they have pierced, and they shall mourn for him, as one mourneth for his only son, and shall be in bitterness for him, as one that is in bitterness for his firstborn."[1368] What does one do when mourning for their firstborn? What did David do? It says, "David fasted, and went in, and lay all night upon the

---

1361 Revelation 18:12,13
1362 Hebrews 4:12
1363 Titus 1:4
1364 Titus 1:3
1365 1 Chronicles 29:18
1366 Luke 24:32
1367 Isaiah 13:7,8
1368 Zechariah 12:10

earth."[1369] When Egypt's men fully understand the blasphemy of their creed and conversation, they will fast from their former conversation, and every "body" of every minister will fall to the earth. This deceased "body" is no literal or physical body, but is that body according to the saying, "Put off concerning the former conversation the old man, which is corrupt according to the deceitful lusts."[1370]

9. With the bodies of the earth's kings fallen, not one man among them will gather any body to his self, but those bodies will remain untouched, for they are food for them that are joined to heaven's assembly. Earth's kings are, by the Word's wrathful impression, quitting their former religious conversation to pick up a new mind of devotion, even as it says, "Put off concerning the former conversation the old man...and be renewed in the spirit of your mind; and that ye put on the new man, which after God is created in righteousness and true holiness."[1371] Thus, the question is asked to the mole and bat, "The great day of his wrath is come; and who shall be able to stand?"[1372] and they are pointed to where it says, "Who may abide the day of his coming? and who shall stand when he appeareth? for he is like a refiner's fire, and like fullers' soap: and he shall sit as a refiner and purifier of silver: and he shall purify the sons of Levi."[1373] Herein the earth's men learn that they may do well only by refining their understanding on heavenly things, for, concerning the illustration of "silver," we read, "How much better is it to get wisdom than gold! and to get understanding rather to be chosen than silver!"[1374] Thus, when in the presence of heaven's converted assembly, earth's men are taught, "Know that ye were not redeemed with corruptible things, as silver and gold, from your vain conversation received by tradition from your fathers."[1375]

10. The aim of this new judgment upon those Gentiles taken out of Error's institution is to purify them for a gift to heaven's stewards, even

---

1369 2 Samuel 12:16
1370 Ephesians 4:22
1371 Ephesians 4:22-24
1372 Revelation 6:17
1373 Malachi 3:2,3
1374 Proverbs 16:16
1375 1 Peter 1:18

as the Levites were that gift to Aaron and his sons; "Thou shalt give the Levites unto Aaron and to his sons: they are wholly given unto him out of the children of Israel,"[1376] says the Spirit, and again, "I, behold, I have taken your brethren the Levites from among the children of Israel: to you they are given as a gift for the LORD, to do the service of the tabernacle of the congregation."[1377] Herein we may understand why John, when hearing Error's men say, "Who shall be able to stand?"[1378] isn't led to believe that redemption's triumphant vision is over. Life doesn't end after the sixth seal, but rather a new age of investigative judgment against the then Gentiles begins, which is why, after the sixth seal, John "saw another angel ascending from the east, having the seal of the living God: and he cried with a loud voice to the four angels, to whom it was given to hurt the earth and the sea, saying, Hurt not the earth, neither the sea, nor the trees, till we have sealed the servants of our God in their foreheads."[1379]

11. When this full period of judgment is over, only one hundred forty-four thousand priests of heaven's Faith will remain to join heaven's ministers for looking after that heavenly Temple's Faith in the new earth. By the third woe of the seventh trumpet, all bodies will drop, and that generation of converts will give heaven's right knowledge as heaven's right assembly, but later on, many will be deceived, and their numbers will decline.

1376 Numbers 3:9
1377 Numbers 18:6
1378 Revelation 6:17
1379 Revelation 7:2,3

25

The One Hundred Forty-Four Thousand

1. After the seventh trumpet pronounces the third woe, a time of "rest" and "refreshing" is revealed to John, who writes, "I saw another angel ascending from the east, having the seal of the living God: and he cried with a loud voice to the four angels, to whom it was given to hurt the earth and the sea, saying, Hurt not the earth, neither the sea, nor the trees, till we have sealed the servants of our God in their foreheads."[1380] This stillness occurs after the third woe has abolished the institution of the serpent's spirit, and after the "dens" and "rocks" of the mountains have fallen on the priests and ministers of that institution. After the seventh plague, the age that we are now entered into is one where they "laid hold on the dragon, that old serpent, which is the Devil, and Satan, and bound him a thousand years, and cast him into the bottomless pit, and shut him up, and set a seal upon him, that he should deceive the nations no more, till the thousand years should be fulfilled."[1381]

1380   Revelation 7:2,3
1381   Revelation 20:2,3

2. A new judgment commences when once Error's religious institution is for ever silenced, and this judgment occurring against them that are taken out of that institution, even as it says, "I will also leave in the midst of thee an afflicted and poor people, and they shall trust in the name of the LORD."[1382] This first judgment of trusting on the living God's name will last for one thousand years, after which the spirit of the serpent will resurrect to pervert the earth's converted host. A second judgment will then commence after this first judgment, leaving only one hundred forty-four thousand faithful ministers to enter into the new heaven and earth with His Spirit's then apostles.

3. The one hundred forty-four thousand make up the number of priests and elders that remain faithful to heaven's faith during the one thousand year absence of the serpent's spirit, and especially after that spirit is resurrected among them. We understand that the one hundred forty-four thousand are priests due to the witness of Scripture, who, for example, reveals the number that David obtained when counting the fit men in Israel and Judah, for "there were in Israel eight hundred thousand valiant men that drew the sword; and the men of Judah were five hundred thousand men."[1383] Again, when numbering the people, Moses records that, for example, of the tribe of Ruben "were forty and six thousand and five hundred";[1384] of Simeon, "fifty and nine thousand and three hundred";[1385] of Zeb'ulun, "fifty and seven thousand and four hundred."[1386] Now, there were, of course, more than fifty-seven thousand people in Zeb'ulun, and more than forty-six thousand people in the tribe of Ruben; these numbers are not for a total sum of people, but are only in relation to the "sons" of the tribes, to individuals "that were able to go forth to war."[1387] Just as Moses and David numbered a specific host for a specific reason; which reason was to tell who could wield the sword; so also John heard, in the Revelation, the number of

---

[1382] Zephaniah 3:12
[1383] 2 Samuel 24:9
[1384] Numbers 1:21
[1385] Numbers 1:23
[1386] Numbers 1:31
[1387] Numbers 1:26

them that, after this full period of sealing, remained faithful to "the sword of the Spirit, which is the word of God."[1388]

4. The one hundred forty-four thousand are them that have not only been faithful to the Word's Faith during the entire period of the thousand year reign of the LORD's throne religion; for at this time "the Lord God omnipotent reigneth";[1389] but also during the years of apostasy afterwards, for "when the thousand years are expired, Satan shall be loosed out of his prison, and shall go out to deceive the nations."[1390] The earth's number of faithful priests to heaven's Faith will dramatically fall after the thousand years are passed, and after a very great devouring of these priests and their negligent religious ideologies occur, a special judgment against them will open, which is why it says, "I saw the dead, small and great, stand before God."[1391] After the first and second resurrection, there will then be "an hundred forty and four thousand, having his Father's name written in their foreheads,"[1392] left to hear, "I will be his God, and he shall be my son."[1393]

5. The entire purpose of the thousand years is to prepare the earth's ministers for handling heavenly things under the new heaven and earth, even as heaven's ministers were beforehand first prepared. The time of the Gentiles begins when the third woe has finished its mission "to execute judgment upon all, and to convince all that are ungodly among them of all their ungodly deeds which they have ungodly committed, and of all their hard speeches which ungodly sinners have spoken against him."[1394] As soon as this annihilation of *bodies* is ended, "After these things,"[1395] writes John, "I saw four angels standing on the four corners of the earth, holding the four winds of the earth, that the wind should not blow on the earth, nor on the sea, nor on any tree."[1396]

1388 Ephesians 6:17
1389 Revelation 19:6
1390 Revelation 20:7,8
1391 Revelation 20:12
1392 Revelation 14:1
1393 Revelation 21:7
1394 Jude 1:15
1395 Revelation 7:1
1396 Revelation 7:1

6. This language confesses to the restraining or imprisonment of chaos, which line of events fit in with the subjection of the serpent's spirit. For a great period of time after the third woe, the earth's ministers will embrace heaven's doctrine, and having the memory of the Spirit's wrathful judgment upon their heart, they will not care to separate from heaven's Word to know any other wisdom. The theme of this age for one thousand years will be "rest," for the saying is fulfilled, "The whole earth is at rest, and is quiet: they break forth into singing."[1397] "And they sing the song of Moses the servant of God, and the song of the Lamb, saying, Great and marvellous are thy works, Lord God Almighty; just and true are thy ways, thou King of saints. Who shall not fear thee, O Lord, and glorify thy name? for thou only art holy,"[1398] for the saying is fulfilled, "Sing unto the LORD a new song: sing unto the LORD, all the earth."[1399] This "song" is the "rest" of the LORD God's renewed religious earth, and concerning the definition of "rest," we read, "Precept must be upon precept, precept upon precept...To whom he said, This is the rest."[1400]

7. "Rest" is not dormant inactivity, but, according to Scripture, is mental activity and spiritual learning. To the Spirit's mind, "rest" is mental and spiritual alleviation by examining and applying self to His words, which is why, concerning His "rest," He says, "Whom shall he teach knowledge? and whom shall he make to understand doctrine?"[1401] Herein we may understand why, after "the vengeance of the LORD our God, the vengeance of his temple,"[1402] it says, "He who smote the people in wrath with a continual stroke, he that ruled the nations in anger, is persecuted, and none hindereth. The whole earth is at rest, and is quiet: they break forth into singing."[1403] With the spirit and philosophy of the serpent bound and cast away, all that remains for priests and elders of the Spirit's earth to do is according to the saying,

---

1397   Isaiah 14:7
1398   Revelation 15:3,4
1399   Psalm 96:1
1400   Isaiah 28:10-12
1401   Isaiah 28:9
1402   Jeremiah 50:28
1403   Isaiah 14:6,7

"Fear God, and give glory to him; for the hour of his judgment is come: and worship him that made heaven, and earth, and the sea, and the fountains of waters."[1404]

8. The song of the earth is the living God's judgment, which judgment is understood by how He says, "A law shall proceed from me, and I will make my judgment to rest for a light of the people."[1405] For one thousand years, "the law of the Spirit of life"[1406] will be the study and employment of the earth's newly converted host to heaven's will and doctrine, but then history will be repeated. It will again be fulfilled, "And the people served the LORD all the days of Joshua, and all the days of the elders that outlived Joshua, who had seen all the great works of the LORD, that he did for Israel. And Joshua the son of Nun, the servant of the LORD, died...And also all that generation were gathered unto their fathers: and there arose another generation after them, which knew not the LORD, nor yet the works which he had done for Israel. And the children of Israel did evil in the sight of the LORD, and served Ba'alim."[1407]

9. Like as the sobriety of the generations failed after Joshua's age, so when the spirit of the serpent is resurrected, the saying will again be fulfilled, "And his tail drew the third part of the stars of heaven, and did cast them to the earth."[1408] Now, "the prophet that teacheth lies, he is the tail,"[1409] for the dragon's angel will arise with a vengeance, and with a desire to stir up another controversy against the name of the Spirit's Chief Priest. With a great period of time without religious error, the sound of the serpent is become a new doctrine to them that have never come in to contact with it. Thus, with great confidence on their religious philosophy of what the earth's doctrine is and should be, a new host of error "went up on the breadth of the earth, and compassed the camp of the saints about, and the beloved city: and fire came down from God

---

1404 Revelation 14:7
1405 Isaiah 51:4
1406 Romans 8:2
1407 Judges 2:7-11
1408 Revelation 12:4
1409 Isaiah 9:15

out of heaven, and devoured them. And the devil that deceived them was cast into the lake of fire and brimstone."[1410]

10. Such a consumption marks the beginning of a second judgment against "the kings of the earth and of the whole world."[1411] Herein priests and ministers; along with their wives and substance; willingly stout to "death," are come up before the face of the living God for understanding if they will "keep the commandments of God, and the faith of Jesus."[1412] Because "the sting of death is sin; and the strength of sin is the law";[1413] "death's" practice involves supporting the religious conversation with what "sin" is, and "having abolished in his flesh the enmity, even the law of commandments contained in ordinances,"[1414] the passing flesh of the Word's Christ on the tree confirms that "the strength of sin is the law."[1415] "Death" is a religious conversation upheld by the religious law and tradition of priests and elders, opening up "death's" adherent "to Jewish fables, and commandments of men, that turn from the truth."[1416] This second judgment is a resurrection of every character of every priest's conversation still reverencing that abolished spirit and persuasion of the serpent, "and whosoever was not found written in the book of life was cast into the lake of fire."[1417]

11. At the end of this full judgment; the judgment of the first and second resurrection; the Book of Life will reveal that "there were sealed an hundred and forty and four thousand of all the tribes of the children of Israel."[1418] Again, them that are sealed are chief ministers capable of wielding the Spirit's sword, who have also remained faithful to that sword in their time. And again, we understand that this number is wholly comprised of priests by how it says, "Now those that sealed were, Nehemi'ah, the Tirsha'tha, the son of Hachali'ah, and Zidki'jah, Sera'iah, Azari'ah, Jeremi'ah...Shema'iah: these were the priests. And

---

1410 Revelation 20:9,10
1411 Revelation 16:14
1412 Revelation 14:12
1413 1 Corinthians 15:56
1414 Ephesians 2:15
1415 1 Corinthians 15:56
1416 Titus 1:14
1417 Revelation 20:15
1418 Revelation 7:4

the Levites...and their brethren...the chief of the people; Pa'rosh, Pa'hath-mo'ab, E'lam."[1419]

11. Of old, them that willingly offered themselves to be sealed, and to seal themselves to the living God for a specific work, were the chief of the priests of Israel and Judah, but "the rest of the people, the priests, the Levites, the porters, the singers, the Neth'inims, and all they that had separated themselves from the people of the lands unto the law of God, their wives, their sons, and their daughters, every one having knowledge, and having understanding; they clave to their brethren, their nobles,"[1420] which "nobles" are the same sealed ones previously mentioned. The one hundred forty-four thousand will be those elect priests and ministers of the Spirit's earth who, not simply during the age of "rest," but during the age of agitation, remain faithful to the face of heaven's High Priest, doing no thing against the God and Father of that High Priest's mediation. Them that pass through this judgment successfully will be given to the ministers of the Spirit's High Priest as a gift to assist with forwarding the rule of the new earth and heaven, for, concerning that religious world to come, "the nations of them which are saved shall walk in the light of it: and the kings of the earth do bring their glory and honour into it."[1421]

[1419] Nehemiah 10:1-14
[1420] Nehemiah 10:28,29
[1421] Revelation 21:24

26

Love's Factor

1. Says Scripture, "He had opened the sixth seal, and, lo, there was a great earthquake; and the sun became black as sackcloth of hair, and the moon became as blood; and the stars of heaven fell unto the earth,"[1422] and this saying describing "the wrath of the Lamb,"[1423] "the day of Christ,"[1424] for in this vision the saying is fulfilled, "The whole land trembled at the sound of the neighing of his strong ones; for they are come, and have devoured the land, and all that is in it; the city, and those that dwell therein."[1425]

2. "As a fig tree casteth her untimely figs, when she is shaken of a mighty wind,"[1426] "I will surely consume them, saith the LORD: there shall be no grapes on the vine, nor figs on the fig tree, and the leaf shall fade."[1427] "Thus saith the LORD, Behold, a people cometh from the north country, and a great nation shall be raised from the sides of the earth. They shall lay hold on bow and spear; they are cruel, and have no

---

1422   Revelation 6:12,13
1423   Revelation 6:16
1424   Philippians 1:10
1425   Jeremiah 8:16
1426   Revelation 6:13
1427   Jeremiah 8:13

mercy; their voice roareth like the sea; and they ride upon horses, set in array as men for war against thee, O daughter of Zion."[1428]

3. The daughter of Zion here mentioned should not be thought of as that House of the Spirit born from out of the Spirit's heavenly Sanctuary, but as rather that counterfeit ministry of error who, by the impression of the Word, will fulfill the vision, "Our hands wax feeble: anguish hath taken hold of us, and pain, as of a woman in travail."[1429] This is spoken against them who fulfill the rebuke, "They have forsaken my law which I set before them, and have not obeyed my voice";[1430] even them that "worship the beast and his image, and receive his mark";[1431] therefore against them the prayer is fulfilled, "Cause thy mighty ones to come down, O LORD,"[1432] and these mighty ones, these strong ones, fulfilling the saying, "The noise of a multitude in the mountains, like as of a great people; a tumultuous noise of the kingdoms of nations gathered together: the LORD of hosts mustereth the host of the battle. They come from a far country, from the end of heaven, even the LORD, and the weapons of his indignation, to destroy the whole land. Howl ye; for the day of the LORD is at hand."[1433]

4. The sixth seal, although concealing the continued events of the order and mission of the pale horse and his rider, and with their companions and agents, is in reality a vision of a clash of riders, wherein heaven's army will "cause to cease from the cities of Judah, and from the streets of Jerusalem, the voice of mirth, and the voice of gladness, the voice of the bridegroom, and the voice of the bride: for the land shall be desolate."[1434] Again, this *Judah* and *Jerusalem*, and the church of their land, is not, in context, the living God's assembly, for this is that denomination where "truth is perished, and is cut off from their mouth."[1435] At this time in the world's ecclesiastical history, this insti-

---

1428   Jeremiah 6:22,23
1429   Jeremiah 6:24
1430   Jeremiah 9:13
1431   Revelation 14:9
1432   Joel 3:11
1433   Isaiah 13:4,5
1434   Jeremiah 7:34
1435   Jeremiah 7:28

tution fulfills the saying, "As a cage is full of birds, so are their houses full of deceit: therefore they are become great, and waxen rich."[1436] Therefore we know this institution because it is said, "Babylon the great is fallen, is fallen, and is become the habitation of devils, and the hold of every foul spirit, and a cage of every unclean and hateful bird."[1437]

5. Who was anciently brought against Babylon? It is written, "The LORD hath raised up the spirit of the kings of the Medes: for his device is against Babylon, to destroy it; because it is the vengeance of the LORD, the vengeance of his temple."[1438] The vengeance of His temple against ancient Babylon is a figurative illustration of "the day of the LORD'S vengeance, and the year of recompences for the controversy of Zion."[1439] For, "I will raise and cause to come up against Babylon an assembly of great nations from the north country,"[1440] says the Spirit. "The LORD hath opened his armoury, and hath brought forth the weapons of his indignation: for this is the work of the Lord GOD of hosts in the land of the Chalde'ans. Come against her from the utmost border, open her storehouses: cast her up as heaps, and destroy her utterly: let nothing of her be left."[1441] "Woe unto them! for their day is come, the time of their visitation."[1442]

6. "Seeing then that all these things shall be dissolved, what manner of persons ought ye to be in all holy conversation and godliness, looking for and hasting unto the coming of the day of God, wherein the heavens being on fire shall be dissolved, and the elements shall melt with fervent heat?"[1443] For at this time, heaven's army says, "'Truly I am full of power by the spirit of the LORD, and of judgment, and of might, to declare unto Jacob his transgression, and to Israel his sin.'[1444] 'Whosoever transgresseth, and abideth not in the doctrine of Christ, hath not

---

1436 Jeremiah 5:27
1437 Revelation 18:2
1438 Jeremiah 51:11
1439 Isaiah 34:8
1440 Jeremiah 50:9
1441 Jeremiah 50:25,26
1442 Jeremiah 50:27
1443 2 Peter 3:11,12
1444 Micah 3:8

God.'[1445] But 'put ye on the Lord Jesus Christ, and make not provision for the flesh, to fulfil the lusts thereof';[1446] 'for God hath not appointed us to wrath, but to obtain salvation by our Lord Jesus Christ.'"[1447]

7. It is a fact that the day of the Spirit is divided into two parts that form one event, and that day beginning with "the vials of the wrath of God upon the earth,"[1448] and after this should take place, then the Spirit's unrestrained wrath will appear to execute "the cup of the wine of the fierceness of his wrath."[1449]

8. With all that heaven has poured out for us, not one person should be a receiver of the Spirit's wrath; not one spirit should be fearful for either of these times; yet unbelief is consistently an active agent in turning away the heart from right duty and learning, for it is as it is said, "Perfect love casteth out fear."[1450] How is love made perfect in the believer? It says, "Whoso keepeth his word, in him verily is the love of God perfected,"[1451] and, "If we love one another, God dwelleth in us, and his love is perfected in us."[1452] There is a twofold work for having the doctrine of the Spirit's love within our inward parts, "and this is his commandment, That we should believe on the name of his Son Jesus Christ, and love one another, as he gave us commandment."[1453] According to His commandment, and as He has charged every reforming mind by the voice of His Son's intercession, belief and love are to be accomplished. For this cause we know that only "through the righteousness of faith"[1454] may it be heard and accomplished, "Whosoever of you will be the chiefest, shall be servant of all."[1455]

9. "If I then, your Lord and Master, have washed your feet; ye also ought to wash one another's feet. For I have given you an example,

---

1445 2 John 1:9
1446 Romans 13:14
1447 1 Thessalonians 5:9
1448 Revelation 16:1
1449 Revelation 16:19
1450 1 John 4:18
1451 1 John 2:5
1452 1 John 4:12
1453 1 John 3:23
1454 Romans 4:13
1455 Mark 10:44,45

that ye should do as I have done to you. Verily, verily, I say unto you, The servant is not greater than his lord; neither he that is sent greater than he that sent him. If ye know these things, happy are ye if ye do them,"[1456] says our High Priest. "A new commandment I give unto you, That ye love one another; as I have loved you, that ye also love one another. By this shall all men know that ye are my disciples, if ye have love one to another."[1457] Therefore "we know that we have passed from death unto life, because we love the brethren. He that loveth not his brother abideth in death."[1458]

10. "Love" is defined by the Spirit's Christ as, "To give his life a ransom for many,"[1459] which is why the apostle wrote, "Hereby perceive we the love of God, because he laid down his life for us: and we ought to lay down our lives for the brethren."[1460] Because there is no advancing education on right kindness as the Spirit has commanded and charged, fear to trust self with the Word's Son and Spirit retards the heart from growth and unity with heaven's course. Again, Scripture says, "Love one another,"[1461] but the reality of this saying means, "Comfort yourselves together, and edify one another,"[1462] that is, "Warn them that are unruly, comfort the feebleminded, support the weak, be patient toward all men. See that none render evil for evil unto any man; but ever follow that which is good, both among yourselves, and to all men."[1463] Therefore "let us not be weary in well doing: for in due season we shall reap, if we faint not. As we have therefore opportunity, let us do good unto all men, especially unto them who are of the household of faith."[1464]

11. The Spirit's will is grounded in liberty of personal union to the Godhead by right benevolence through a faith strengthened by understanding. No one can profess communion with the living God and yet

---

1456 John 13:14-17
1457 John 13:34,35
1458 1 John 3:14
1459 Mark 10:45
1460 1 John 3:16
1461 1 Thessalonians 4:9
1462 1 Thessalonians 5:11
1463 1 Thessalonians 5:14,15
1464 Galatians 6:9,10

remain without His Spirit, which Spirit provokes the heart to earnestly desire a means to achieve heaven-appointed unity; first inwardly and then externally. The Spirit's doctrine is a law of "charity out of a pure heart, and of a good conscience, and of faith unfeigned,"[1465] and to accept this saying is to accept the personal and inward marks of the course of this counsel. Fear in the heart is magnified by the imagination because there is a refusal to acknowledge the fact of the revelation and nature of the words of God's Christ. The immediate result of accepting the name of His Christ within the heart freely places a bounty on the mind for the Word's Spirit to capture, to the end "he might sanctify and cleanse it with the washing of water by the word,"[1466] even as He Himself says, "Ye are clean through the word which I have spoken unto you."[1467] This is why it does not first say, "Love," and then, "Believe," but rather, "Believe on the virtue of His name,"[1468] and then, "As the Father gave us a charge by His name, let us edify and comfort one another in and by that name."[1469]

12. For this cause, "Above all these things put on charity, which is the bond of perfectness,"[1470] says the apostle, and this is well to observe, yet this charge cannot take root within the mind without first hearing, "But put ye on the Lord Jesus Christ, and make not provision for the flesh."[1471] Without accepting that righteousness born from learning of and doing the words of heaven's Spirit, not one soul may know of the "exceeding great and precious promises"[1472] that come by exercising faith on His voice, for these things are added and then multiplied to our account when once there is a mind to leave off "the corruption that is in the world through lust."[1473] In order for the heart to hear the wisdom of His mediation, it is no surprise that the heart itself must be suppressed and re-educated by the will of the person through the will and under-

---

1465   1 Timothy 1:5
1466   Ephesians 5:26
1467   John 15:3
1468   1 John 3:23
1469   1 John 3:23
1470   Colossians 3:14
1471   Romans 13:14
1472   2 Peter 1:4
1473   2 Peter 1:4

standing of the Spirit. The conversation's conscience needs the righteousness of His Christ's name, for no thing done by any religious law or policy of the heart may replace the necessary effort to receive any benefit from heaven's ministry. After the heart has heard whatever it has heard of the Word and of His Son, to then turn whatever is in it to His name, know that whosoever "believeth on him that justifieth the ungodly, his faith is counted for righteousness."[1474]

13. Scripture counsels, "The wrath of God is revealed from heaven against all ungodliness and unrighteousness of men, who hold the truth in unrighteousness,"[1475] and the way ungodliness is kept alive, and within the members of the mind of the body, is that for some presumptuously secret error within the heart against the living God, that body must have "changed the truth of God into a lie, and worshipped and served the creature more than the Creator."[1476] Due to a lack of faithfulness towards the Spirit's voice, the heart stands still within self, and although the individual may confess the *ministry* of *the LORD's Priest* as their *peace*, it will always be that "in works they deny him,"[1477] for the Spirit explains, "If ye were Abraham's children, ye would do the works of Abraham."[1478]

14. "By faith Abraham, when he was called to go out into a place which he should after receive for an inheritance, obeyed; and he went out, not knowing whither he went."[1479] "He staggered not at the promise of God through unbelief,"[1480] "therefore it was imputed to him for righteousness. Now it was not written for his sake alone, that it was imputed to him; but for us also, to whom it shall be imputed, if we believe on him that raised up Jesus our Lord from the dead; who was delivered for our offences, and was raised again for our justification."[1481]

1474 Romans 4:5
1475 Romans 1:18
1476 Romans 1:25
1477 Titus 1:16
1478 John 8:39
1479 Hebrews 11:8
1480 Romans 4:20
1481 Romans 4:22-25

15. Transgression against the doctrine of Christ occurs through the belief that "righteousness come by the law"[1482] of priests and elders; that all are "justified by the law"[1483] of ministers; when the fact of the matter is that "no man is justified by the law in the sight of God"[1484] because "the law is not of faith,"[1485] that is, the laws and traditions cultivated and inherited of men, and of the natural self, are empty and without weight before the living God. For, "according to the truth of the gospel,"[1486] "we might be justified by the faith of Christ, and not by the works of the law,"[1487] which is why it says, "Ye are sanctified, but ye are justified in the name of the Lord Jesus, and by the Spirit of our God."[1488] Notice that one is justified; or sanctified; in the name of God's Christ, which name is the will and knowledge of the LORD's Spirit, which is why the reformer is blessed "through sanctification of the Spirit and belief of the truth."[1489] An experimental faith on the Spirit's voice will qualify the believer for heaven-appointed purification as they actively take hold of the virtue and charge of His Christ's mediation by faith. A personal religion with His name by obeying His Faith's precepts will bring the hearer to receive and acknowledge the precepts of the LORD His Father, and as His Spirit fills the heart with His wisdom concerning creation, the mind of His Spirit's intention will move the person to sincerely love the LORD of that wisdom, "and this is love, that we walk after his commandments."[1490]

16. "Ungodliness" is pushed out of the soul by the Spirit's system of regeneration. "The LORD hath made all things for himself: yea, even the wicked for the day of evil,"[1491] and herein it is observed that the *wicked* are not them that do not know the LORD's Word, nor are they them that have not had a fair chance to know His voice,

---

1482 Galatians 2:21
1483 Galatians 5:4
1484 Galatians 3:11
1485 Galatians 3:12
1486 Galatians 2:14
1487 Galatians 2:16
1488 1 Corinthians 6:11
1489 2 Thessalonians 2:13
1490 2 John 1:6
1491 Proverbs 16:4

but are them "that obey not the gospel of our Lord,"[1492] to do it. For some thing in them, whether "being more exceedingly zealous of the traditions"[1493] of their family or "art in the gall of bitterness, and in the bond of iniquity,"[1494] "I have written to him the great things of my law, but they were counted as a strange thing,"[1495] says the Spirit of error's subject; the enemies of the Spirit's law are them that He has described as, "Those mine enemies, which would not that I should reign over them."[1496] The reign of the Spirit's voice over the spirit of the mind, the heart, the soul temple, and over the members of the body of our faith, is found in that His righteousness suffocates our inherited conversation in to certain newness. If there is not a willingness to abandon self to His Priest's Spirit, there is plainly a rejection of His ministry, and that rejection had only by unbelief, and that unbelief upheld by a love for "ungodliness," which vanity is "after the commandments and doctrines of men."[1497]

17. The name of God's Priest will come to His LORD and Father's earth at the appointed time in unimaginable glory, and it is well for us to understand that only "the spirit may be saved in the day of the Lord Jesus."[1498] The spirit saved at the day of this manifestation is not the spirit saved or ransomed at this present day. Remember, in order to even be joined to the events of that great year, one must survive the season of the Spirit's plagues. In order to survive that day of His wrath, one must be able to stand against the then institution that first procures a wrath against heaven's host, and in order to stand against that final institution of the religious world's history, one must be able, before all of this, to stand up for the Spirit in a time when the earth beast; that new two-horned pagan apostate religious State; should command itself under the image of the leopard beast before it, that is, under a church and State government. In order to be able to stand for heaven's will in

---

1492   2 Thessalonians 1:8
1493   Galatians 1:14
1494   Acts 8:23
1495   Hosea 8:12
1496   Luke 19:27
1497   Colossians 2:22
1498   1 Corinthians 5:5

the time of an openly and further apostatized religious denomination taking the LORD's name out of context, one must, before this time, which time is now, admit the heart in to the higher education of His Spirit's will and learning, and from surrendering our will to His name, go on "speaking the truth in love,"[1499] to "grow up into him in all things"[1500] "unto a perfect man, unto the measure of the stature of the fulness of Christ."[1501]

18. There is a present work for the believer, and it is in fact "the work of righteousness";[1502] this is His commandment concerning the present duty of His congregation: "Ye shall afflict your souls, and offer an offering made by fire unto the LORD...Ye shall do no work...Whatsoever soul it be that doeth any work in that same day, the same soul will I destroy from among his people."[1503] It is for this reason that this counsel is an ever-present fact to be observed: "To him that worketh is the reward not reckoned of grace, but of debt. But to him that worketh not, but believeth on him that justifieth the ungodly, his faith is counted for righteousness."[1504] Thus, every right student of heaven's will should individually know that "God imputeth righteousness without works."[1505]

19. The great revelation of the name of God's Priest; which name will appear in the glory of the LORD His Father's throne; will gather together all who have accepted their reconciliation to the Spirit of this same LORD by the ministry of His Son, and who, from that acceptance, have by faith sought His face to "know him, and the power of his resurrection, and the fellowship of his sufferings, being made conformable unto his death."[1506] The only thing that will keep the reformer from joining the ranks of "the clusters of the vine of the earth"[1507] is

---

1499   Ephesians 4:15
1500   Ephesians 4:15
1501   Ephesians 4:13
1502   Isaiah 32:17
1503   Leviticus 23:28-30
1504   Romans 4:4,5
1505   Romans 4:6
1506   Philippians 3:10
1507   Revelation 14:18

a "faith which worketh by love."[1508] Again, how is love perfected? By a faithful adherence to the voice and commandments of the Spirit to grow fond of His name, and while being comforted by the Spirit with all of His fullness, applying the heart to further overcome self to obtain wisdom and knowledge not only to govern self, or to serve heaven's voice, but to also "follow after the things which make for peace, and things wherewith one may edify another."[1509] From such "fellowship of the Spirit,"[1510] precepts will be given of the Word in relation to "the law of Christ,"[1511] and these things are given to the heart of our conversation that it may be fulfilled, "I will put my law in their inward parts."[1512]

20. Them that do not learn of and do the Spirit's course will suffer through both phases of the Spirit's wrath in agony. As His vengeance will appear to gather His faithful together, He will come, as it was depicted of old, to fulfill the saying, "I will cut off thy horses out of the midst of thee, and I will destroy thy chariots: and I will cut off the cities of thy land, and throw down all thy strong holds: and I will cut off witchcrafts out of thine hand; and thou shalt have no more soothsayers: thy graven images also will I cut off, and thy standing images out of the midst of thee; and thou shalt no more worship the work of thine hands. And I will pluck up thy groves out of the midst of thee: so will I destroy thy cities. And I will execute vengeance in anger and fury upon the heathen, such as they have not heard."[1513]

21. There will be "a voice of noise from the city, a voice from the temple, a voice of the LORD that rendereth recompence to his enemies."[1514] "And, lo, there was a great earthquake; and the sun became black as sackcloth of hair, and the moon became as blood; and the stars of heaven fell unto the earth, even as a fig tree casteth her untimely figs, when she is shaken of a mighty wind. And the heaven departed as

---

1508 Galatians 5:6
1509 Romans 14:19
1510 Philippians 2:1
1511 Galatians 6:2
1512 Jeremiah 31:33
1513 Micah 5:10-15
1514 Isaiah 66:6

a scroll when it is rolled together; and every mountain and island were moved out of their places."[1515] "The carcases of men shall fall as dung upon the open field, and as the handful after the harvestman, and none shall gather them."[1516] "The carcases of this people shall be meat for the fowls of the heaven, and for the beasts of the earth; and none shall fray them away."[1517]

1515 Revelation 6:12-14
1516 Jeremiah 9:22
1517 Jeremiah 7:33

27

The Last Trump

1. "In the days of the voice of the seventh angel, when he shall begin to sound, the mystery of God should be finished, as he hath declared to his servants the prophets."[1518]

2. The Spirit's mystery will be finished at the sounding of the seventh angel, even as the Word has spoken through His men of old. Another minister of the Spirit, highlighting the LORD's Faith, uses language similar to John's, in that he says, "Surely the Lord GOD will do nothing, but he revealeth his secret unto his servants the prophets."[1519] That written by John and Amos is synonymous, the only difference being in the words, "secret," and, "mystery." This secret and mystery cannot be any thing else than what is written according to how it says, "Then was the secret revealed unto Daniel in a night vision,"[1520] and, "There is a God in heaven that revealeth secrets, and maketh known"[1521] "what shall be in the latter days."[1522] Daniel utters Amos and John's words, namely, "That revealeth," and, "Hath declared." Thus, it is fair to conclude that the Spirit's mystery should be finished by the time of some great declaration and revelation of the living God. The sounding

---

1518 Revelation 10:7
1519 Amos 3:7
1520 Daniel 2:19
1521 Daniel 2:28
1522 Daniel 2:28

of this seventh angel is therefore marked by a vision regarding the estate of ministers in the latter days.

3. It should be noted and fairly considered that, if the fifth angel and first woe, and the sixth angel and second woe, were not separated by any drastic period of time, it cannot be expected that the seventh angel sounding his trumpet, and the third woe that should follow after, are separated by any drastic period of time. Wasted or elapsed time is not the Spirit's pattern concerning the two woes and trumpets before the seventh trumpet and third woe.

4. When we read the eleventh chapter of the Revelation, verses fifteen to nineteen, John's voice does not enter into the vision until the nineteenth verse. Verses fifteen to eighteen are not spoken by John, but are rather a recording or rehearsal of what exclamation John hears. It is after these voices have spoken that John then reports, "The temple of God was opened in heaven, and there was seen in his temple the ark of his testament."[1523] The entire context of the vision changes as the perspectives change. And if that is the case; and it is; verse nineteen should have nothing to do with the four previous verses before it, for in verse nineteen, John is giving a discourse of his own personal encounter, whereas in verses fifteen to eighteen, the experience is not his own, but the encounter is rather a summary of events revealing the marked path of joy from ones directly before the LORD God and His Son, who personally see, and have prior knowledge of, some thing occurring among the earths priests and ministers.

5. John writes, "There were great voices in heaven,"[1524] and because no thing in the vision given to John is real, but is rather a figurative delineation explaining a sure reality, the voices in heaven come from none other source but human beings. John would again write, "I heard the voice of harpers harping with their harps: and they sung as it were a new song,"[1525] and, "I saw another angel fly in the midst of heaven, having the everlasting gospel to preach unto them that dwell on the earth."[1526] These voices in heaven are born from men and women on

---

1523 Revelation 11:19
1524 Revelation 11:15
1525 Revelation 14:2
1526 Revelation 14:6

the earth whose mind and conversation is found within the heavenly Sanctuary, that is, these are "them that dwell in heaven."[1527] Concerning these ministers, it is said of them, "Thou heaven, and ye holy apostles and prophets,"[1528] for them in heaven are of "the general assembly and church of the firstborn, which are written in heaven,"[1529] who exist in spirit by faith within "mount Si'on,"[1530] "the city of the living God, the heavenly Jerusalem."[1531]

6. Them that confess, "The kingdoms of this world are become the kingdoms of our Lord,"[1532] are them within "the temple of God"[1533] and "that worship therein."[1534] These have long since confessed, "We have such an high priest, who is set on the right hand of the throne of the Majesty in the heavens; a minister of the sanctuary, and of the true tabernacle, which the Lord pitched, and not man,"[1535] for they have acknowledged exactly what John sees concerning both rooms within the heavenly Temple. And yet, these who make such a confession of what they currently behold and have seen are distinct from the ones who confess, "The Word's second Room was opened and His ark was observed therein."[1536] A period of time passes from the vision of the most holy to the vision of the LORD's Spirit conquering the denominations of the religious world, and what is written confesses that them who exist in the period of the second ministration may not be them that exist at the glorious appearing of the Spirit's fury, even though both take residence under the same faith within the same House.

7. It is most certainly interesting to notice the language of certain verses within the eleventh chapter of the Revelation. Verses fifteen and seventeen of the eleventh chapter of the Revelation are spoken from two different perspectives relative to time. Them in heaven say,

---

1527   Revelation 13:6
1528   Revelation 18:20
1529   Hebrews 12:23
1530   Hebrews 12:22
1531   Hebrews 12:22
1532   Revelation 11:15
1533   Revelation 11:1
1534   Revelation 11:1
1535   Hebrews 8:1,2
1536   Revelation 11:19

"He shall reign,"[1537] while them before the presence of God say, "And hast reigned."[1538] At this point in time, from the perspective of them in heaven before the LORD and His Priest, and them in heaven while constrained to earth, the word is fulfilled, "Thou hast taken to thee thy great power, and hast reigned,"[1539] for it is fulfilled, "I heard a great voice of much people in heaven, saying, Allelu'ia; Salvation, and glory, and honour, and power, unto the Lord our God: for true and righteous are his judgments: for he hath judged the great whore, which did corrupt the earth with her fornication, and hath avenged the blood of his servants at her hand."[1540]

8. Again, in the eighteenth verse of the eleventh chapter of the Revelation, language becomes important. Them before the Word's throne say, "The nations were angry,"[1541] but then go on to say, "And thy wrath is come."[1542] These two words, "were," and, "is," denote periods of time, where "were" is past and over, and where "is" is yet present and current. The voices of the elders speak in reference to time according to what has just been accomplished before them from what they see transpiring on earth. The strange behavior of the nations, or of the families of religious denominations professing service to *the LORD* and *His Son*; as it says, "The kindreds of the nations";[1543] has long since occurred, along with the seven last plagues, for at this time "the sun became black as sackcloth of hair, and the moon became as blood; and the stars of heaven fell unto the earth."[1544] "The great day of his wrath is come,"[1545] "and the heaven departed as a scroll when it is rolled together."[1546]

9. It is then apparent that the eleventh chapter of the Revelation, verses fifteen to seventeen, are a direct fulfillment of the nineteenth

---

1537 Revelation 11:15
1538 Revelation 11:17
1539 Revelation 11:17
1540 Revelation 19:1,2
1541 Revelation 11:18
1542 Revelation 11:18
1543 Psalms 22:27
1544 Revelation 6:12,13
1545 Revelation 6:17
1546 Revelation 6:14

chapter of the Revelation, verses eleven to nineteen, wherein it is fulfilled, "Behold, the Lord cometh with ten thousands of his saints, to execute judgment upon all, and to convince all that are ungodly."[1547] Thus, as it says, "The kingdoms of this world,"[1548] and, "The kindreds of the nations,"[1549] these are synonymous with how it is said, "The kings of the earth,"[1550] or rather, the priests of the earth, and these "priests" are linked to how it is said, "O ye kings,"[1551] and, "Ye judges of the earth."[1552]

10. The seventh trumpet is yet sounding during the Word's omnipotent appearing, and this event is a direct fulfillment of how it is said, "Rejoice over her, thou heaven, and ye holy apostles and prophets; for God hath avenged you on her."[1553] There is therefore no other reason why the seventh angel should not begin to sound at the point where heaven's host confesses, "The kingdoms of this world are become the kingdoms of our LORD and His Christ."[1554] The fury of the denominations; as it says, "The nations were angry";[1555] appears to be that leading force and agenda moving the Spirit to pour out His wrath at the appointed time.

11. It does not make sense to link the passing of the LORD's Christ in to the second door of the Spirit's Temple to the seventh angel because, first of all, none of the other two angels with their woes are found doing any good or bad thing for heaven's assembly, but were born to serve the LORD's cause against the ungodly, and were to even serve as the announcement for the Spirit's soon appearing in unspeakable glory. Second, if each of the angels with woes were immediately joined by the woe pronounced after their sounding, and if these woes were a blatant detestation of the spirit within the religious world by the LORD's Spirit, then when the seventh sounds, the third woe should be

---

1547   Jude 1:14,15
1548   Revelation 11:15
1549   Psalm 22:27
1550   Revelation 19:19
1551   Psalms 2:10
1552   Psalms 2:10
1553   Revelation 18:20
1554   Revelation 11:15
1555   Revelation 11:18

immediately declared against the same ungodly mind and persuasion. The first two woes were against an institution that refused to learn of and do repentance,[1556] which institution was the Papacy. If the first two woes were against the perverse and apostate ecclesiastical government of Rome, then the final woe should also be against the same spirit of the like ecclesiastical institution. Where there is no sight of the full spirit of this institution, there is no third woe or sounding of the seventh angel.

12. These judgments of the LORD's Spirit brought against Rome; in the form of trumpets and woes; were to silence her into the dust for her open defamation against the throne of heaven's LORD. She did not repent,[1557] and even after she had suffered a wound to the head of her political prowess, she still has yet to reform her thoughts and feelings. These things were imperfectly accomplished against that great erroneous spirit and understanding. The Spirit has confirmed that "he will make an utter end: affliction shall not rise up the second time";[1558] allowing us to understand that what was done by the first two woes through flesh, the LORD God, by His Spirit, will personally accomplish in the third, and by His own hand and voice without restraint upon the conscience of men.

13. The trumpets and the woes before the third woe and the seventh trumpet served to destroy that mind found in the thirteenth chapter of the Revelation, verses five to seven. In the eleventh chapter of the Revelation, verse fifteen, the seventh angel does most emphatically sound, and it is not long before the third woe commences thereafter, and this word of that woe being, "The kingdoms of the religious age now belong to our LORD and to the knowledge of His Son,"[1559] is but the fulfillment of the saying, "The Lord himself shall descend from heaven with a shout, with the voice of the archangel, and with the trump of God."[1560] It is the Spirit's sword that does accomplish the third woe, for the sign of the plagues will be a testimony to the appearing of

---

1556 Revelation 2:21
1557 Revelation 9:20,21
1558 Nahum 1:9
1559 Revelation 11:17
1560 1 Thessalonians 4:16

a vengeful knowledge, wherefore the seventh trumpet cannot escape pronunciation outside of the saying, "I saw heaven opened, and behold a white horse."[1561]

14. Them alive at this point in earth's history, when they observe the clear fulfillment of the first of seven last plagues, will say, "All things in heaven and earth now belong to the LORD, and He will soon reign by the wisdom of His Son." The day is then near, at this time, when it will be that "great Babylon came in remembrance before God, to give unto her the cup of the wine of the fierceness of his wrath."[1562] According to what is written in the seventh verse of the tenth chapter of the Revelation, before these things occur on the earth, the Word will have a people sealed and known only to His LORD and Father. The mystery and secret of the Spirit should be finished at the time of the sounding of the seventh angel, and if the Spirit's "secret" is synonymous with the Spirit's "mystery"; and it is; and this secret relating to the historic events of the earth; and it is; then the voice of the seventh angel should begin to sound when a known people consciously refuse to cooperate with heaven's throne religion. When the Word's *Hebrew* worthies refuse to worship the golden image of the earth beast, it is then that this last angel may prepare to soon sound, but not after judgment against the Spirit's *household*, and then against them within the land of the living that will not repent.

15. When the first two woes issued, that destroying agent was told not to hurt them that were sealed to the living God.[1563] The angel will sound the seventh time, and at the time of the third woe, them that have the Father's seal will not be touched by what He Himself has decreed for the then ungodly. These patterns of His Word concerning the trumpets and their woes cannot be overlooked.

16. Since the day of the Spirit's wrath cannot begin until Christ's ministration is finished in heaven's second apartment, from the first plague until the appearing of His name in the clouds, and then beyond that time, the LORD will have a host untouched by what is poured out

---

1561 Revelation 19:11
1562 Revelation 16:19
1563 Revelation 9:4

against the stubborn. There was not a period of healing during the first two woes and trumpets, for God Himself already knew who should not be attacked by the terror He pronounced; for they were sealed and known to Him; and it cannot, and should not be expected to fall any differently under the seventh trumpet and third woe. This is why, again, the events concerning the first opening of the second room within the heavenly Sanctuary cannot be linked to that of the seventh trumpet. The Spirit and his assembly are not prominent figures for suffering wrath in any of the previous trumpet devastations or woes; the Spirit's pattern for executing these things cannot be broken, for the LORD establishes them. Just because the first two woes were accomplished by a tribe of people, and the first six trumpets also by tribes of people, this does not deter from the underlying point of the woes and their trumpets, whose aim is the destruction of a false religious institution "who opposeth and exalteth himself above all that is called God, or that is worshipped."[1564] If this is so, and if the seventh trumpet announces the victory accomplished by the third woe; and it does; then the system erected by LORD's Spirit maintains itself without flaw.

17. The tribe of the third woe will be ministers that fulfill the saying, "Babylon, the glory of kingdoms, the beauty of the Chal'dees' excellency, shall be as when God overthrew Sodom and Gomor'rah."[1565] "I have commanded my sanctified ones, I have also called my mighty ones for mine anger, even them that rejoice in my highness. The noise of a multitude in the mountains, like as of a great people; a tumultuous noise of the kingdoms of nations gathered together: the LORD of hosts mustereth the host of the battle. They come from a far country, from the end of heaven, even the LORD, and the weapons of his indignation, to destroy the whole land,"[1566] says the Spirit. This is why it says, "Assemble yourselves, and come, all ye heathen, and gather yourselves together round about: thither cause thy mighty ones to come down, O LORD."[1567]

1564 2 Thessalonians 2:4
1565 Isaiah 13:19
1566 Isaiah 13:3-5
1567 Joel 3:11

18. This is that tribe "ascending from the east, having the seal of the living God,"[1568] who will fulfill the saying, "As God overthrew Sodom and Gomor'rah and the neighbour cities thereof, saith the LORD; so shall no man abide there, neither shall any son of man dwell therein. Behold, a people shall come from the north, and a great nation, and many kings shall be raised up from the coasts of the earth. They shall hold the bow and the lance: they are cruel, and will not shew mercy: their voice shall roar like the sea, and they shall ride upon horses, every one put in array, like a man to the battle, against thee, O daughter of Babylon."[1569] Herein are "the kings of the east."[1570]

19. "Behold, I am against thee, O destroying mountain, saith the LORD, which destroyest all the earth: and I will stretch out mine hand upon thee, and roll thee down from the rocks, and will make thee a burnt mountain. And they shall not take of thee a stone for a corner, nor a stone for foundations; but thou shalt be desolate for ever, saith the LORD. Set ye up a standard in the land, blow the trumpet among the nations, prepare the nations against her, call together against her the kingdoms of A'rarat, Min'ni, and Ash'chenaz; appoint a captain against her; cause the horses to come up as the rough caterpillers. Prepare against her the nations with the kings of the Medes, the captains thereof, and all the rulers thereof, and all the land of his dominion. And the land shall tremble and sorrow: for every purpose of the LORD shall be performed against Babylon, to make the land of Babylon a desolation without an inhabitant."[1571]

20. These are them that fulfill the word, "The LORD shall utter his voice before his army: for his camp is very great: for he is strong that executeth his word: for the day of the LORD is great and very terrible; and who can abide it?"[1572] For it says, "A voice of noise from the city, a voice from the temple, a voice of the LORD that rendereth recompence to his enemies."[1573] "For by fire and by his sword will the LORD

1568 Revelation 14:2
1569 Jeremiah 50:40-42
1570 Revelation 16:12
1571 Jeremiah 51:25-29
1572 Joel 2:11
1573 Isaiah 66:6

plead with all flesh: and the slain of the LORD shall be many."[1574] Thus, we are brought to view, and with the man of the Revelation, "heaven opened, and behold a white horse; and he that sat upon him was called Faithful and True, and in righteousness he doth judge and make war."[1575] "And the armies which were in heaven followed him upon white horses, clothed in fine linen, white and clean."[1576]

21. The first woe did only hurt them that did not possess the LORD's seal, but the second woe did kill them, albeit they remained impenitent, for that sentence of death was imperfect. Therefore the third woe, being entirely of the Word, will contain the perfect fulfillment of the two, and "perfect, as pertaining to the conscience."[1577] It is for this reason that the seventh angel cannot sound at any other time apart from the vibration of the Spirit's wrath in unrestrained vengeance, for the woes of the other two previous trumpets quickly followed after their trumpets.

22. When the denominations should become upset and offended at the Spirit's assembly, and after it should be fulfilled, "He spake as a dragon,"[1578] then should that seventh angel be expected to sound. The period from the disturbed church factions; for it will take time for the earth beast to build up its oppressive voice; until the first of the last seven plagues, the announcement of the soon and permanent destruction of Error's institution, and the pure judgment of His Son's name against them that remain negligent to the Spirit's will and doctrine, is imperfectly understood, but these events will follow one after other, and without fail. Yet, when the kindreds of the nations are no longer frustrated, but are now become angry with the Spirit's commandment keeping people, then the nearness of the seventh angel will be apparent, for, soon after these things, the final trumpet will sound, and the last woe will be accomplished. Then it will be said, "The kingdoms of the religious world now belong to the LORD and to His Spirit."[1579]

1574 Isaiah 66:16
1575 Revelation 19:11
1576 Revelation 19:14
1577 Hebrews 9:9
1578 Revelation 13:11
1579 Revelation 11:15

23. Now is the time that every one who sincerely cares for knowledge of heaven's voice and ministry should personally know the name of His Son's mediation. The season that we now live in is under the commandment, "Be renewed in the spirit of your mind."[1580] When the seventh angel begins to sound, this sealing period for those found within His heavenly Temple will be finished, for they will immediately be put to a terrible test in the greatest period of the earth's religious history. Whether we live to see these things at the end of today's current period of atonement, or are passed away from the earth, it is apparently clear that the soul who feels after heaven's intention should hear the counsel, "Is not this the fast that I have chosen? to loose the bands of wickedness, to undo the heavy burdens, and to let the oppressed go free, and that ye break every yoke?"[1581] "Afflict your souls, and offer an offering made by fire unto the LORD,"[1582] counsels the Spirit. "Do no work in that same day: for it is a day of atonement, to make an atonement for you before the LORD your God."[1583]

24. It is time to know the living God on a more personal level. We should daily move the LORD to say of us, "Who is this that engaged his heart to approach unto me?"[1584] yet what is the current position of *His* people? It is written, "They said, There is no hope: but we will walk after our own devices, and we will every one do the imagination of his evil heart."[1585] "The wrath of God is revealed from heaven against all ungodliness and unrighteousness of men, who hold the truth in unrighteousness,"[1586] and these ministers are them "which had the mark of the beast"[1587] and "which worshipped his image."[1588] The LORD would have no one found in such a condition for wrath; whether now, or at that later time; but would rather "have all men to be saved,

---

1580 Ephesians 4:23
1581 Isaiah 58:6
1582 Leviticus 23:27
1583 Leviticus 23:28
1584 Jeremiah 30:21
1585 Jeremiah 18:12
1586 Romans 1:18
1587 Revelation 16:2
1588 Revelation 16:2

and to come unto the knowledge of the truth."[1589] This "saving," this "redeeming," and this "deliverance" preached through the name of His Son, it is "salvation through sanctification of the Spirit and belief of the truth"[1590] within our conversation's conscience. The inward faculties are to be regenerated to uphold the name of His Son with His Spirit's laws and Faith in truth, in deed, and within the spirit of our mind in right benevolence.

25. There is no other time to receive inward correction for heaven's self-effacing good than now. The instruction is, "Humble yourselves in the sight of the Lord,"[1591] and, "Cleanse your hands, ye sinners; and purify your hearts, ye double minded. Be afflicted, and mourn, and weep: let your laughter be turned to mourning, and your joy to heaviness."[1592] Reverently searching after the Spirit's sayings for a beneficial self-examination for the purpose of self-development, and by the precious gifts and promises given to us for an experimental faith in our atonement to the LORD's right hand by His Son's mediation, is to swallow up our heart and mind today, for unimaginable movements provoked by thoughtless and unsanctified priests will soon inevitably surface.

1589   1 Timothy 2:4
1590   2 Thessalonians 2:13
1591   James 4:10
1592   James 4:8,9

28

Heaven's Eminent Reign

1. "And the seventh angel sounded; and there were great voices in heaven, saying, The kingdoms of this world are become the kingdoms of our Lord, and of his Christ; and he shall reign for ever and ever."[1593]

2. John sees, in vision, the image of the Spirit's sealed host protected from harm by their Captain's voice. What these have, up until this point, endured, is best summarized by the saying, "The dragon was wroth with the woman, and went to make war with the remnant of her seed."[1594] Before this time of deliverance, there was a period where "the nations were angry"[1595] against heaven's host, for they would not honor the earth's Regime, therefore when they could no longer suffer the spirit of these then Hebrews, "at that time certain Chalde'ans came near, and accused the Jews."[1596] Before this time of accusation, "there rose up certain of the sect of the Pharisees which believed"[1597] on *the Spirit's name* to prominence within the State of the new earth beast. These are them "of the synagogue of Satan, which say they are Jews, and

---

1593 Revelation 11:15
1594 Revelation 12:17
1595 Revelation 11:18
1596 Daniel 3:8
1597 Acts 15:5

are not, but do lie,"[1598] and have, out of a perversely ambitious heart for the elevation of their *God*; who is "another Jesus"[1599] of "another gospel";[1600] fulfilled the saying, "Thou hast there them that hold the doctrine of Ba'laam, who taught Ba'lac to cast a stumblingblock."[1601]

3. After the earth suffered a rent, a two-horned beast came up out of her. Such a beast was after the image of the beast before it, and this earth beast willfully suffered abuse to its conscience, placing a woman over its hands and thoughts, conceiving confusion, even as it says, "Neither shall any woman stand before a beast to lie down thereto: it is confusion."[1602] Such events happened due to a union of philosophical and ideological religious doctrines among certain sects and ministers of the earth. The canon of these *Pharisaical Chalde'ans* is eventually found in the secular laws and lawmakers of the land; their notions sealed with the authority of the State; and because there is a certain group of commandment keepers who had beforehand experienced the Spirit's Faith to know their Father, it is fulfilled, "The people that do know their God shall be strong, and do exploits."[1603]

4. This ecclesiastical empire grew tired of this host because they would not honor the image of their imagination, that is, the image of the first beast before them. They were repeat violators of the religion of the State, which meant that they were enemies of the State. This sect of individuals that sat in the presence of the king of the land "had power to give life unto the image of the beast, that the image of the beast should both speak, and cause that as many as would not worship the image of the beast should be killed,"[1604] for when they perceived a people stealing bodies from their congregation, the word was fulfilled, "They hate him that rebuketh in the gate, and they abhor him that speaketh uprightly."[1605] After passing petty legislative restrictions and

---

1598 Revelation 3:9
1599 2 Corinthians 11:4
1600 2 Corinthians 11:4
1601 Revelation 2:14
1602 Leviticus 18:23
1603 Daniel 11:32
1604 Revelation 13:15
1605 Amos 5:10

decrees against this people, when they observed that they would even suffer jail and prison for their conscience's testimony, they said to the king, "There are certain Jews,"[1606] "O king,"[1607] that "have not regarded thee: they serve not thy gods, nor worship the golden image which thou hast set up."[1608]

5. To regard the king is to obey the laws of the land, for the throne is but a symbol of civil government. The Spirit counsels His host, "Serve the king of Babylon, and it shall be well with you,"[1609] but when the State erects a standard directly compromising heaven's will, His instruction for compliance with the State finds itself changed. For, every king is told, "The God of heaven hath given thee a kingdom, power, and strength, and glory,"[1610] and this is why Paul writes, "Render therefore to all their dues: tribute to whom tribute is due; custom to whom custom; fear to whom fear; honour to whom honour."[1611] Obedience to the laws of the land will secure to every person a quiet existence, for their daily endeavors and personal goals will find themselves without State encroachment or harassment. But just as the citizen is culpable for his or her own self, so too the State has been given a restriction by the LORD's wisdom, for "the most High ruleth in the kingdom of men."[1612]

6. As time passes on that earth under a new national religious rule, the beast of the earth exercises "all the power of the first beast before him,"[1613] and then "causeth the earth and them which dwell therein to worship the first beast."[1614] This earth beast embraces the spirit of that injurious church and State government before it, and after compromising the conscience of his citizens, he eventually fulfills the saying, "All the world wondered after the beast."[1615] This is that "false prophet

---

1606 Daniel 3:12
1607 Daniel 3:12
1608 Daniel 3:12
1609 Jeremiah 40:9
1610 Daniel 2:37
1611 Romans 13:7
1612 Daniel 4:17
1613 Revelation 13:12
1614 Revelation 13:12
1615 Revelation 13:3

that wrought miracles before him"[1616] that is healed, and because there is a band scattered across the land that does not care to worship this pagan apostate government, it is said of the two-horned State, "The form of his visage was changed."[1617]

7. After a period of gross abuse and harassment, after "Sha'drach, Me'shach, and Abed'-nego, fell down bound into the midst of the burning fiery furnace";[1618] and these things done while the Spirit's plagues are falling against them that afflict them; a melody flows across the canvas of the earth, and every eye that is made to comprehend; as it says, "As many as were ordained to eternal life believed";[1619] announces, "The kingdoms of this world are become the kingdoms of our Lord, and of his Christ; and he shall reign for ever and ever."[1620] Them that have been defiled by the dragon at the word of the nations are finally rescued. Then "the king was astonied, and rose up in haste, and spake, and said unto his counsellors, Did not we cast three men bound into the midst of the fire? They answered and said unto the king, True, O king."[1621] Them that are *alive* have honored the living God above the king of the earth, and their confession is evidence that these are them "that had gotten the victory over the beast, and over his image, and over his mark, and over the number of his name."[1622]

8. Before this time, "men, who hold the truth in unrighteousness,"[1623] burned and distressed the earth and her members with coarse sayings. These priests abused the character of *God's Faith*, and the simplicity of *His voice*, while also holding *the LORD's name* in vain due to the persuasion of their polytheistic religion, and the strange ambition of their heart. Distraught and frustrated by the Spirit's Hebrews, these false Jews persecuted the seed of God's Son and their converts through the body of their State. When the cup of their wickedness had reached

---

1616   Revelation 19:20
1617   Daniel 3:19
1618   Daniel 3:23
1619   Acts 13:48
1620   Revelation 11:15
1621   Daniel 3:24
1622   Revelation 15:2
1623   Romans 1:18

its height, when these consciously advocated the defamation of the living God's name and body of knowledge, and by law sought the eradication of *heretics* from the earth, then fell the first of the Spirit's seven final plagues upon their inwards, and being the only sufferers of this sorrow, and while clueless of their suffering at the same time, their fury against the Spirit's creation grew worse and worse. But eventually their anger is halted; all are made to hear the saying, "After the glory hath he sent me unto the nations which spoiled you: for he that toucheth you toucheth the apple of his eye."[1624]

9. The confession that John hears of the Spirit's reign is a direct testimony to the fact that the obedient have not perished by the ecclesiastical institution of their day. How many generations have passed from the beginning of the earth's division until the revelation of the seventh angel is not known, but the words of these servants are a blatant witness that the LORD's Spirit does in fact rule in the religious assembles of earth's men. No man or government is above the LORD's ten immutable precepts, and the laws and authority entrusted to a State for the good of the human body and conscience is not above the LORD's voice. The saying, "All kingdoms are now of the Spirit and of His Christ's name,"[1625] is a tribute to the Word's spiritual power over the power of any State commandment and doctrine of priests and ministers, and is a witness to the faithfulness that He holds towards any one who executes His voice when confronted with oppressive legislative decrees that violate the conscience of their service to His name, even as He protected His three Hebrew stewards.

10. As the two previous trumpets were followed by their woes, so when the seventh angel sounds his seventh trumpet, it will not take long until the third woe takes to the scene of conflict, finishing the work that the other two failed to do. The word of the Word's servants that John hears announces the final exclamation of grief from those priests and elders not killed by the seven last plagues, and that did not repent of their inventions against heaven's will, for "neither repented they of their murders, nor of their sorceries, nor of their fornication,

---

1624 Zechariah 2:8
1625 Revelation 11:15

nor of their thefts."[1626] The Spirit's plagues do not fully destroy Error's name and assembly, for even while the final plague pours out, "men blasphemed God because of the plague."[1627] Nevertheless, as the first woe only hurt men that did not have the Spirit's seal, and as the second served to kill them for repentance, but failed to do so perfectly, so the third woe must come after plagues greater than those plagues previously executed by flesh to execute a more perfect justice then ever before, and for a more perfect penitence.

11. At the time appointed, "there came a great voice out of the temple of heaven, from the throne, saying, It is done,"[1628] "and great Babylon came in remembrance before God, to give unto her the cup of the wine of the fierceness of his wrath."[1629] "There was a great earthquake; and the sun became black as sackcloth of hair, and the moon became as blood; and the stars of heaven fell unto the earth";[1630] "the heaven departed as a scroll."[1631] And when "every mountain and island were moved out of their places,"[1632] then "the four and twenty elders, which sat before God on their seats, fell upon their faces, and worshipped God, saying, We give thee thanks, O Lord God Almighty, which art, and wast, and art to come; because thou hast taken to thee thy great power, and hast reigned."[1633]

1626 Revelation 9:21
1627 Revelation 16:21
1628 Revelation 16:17
1629 Revelation 16:19
1630 Revelation 6:12,13
1631 Revelation 6:14
1632 Revelation 6:14
1633 Revelation 11:16,17

29

The Earth's Sorrow

1. John writes, "I beheld, and heard an angel flying through the midst of heaven, saying with a loud voice, Woe, woe, woe, to the inhabiters of the earth."[1634]

2. This word, "woe," is better understood from how Ezekiel speaks of that food given him to eat by the Spirit, and he says, "There was written therein lamentations, and mourning, and woe."[1635] The phrase that John heard uttered by the Spirit is better said as, "Lamentation, Lamentation, Lamentation," or, "Mourning, Mourning, Mourning," for them that dwell within the religious earth's confidence. Each of the Revelation's woes involve a particular mourning and lamentation held to a particular earth, or sphere, or terrain. In this case, seeing as how no thing of the vision given to John is real within itself; but is rather a spiritual transcription of a sure reality; there is not a literal surface of the earth to look to, but rather the earth and ground of a particular religious institution.

3. The institution that fulfills the word, "The inhabiters of the earth,"[1636] and, "Them that dwell on the earth,"[1637] in the language of

---

1634   Revelation 8:13
1635   Ezekiel 2:10
1636   Revelation 8:13
1637   Revelation 6:10

Scripture, are them that fulfill the word, "Those men which have not the seal of God in their foreheads."[1638] The fact of the Spirit's woe, and for who that woe is particularly constrained, cannot be refuted or argued against. The Spirit's intention and purpose of the woe is against a particular faction of priests that do not know His name without perverting His name, for they do "not like to retain God in their knowledge."[1639] The woes cannot break their purpose, for the Spirit has ordained their mission, and every one of the three woes declared by the angel is to occur against the same faction to produce the same end, that is, lamentation and mourning.

4. Concerning the agent of the first woe, it says, "It was given that they should not kill,"[1640] nevertheless "their power was to hurt men five months."[1641] But the second woe confesses that, in it, by the agents of this woe, death was sanctioned, and by them was "the third part of men killed, by the fire, and by the smoke, and by the brimstone, which issued out of their mouths."[1642]

5. The individuals who were the Spirit's agents for the first two woes were of the seed of Ishmael, who dwelt in the deserts of the east, and the particular object of their anger was that brand of apostate Christianity upheld by Papal Rome, for their attacks were against the ecclesiastical State of Rome during Catholicism's reign over the then State of the then world. The agents of the woes are viewed as having the form of locusts that look like horses upon a closer inspection, for of the locust it is said, "They covered the face of the whole earth, so that the land was darkened; and they did eat every herb of the land, and all the fruit of the trees which the hail had left,"[1643] which is why John wrote of these people at the time they should appear in world and ecclesiastical history, "There came out of the smoke locusts upon the earth."[1644]

1638 Revelation 9:4
1639 Romans 1:28
1640 Revelation 9:5
1641 Revelation 9:10
1642 Revelation 9:18
1643 Exodus 10:14,15
1644 Revelation 9:3

6. Since the earth is, in the first six trumpets, Papal Rome, and since the locusts have had their mission against this institution, it serves as a fact that when the third woe should come in to the scene of action, it should cause lamentation and mourning to the spirit of this same institution. The second woe did not destroy the earth or the earth's men, but it did kill a part of its priesthood. Because only a part of her men were killed by the second woe, the third woe should serve to deliver the final blow to that priesthood. It is because of this that, in the third woe, the word is fulfilled that says,

7. "I raise up the Chalde'ans, that bitter and hasty nation, which shall march through the breadth of the land, to possess the dwellingplaces that are not theirs. They are terrible and dreadful: their judgment and their dignity shall proceed of themselves. Their horses also are swifter than the leopards, and are more fierce than the evening wolves: and their horsemen shall spread themselves, and their horsemen shall come from far; they shall fly as the eagle that hasteth to eat. They shall come all for violence: their faces shall sup up as the east wind, and they shall gather the captivity as the sand. And they shall scoff at the kings, and the princes shall be a scorn unto them: they shall deride every strong hold; for they shall heap dust, and take it."[1645]

8. It should be remembered that when the woes strike, the Spirit makes a distinction between them that know Him and them that do not know Him. This vision of the Chalde'ans is, as it is here introduced, not literal, but is wholly figurative, as is the vision of the Revelation. These Chalde'ans, and this vision, are but an illustration of how it will be fulfilled,

9. "I will bring upon Tyrus Nebuchadrez'zar king of Babylon, a king of kings, from the north, with horses, and with chariots, and with horsemen, and companies, and much people. He shall slay with the sword thy daughters in the field: and he shall make a fort against thee, and cast a mount against thee, and lift up the buckler against thee. And he shall set engines of war against thy walls, and with his axes he shall break down thy towers. By reason of the abundance of his horses their dust shall cover thee: thy walls shall shake at the noise of the

---

1645 Habakkuk 1:6-10

horsemen, and of the wheels, and of the chariots, when he shall enter into thy gates, as men enter into a city wherein is made a breach. With the hoofs of his horses shall he tread down all thy streets: he shall slay thy people by the sword, and thy strong garrisons shall go down to the ground. And they shall make a spoil of thy riches, and make a prey of thy merchandise: and they shall break down thy walls, and destroy thy pleasant houses: and they shall lay thy stones and thy timber and thy dust in the midst of the water. And I will cause the noise of thy songs to cease; and the sound of thy harps shall be no more heard."[1646]

10. Such an event will fulfill the saying against the earth, "The light of a candle shall shine no more at all in thee; and the voice of the bridegroom and of the bride shall be heard no more at all in thee."[1647]

11. Because the woes are against a particular religious institution, the woes, and the trumpets associated to them, cannot fall unless that institution is fully operational. And because the first two woes occurred at a time when the LORD observed, and He Himself certified, His house divided from other folds, the third woe cannot fall until His Word's assembly is again clearly recognized by Him as being fully separated from the other folds mishandling His name. Thus, *Nebuchadnez'zar* and the host of the *Chalde'ans*; who are but representatives of heaven's assembly headed by the law and doctrine of their High Priest; will execute judgment upon the ungodly.[1648] That true king of the north; who is the Faith and Counsel of the living God; will be the one to deal the final blow to that institution suffering to the final woe. This final woe can only occur when the Word's Spirit has sealed His own host within their foreheads, when the high priestly ministration of His Son is become swallowed up by the furious glory of His LORD's face, and when the Word's final seven plagues have been fully poured out. When the plagues have ended their season, "It is done,"[1649] says that LORD on heaven's throne. Then will it be said, "Great Babylon came in remembrance before God."[1650]

1646   Ezekiel 26:7-13
1647   Revelation 18:23
1648   Jude 1:15
1649   Revelation 16:17
1650   Revelation 16:19

12. These judgments are designed to inflict mourning and lamentation upon a particular religious tribe of people, and more specifically, "the men which had the mark of the beast, and upon them which worshipped his image."[1651] Until the era of that new republic after the image of the leopard beast is born, and until that pagan apostate ecclesiastical government joins hands with the spirit and philosophy that was wounded, heaven's final woe should not expect to fall, for it will only fall on the seed and lineage of the earth's host. This is why, at the time of her execution by that right Spirit of the north, and through His host; even by the voice and army of heaven's sanctified priests; many will say, "Alas, alas";[1652] that is, Woe, woe; "that great city Babylon, that mighty city!"[1653] "Alas, alas";[1654] that is, Mourn, mourn; "that great city, that was clothed in fine linen, and purple."[1655] "Alas, alas";[1656] that is, Lament, lament; "that great city, wherein were made rich all that had ships in the sea."[1657]

13. When the Spirit unleashes this third woe by His own voice, the institution supported by the original apostate spirit of the LORD's heavenly Government will no longer be in existence. For, says this Spirit, "I will also make the multitude of Egypt to cease by the hand of Nebuchadrez'zar king of Babylon. He and his people with him, the terrible of the nations, shall be brought to destroy the land: and they shall draw their swords against Egypt, and fill the land with the slain. And I will make the rivers dry, and sell the land into the hand of the wicked: and I will make the land waste, and all that is therein, by the hand of strangers: I the LORD have spoken it."[1658] This "wicked" band, these "strangers," these are "them that turn the battle to the gate"[1659] of "the land of Assyria with the sword, and the land of Nimrod in the

---

1651 Revelation 16:2
1652 Revelation 18:10
1653 Revelation 18:10
1654 Revelation 18:16
1655 Revelation 18:16
1656 Revelation 18:19
1657 Revelation 18:19
1658 Ezekiel 30:10-12
1659 Isaiah 28:6

entrances thereof,"¹⁶⁶⁰ for we shouldn't forget how it is written of that devastation against ancient Egypt, how "he cast upon them the fierceness of his anger, wrath, and indignation, and trouble, by sending evil angels among them."¹⁶⁶¹ These angels or messengers are only evil because they speak against Pharaoh, which is why they are told by Pharaoh's men, "Prophesy not again any more at Beth'-el: for it is the king's chapel, and it is the king's court."¹⁶⁶²

14. "Woe worth the day! For the day is near, even the day of the LORD is near, a cloudy day; it shall be the time of the heathen."¹⁶⁶³ "The pomp of her strength shall cease in her: as for her, a cloud shall cover her, and her daughters shall go into captivity. Thus will I execute judgments in Egypt: and they shall know that I am the LORD,"¹⁶⁶⁴ says His Spirit.

1660 Micah 5:6
1661 Psalm 78:49
1662 Amos 7:13
1663 Ezekiel 30:2,3
1664 Ezekiel 30:18,19

30

A Judgment Of Deliverance

1. Says Scripture, "In the days of the voice of the seventh angel, when he shall begin to sound, the mystery of God should be finished, as he hath declared to his servants the prophets."[1665]

2. "Days" are better understood as being "times," as it says, "The vision that he seeth is for many days to come, and he prophesieth of the times that are far off."[1666] Although the Spirit has confessed, "There should be time no longer,"[1667] it is an open fact that there will return to the earth certain of the "times or the seasons, which the Father hath put in his own power."[1668] When the seventh angel sounds his trumpet, a special revelation will commence to forward a season of potent power from heaven's throne. Wherefore "we shall see no war, nor hear the sound of the trumpet, nor have hunger of bread";[1669] "not a famine of bread, nor a thirst for water, but of hearing the words of the LORD";[1670] until that which the living God has spoken by His prophets shall begin.

1665 Revelation 10:7
1666 Ezekiel 12:27
1667 Revelation 10:6
1668 Acts 1:7
1669 Jeremiah 42:14
1670 Amos 8:11

And this phrase, "By His servants those prophets,"[1671] is quite interesting. The word that these men speak of reports the sounding of a trumpet, an alarm of war against hosts, for at this time of warning, the final work of engraving the name of the Word's Son within His LORD's earth and people will be finished.

3. We may mark the beginning of the voice of this seventh trumpet according to what those prophets of old confessed. We read: "And the LORD spake by his servants the prophets, saying, Because Manas'seh king of Judah hath done these abominations, and hath done wickedly above all that the Am'orites did, which were before him, and hath made Judah also to sin with his idols: therefore thus saith the LORD God of Israel, Behold, I am bringing such evil upon Jerusalem and Judah, that whosoever heareth of it, both his ears shall tingle. And I will stretch over Jerusalem the line of Sam'aria, and the plummet of the house of Ahab: and I will wipe Jerusalem as a man wipeth a dish, wiping it, and turning it upside down. And I will forsake the remnant of mine inheritance, and deliver them into the hand of their enemies; and they shall become a prey and a spoil to all their enemies; because they have done that which was evil in my sight, and have provoked me to anger, since the day their fathers came forth out of Egypt, even unto this day."[1672]

4. Again: "The LORD sent against him bands of the Chal'dees, and bands of the Syrians, and bands of the Mo'abites, and bands of the children of Ammon, and sent them against Judah to destroy it, according to the word of the LORD, which he spake by his servants the prophets. Surely at the commandment of the LORD came this upon Judah, to remove them out of his sight, for the sins of according to all that he did."[1673]

5. Again: "The LORD turned not from the fierceness of his great wrath, wherewith his anger was kindled against Judah, because of all the provocations that Manas'seh had provoked him withal. And the LORD said, I will remove Judah also out of my sight, as I have removed Israel, and will cast off this city Jerusalem which I have chosen, and the

---

1671 Revelation 10:7
1672 2 Kings 21:10-15
1673 2 Kings 24:1-3

house of which I said, My name shall be there."[1674] "I will raise up thy lovers against thee, from whom thy mind is alienated, and I will bring them against thee on every side,"[1675] says the Spirit, "the Babylonians, and all the Chalde'ans, Pe'kod, and Sho'a, and Ko'a, and all the Assyrians with them: all of them desirable young men, captains and rulers, great lords and renowned, all of them riding upon horses."[1676]

6. Part of the message contained within that declared unto the Word's stewards, and to His prophets, was destruction against the land and structure of *His* apostate people. The LORD's men confess that, like the house of Ahab; which is called Sama'ria; Jerusalem will also be handled. Of this house or church, the Spirit says, "I gave her space to repent of her fornication; and she repented not. Behold, I will cast her into a bed, and them that commit adultery with her into great tribulation, except they repent of their deeds."[1677] Thus, the word will be repeated against the then house of Judah headed by *Manas'seh*, "Thy wife shall be an harlot in the city, and thy sons and thy daughters shall fall by the sword, and thy land shall be divided by line; and thou shalt die in a polluted land: and Israel shall surely go into captivity forth of his land."[1678]

7. "Thou shalt be filled with drunkenness and sorrow, with the cup of astonishment and desolation, with the cup of thy sister Sama'ria,"[1679] promises the Spirit to this hypocritical host. "They shall come against thee with chariots, wagons, and wheels, and with an assembly of people, which shall set against thee buckler and shield and helmet round about: and I will set judgment before them, and they shall judge thee according to their judgments. And I will set my jealousy against thee, and they shall deal furiously with thee: they shall take away thy nose and thine ears; and thy remnant shall fall by the sword: they shall take thy sons and thy daughters; and thy residue shall be devoured by the fire. They

---

1674   2 Kings 23:26,27
1675   Ezekiel 23:22
1676   Ezekiel 23:22,23
1677   Revelation 2:21,22
1678   Amos 7:17
1679   Ezekiel 23:33

shall also strip thee out of thy clothes, and take away thy fair jewels."[1680] Therefore He says, "Remove the diadem, and take off the crown,"[1681] and, "I, even I, am against thee, and will execute judgments in the midst of thee in the sight of the nations."[1682]

8. It was the anticipated fury of His Spirit against *His* Ba'al worshipping house that compelled the prophet to exclaim, "Thou hast heard, O my soul, the sound of the trumpet, the alarm of war. Destruction upon destruction is cried."[1683] This is why the Spirit told another, "Sigh therefore, thou son of man, with the breaking of thy loins; and with bitterness sigh before their eyes."[1684] "Cry and howl, son of man: for it shall be upon my people, it shall be upon all the princes of Israel: terrors by reason of the sword shall be upon my people: smite therefore upon thy thigh. Because it is a trial."[1685] This "trial" is that bitter judgment of His name executed against an apostate religious institution for their perpetual disobedience towards His throne's will and wisdom, especially when her leaders, after receiving word from His men; for "they mocked the messengers of God, and despised his words, and misused his prophets";[1686] should have openly "humbled her that was set apart for pollution."[1687] Thus, because of her spiritual errors, He promises, "So will I send upon you famine and evil beasts, and they shall bereave thee; and pestilence and blood shall pass through thee; and I will bring the sword upon thee."[1688]

9. These things will not be done in secret, for the LORD promises to do these things openly against that house speaking against His name and throne. When this time should commence, the Spirit says, concerning this assembly, "I made thee a reproach unto the heathen, and a mocking to all countries. Those that be near, and those that be

---

1680 Ezekiel 23:24-26
1681 Ezekiel 21:26
1682 Ezekiel 5:8
1683 Jeremiah 4:19,20
1684 Ezekiel 21:6
1685 Ezekiel 21:12,13
1686 2 Chronicles 36:16
1687 Ezekiel 22:10
1688 Ezekiel 5:17

far from thee, shall mock thee, which art infamous and much vexed."[1689] Thus, at this time of judgment against error's negligent house; as it says, "Strong is the Lord God who judgeth her";[1690] the saying will be fulfilled, "God, the heathen are come into thine inheritance; thy holy temple have they defiled; they have laid Jerusalem on heaps. The dead bodies of thy servants have they given to be meat unto the fowls of the heaven, the flesh of thy saints unto the beasts of the earth. Their blood have they shed like water round about Jerusalem; and there was none to bury them. We are become a reproach to our neighbours, a scorn and derision to them that are round about us."[1691] This "heathen," this is the Spirit's host; "the armies which were in heaven";[1692] and they are against the temple of error's *God*, even against them "with their backs towards the temple of the LORD, and their faces toward the east,"[1693] who "worshipped the sun toward the east."[1694]

10. The period that we have entered upon is that time confessing to the aftermath of when "the nations were angry,"[1695] for their vexation will fulfill the saying, "The dragon was wroth with the woman, and went to make war with the remnant of her seed."[1696] A trumpet is a sound of war, it a sign of coming calamity, and when the seventh trumpet sounds, utter terror and distress will follow against them that have consciously refused heaven's hand, and while they trouble heaven's host, even as was the case for the previous trumpets before it. It will be fulfilled, against heaven's host, at this time by heaven's challengers, "This day is a day of trouble, and of rebuke, and blasphemy: for the children are come to the birth, and there is not strength to bring forth."[1697] But this time and season will not last. As soon as one will say, "How long, LORD? wilt thou be angry for ever?"[1698] and, "Pour out thy wrath upon

---

1689 Ezekiel 22:4,5
1690 Revelation 18:8
1691 Psalms 79:1-5
1692 Revelation 19:14
1693 Ezekiel 8:16
1694 Ezekiel 8:16
1695 Revelation 11:18
1696 Revelation 12:17
1697 2 Kings 19:3
1698 Psalm 79:5

the heathen that have not known thee, and upon the kingdoms that have not called upon thy name,"[1699] in response they will hear, "Shall I bring to the birth, and not cause to bring forth? saith the LORD: shall I cause to bring forth, and shut the womb? saith thy God."[1700]

11. When this final purging is complete; for the Spirit says, "I make thy lewdness to cease from thee, and thy whoredom,"[1701] and, "Judgment must begin at the house of God,"[1702]; the Spirit says, "Therein shall be left a remnant that shall be brought forth, both sons and daughters: behold, they shall come forth unto you, and ye shall see their way and their doings: and ye shall be comforted concerning the evil that I have brought upon Jerusalem, even concerning all that I have brought upon it. And they shall comfort you, when ye see their ways and their doings: and ye shall know that I have not done without cause all that I have done in it."[1703] Heaven's Temple will at this time have a new and final remnant church to sound mercy's great message. For, "the remnant of Jacob shall be in the midst of many people as a dew from the LORD, as the showers upon the grass, that tarrieth not for man, nor waiteth for the sons of men. And the remnant of Jacob shall be among the Gentiles in the midst of many people as a lion among the beasts of the forest, as a young lion among the flocks of sheep."[1704]

12. The plagues conferred to the Word's house; which three plagues begin before the final seven do fall; executed by Error's assembly, will not cease until the seventh trumpet sounds the third and final woe. Even while the seven last plagues fall on them that have rejected the binding and perpetual laws of heaven's LORD, along with the plain authority of His voice, persecution will still be committed against heaven's modern reformers and their converts. It is during this chaotic time; from the first of the seventh plague, and until the last; that the entire purpose of the LORD's Spirit will be accomplished, ushering in the complete reign of His throne before heaven and earth. Them

---

1699   Psalm 79:6
1700   Isaiah 66:9
1701   Ezekiel 23:27
1702   1 Peter 4:17
1703   Ezekiel 14:22,23
1704   Micah 5:7,8

"redeemed from among men, being the firstfruits unto God and to the Lamb,"[1705] will exist in a time that our imagination cannot yet fully comprehend. Because such an unstable period of apostate degeneracy is but preparing itself to burst onto the scene of action, it is for every one to know the name of the living God, and of His Christ our High Priest, that we would not be forgotten of the Godhead when earth's error begins to capture spirits for wrath, but that we may stand apart, and under the banner given them that fear His name through the knowledge of His Son's mediation.

13. For, concerning the then established house of error's spirit, "Thus saith the Lord GOD; I will bring up a company upon them, and will give them to be removed and spoiled. And the company shall stone them with stones, and dispatch them with their swords; they shall slay their sons and their daughters, and burn up their houses with fire. Thus will I cause lewdness to cease out of the land, that all women may be taught not to do after your lewdness. And they shall recompense your lewdness upon you, and ye shall bear the sins of your idols: and ye shall know that I am the Lord GOD."[1706]

14. At this time, the Spirit's counsel will fall on *His* house, saying, "Therefore also now, saith the LORD, turn ye even to me with all your heart, and with fasting, and with weeping, and with mourning: and rend your heart, and not your garments, and turn unto the LORD your God: for he is gracious and merciful, slow to anger, and of great kindness, and repenteth him of the evil."[1707] "Let the priests, the ministers of the LORD, weep between the porch and the altar, and let them say, Spare thy people, O LORD, and give not thine heritage to reproach, that the heathen should rule over them: wherefore should they say among the people, Where is their God? Then will the LORD be jealous for his land, and pity his people. Yea, the LORD will answer and say unto his people, Behold, I will send you corn, and wine, and oil, and ye shall be satisfied therewith: and I will no more make you a reproach among the heathen."[1708]

1705 Revelation 14:4
1706 Ezekiel 23:46-49
1707 Joel 2:12,13
1708 Joel 2:17-19

15. The name of heaven's Chief Priest, while grossly handling the inwards of Egypt's men, will nourish and alleviate His faithful. That last trumpet will sound against the then registered ungodly, and the Spirit will say, "I will remove far off from you the northern army, and will drive him into a land barren and desolate,"[1709] and the Spirit's host will confess, "The kingdoms of this world are become the kingdoms of our Lord, and of his Christ."[1710] For, "Egypt shall be a desolation, and Edom shall be a desolate wilderness, for the violence against the children of Judah, because they have shed innocent blood in their land."[1711]

16. This is why it says, "Thus saith the Lord GOD; When I shall have gathered the house of Israel from the people among whom they are scattered, and shall be sanctified in them in the sight of the heathen, then shall they dwell in their land that I have given to my servant Jacob. And they shall dwell safely therein, and shall build houses, and plant vineyards; yea, they shall dwell with confidence, when I have executed judgments upon all those that despise them round about them; and they shall know that I am the LORD their God."[1712]

1709 Joel 2:20
1710 Revelation 11:15
1711 Joel 3:19
1712 Ezekiel 28:25,26

31

In Righteousness

1. It is well for us to properly comprehend the manner in which the Spirit relays the appearance of His Son. The witness given of Scripture reports, "The hills melt, and the earth is burned at his presence, yea, the world, and all that dwell therein,"[1713] and the means whereby this devastation is accomplished is according to the saying, "He cometh, for he cometh to judge the earth: he shall judge the world with righteousness, and the people with his truth."[1714]

2. A very great burning is promised to occur against them that falsely hold the name of the living God, "for the wrath of God is revealed from heaven against all ungodliness and unrighteousness of men, who hold the truth in unrighteousness."[1715] Immediately we are made to understand, through Paul, that this fury is against them that hold the Spirit's Faith in "unrighteousness," wherefore it is well to know that "all unrighteousness is sin."[1716] Whatever "unrighteousness" is, it is that "sin" to be warred against by the Spirit of the LORD God, "and the

---

1713 Nahum 1:5
1714 Psalm 96:13
1715 Romans 1:18
1716 1 John 5:17

strength of sin is the law."[1717] This "law" spoken of is the handwritten religious law and tradition of priests and elders, for, "having abolished in his flesh the enmity, even the law of commandments contained in ordinances,"[1718] this LORD's Christ has openly defined what "sin" is, even as "the handwriting of ordinances."[1719] To continue in what this Christ's sacrifice marks as "sin" against heaven's Faith is to hold that Faith in "unrighteousness," which is why, when priests and ministers reach their height of unrighteousness against His name, it is that "in righteousness he doth judge and make war."[1720] This "war" is herein understood to be no literal warfare, seeing as how it is "against spiritual wickedness in high places."[1721]

3. For this cause, "when the Lord Jesus shall be revealed from heaven,"[1722] it will not, and cannot be any literal or physical celestial event, seeing as how it is written, "The hills melted like wax at the presence of the LORD, at the presence of the Lord of the whole earth."[1723] It is this "Lord" of the LORD God that will melt them that hold His name in unrighteousness, and if it is written, "He shall judge the world with righteousness, and the people with his truth,"[1724] it is blatantly evident that the "Lord" fulfilling the saying, "The elements shall melt with fervent heat, the earth also and the works that are therein shall be burned up,"[1725] is in reality the LORD's "truth," which "truth" is the righteousness of His Spirit. Now, "the Spirit of life"[1726] is "the Word of life";[1727] the Word is the living God's Spirit. That great "coming" and "appearing" of the living God's "Lord" is actually a vengeful manifestation and demonstration of the Word of the LORD's Spirit, and seeing

---

1717 1 Corinthians 15:56
1718 Ephesians 2:15
1719 Colossians 2:14
1720 Revelation 19:11
1721 Ephesians 6:12
1722 2 Thessalonians 1:7
1723 Psalm 97:5
1724 Psalm 96:13
1725 2 Peter 3:10
1726 Revelation 11:11
1727 1 John 1:1

as how "a spirit hath not flesh and bones,"[1728] when thinking on that anticipated "appearing," it is well to understand that "the Lord Jesus Christ our Saviour"[1729] is, in reality, "the commandment of God our Saviour."[1730] That "Lord" destroying the earth is the "truth" and "righteousness" of the Spirit's Word consuming the religious world, allowing us to understand that this warfare is not literal or physical, but rather mental and spiritual.

4. Seeing as how "God is the LORD,"[1731] and that "God is a Spirit,"[1732] when hearing, "He cometh,"[1733] it is not lawful to fix this appearing to any literal or tangible event, seeing as how "a spirit hath not flesh and bones."[1734] "In the beginning was the Word, and the Word was with God, and the Word was God,"[1735] and ever since creation, and for ever more, the Word will always be God; "whatsoever God doeth, it shall be for ever: nothing can be put to it, nor any thing taken from it."[1736] Words are not firstly physical. Words are not ultimately tangible. That "Lord" foreshadowed to overthrow that pagan apostate religion falsely calling on the *Spirit's name* is His "word of righteousness,"[1737] "because the Spirit is truth."[1738] The psalmist tells us that "he shall judge the world with righteousness, and the people with his truth,"[1739] and if His Spirit is that "truth," then that "truth" must represent the fact of His "righteousness," even "the knowledge of his will in all wisdom and spiritual understanding."[1740] Thus, concerning this "truth," we read, "Thy word is truth,"[1741] and, "Thy law is the truth."[1742] That "Lord"

1728 Luke 24:39
1729 Titus 1:4
1730 Titus 1:3
1731 Psalm 118:27
1732 John 4:24
1733 Psalm 96:13
1734 Luke 24:39
1735 John 1:1
1736 Ecclesiastes 3:14
1737 Hebrews 5:13
1738 1 John 5:6
1739 Psalm 96:13
1740 Colossians 1:9
1741 John 17:17
1742 Psalm 119:142

to appear to judge the religious world is no literal man, but is, in right context, "the law of truth,"[1743] "the law of the Spirit of life."[1744] It then makes sense why the Spirit will war by the law of His righteousness, for the goal is to utterly end unrighteousness, which "unrighteousness" is "sin" against His LORD's Word, "and the strength of sin is the law."[1745]

5. It therefore helps us to understand just what the Word's righteousness is, or else we will vainly and sensually concoct traditions and superstitions where there need not be any. The doctrine of physical harm or slaughter against humanity from *the heavens* is utterly debunked by the Word's Christ Himself, who, when with His men and passing through a certain place, and was not accepted, was asked by His men, "Wilt thou that we command fire to come down from heaven, and consume them, even as Eli'as did? But he turned, and rebuked them, and said, Ye know not what manner of spirit ye are of. For the Son of man is not come to destroy men's lives, but to save them?"[1746]

6. It is not of this Christ's Spirit to carnally execute any thing against any human being, for this Christ knows that "though we walk in the flesh, we do not war after the flesh,"[1747] which is why He preaches, "That which is born of the Spirit is spirit."[1748] The "life" that this Christ preached deliverance from is herein understood to not be that temporal or natural life, seeing as how "the spirit giveth life,"[1749] and that "if ye through the Spirit do mortify the deeds of the body, ye shall live."[1750] This "life" and "body" is, in no way, a reference to the natural life of the human being, but to the conscience of the religious conversation, and to the body of one's personal faith. The "life" to be delivered from is that conversation of the heart's sensual devotion to *heavenly things*; in other words, "your vain conversation received by tradition";[1751] seeing

---

1743   Malachi 2:6
1744   Romans 8:2
1745   1 Corinthians 15:56
1746   Luke 9:54-56
1747   2 Corinthians 10:3
1748   John 3:6
1749   2 Corinthians 3:6
1750   Romans 8:13
1751   1 Peter 1:18

as how it is the Spirit's will to "purge your conscience from dead works to serve the living God."[1752]

6. Herein is witnessed the Word's righteousness, which "truth" is summed up in the saying: "The law of the Spirit of life in Christ Jesus hath made me free from the law of sin and death."[1753] It is the mission of the Spirit's law and commandment to resurrect the spirit of the mind from "sin" against the living God's name and science, "and the strength of sin is the law."[1754] He or she properly learning of and executing the Spirit's Faith will understand what "sin" is, and regenerating from that spirit of error, will hear the counsel, "Be dead with Christ from the rudiments of the world,"[1755] for "if Christ be in you, the body is dead because of sin."[1756] Again, we cannot lose sight of the fact that, concerning this "Christ" referenced, that "the Lord Jesus Christ our Saviour"[1757] is, in reality, "the commandment of God our Saviour."[1758] "Sin" is annihilated by the Spirit's commandment within the conversation's conscience, allowing the inwards to "seek those things which are above, where Christ sitteth on the right hand of God."[1759] Learning of and doing the Spirit's law of creation is blessed to elevate "the eyes of your understanding"[1760] heavenward for knowledge of redemption's course, for, "through knowledge shall the just be delivered."[1761] Because "the law is spiritual,"[1762] heaven's will and doctrine is "spiritually discerned"[1763] for a perfect conversation, and "perfect, as pertaining to the conscience."[1764] The Spirit is concerned with the inward parts of the heart, for with His voice dressing our mind's organs, we can soberly and benevolently love His name, self, and the spirits of others, better.

1752 Hebrews 9:14
1753 Romans 8:2
1754 1 Corinthians 15:56
1755 Colossians 2:20
1756 Romans 8:10
1757 Titus 1:4
1758 Titus 1:3
1759 Colossians 3:1
1760 Ephesians 1:18
1761 Proverbs 11:9
1762 Romans 7:14
1763 1 Corinthians 2:14
1764 Hebrews 9:9

7. When the third woe is unleashed upon them that consciously will to hold the living God's name in vain, a very great burning will indeed occur, and according to how it says, "Every heart shall melt, and all hands shall be feeble, and every spirit shall faint, and all knees shall be weak as water,"[1765] and, "He also that is valiant, whose heart is as the heart of a lion, shall utterly melt."[1766] The heart of ministers contrary to the living God's science "shall stumble, and fall, and be broken, and be snared, and be taken"[1767] "before the LORD; for he cometh to judge the earth: with righteousness shall he judge the world, and the people with equity."[1768] This judging will not be any thing but a furious conviction of the inwards by the law of His righteousness, even as it says, "To execute judgment upon all, and to convince all that are ungodly among them of all their ungodly deeds which they have ungodly committed, and of all their hard speeches which ungodly sinners have spoken against him."[1769] The issue at hand is "deeds" and "sayings" of "sinners" against His name, and with the LORD's Christ "having abolished in his flesh the enmity, even the law of commandments contained in ordinances,"[1770] "sinners"; both now and then; are them that willingly ignore the fact that "the strength of sin is the law."[1771] Thus, with this warfare over "sin," it is clear that every "body" at this time will have "Christ" within it, for then the body is dead to "serve in newness of spirit."[1772]

8. It is for this cause that we cannot forget that the Spirit will slaughter Error's institution, along with the spirit of her men, "with the spirit of his mouth."[1773] The spirit of the LORD's mouth is the sword of His Word's will and commandment, which "sword" He defines for us by saying, "A law shall proceed from me, and I will make my

---

1765 Ezekiel 21:7
1766 2 Samuel 17:10
1767 Isaiah 8:15
1768 Psalm 98:9
1769 Jude 1:15
1770 Ephesians 2:15
1771 1 Corinthians 15:56
1772 Romans 7:6
1773 2 Thessalonians 2:8

judgment to rest for a light of the people."[1774] This law that is His judgment is "the sword of the Spirit, which is the word of God."[1775] When the third woe falls, it is this judgment that "the Lord Jesus Christ our Saviour";[1776] which "Lord" and "Savior" is "the commandment of God our Saviour";[1777] will execute to convince every mind of its unrighteousness, even as it says concerning "convincing," "By sound doctrine both to exhort and to convince the gainsayers."[1778] What the Spirit reveals by His Revelation is the greatest spiritual resurrection and reform movement ever experienced among priests and ministers within the religious world, which is why it says, "And there was a great earthquake, such as was not since men were upon the earth, so mighty an earthquake, and so great."[1779] At this time, the religious world is violently shaking at the revelation of the Word's righteousness in omnipotent glory; "in that day, that the LORD shall punish the host of the high ones that are on high, and the kings of the earth upon the earth."[1780]

9. This "punishing," because "God is a Spirit,"[1781] and because this wrath is the Spirit's vengeance, is no literal slaughter; the spirit of the LORD's mouth will get His throne the victory. This great battle is against "the course of this world, according to the prince of the power of the air, the spirit that now worketh in the children of disobedience,"[1782] which is why, when "the seventh angel poured out his vial into the air,"[1783] the saying is fulfilled against that spirit and philosophy holding the LORD's earth hostage, "Wilt thou yet say before him that slayeth thee, I am God? but thou shalt be a man, and no God, in the hand of him that slayeth thee."[1784] A "king," in Scripture, is a priest; as it says,

---

1774 Isaiah 51:4
1775 Ephesians 6:17
1776 Titus 1:4
1777 Titus 1:3
1778 Titus 1:9
1779 Revelation 16:18
1780 Isaiah 24:21
1781 John 4:24
1782 Ephesians 2:2
1783 Revelation 16:17
1784 Ezekiel 28:9

"And hast made us unto our God kings and priests."[1785] The Spirit's wrathful Word is against the spirit and strength of priests and elders, and like as Ezekiel, in vision, spoke of Nebuchadnez'zar and his host, so Nebuchadnez'zar and his army figuratively illustrate "them that turn the battle to the gate"[1786] at the time appointed. The Spirit's Word will go forward by the conscience and testimony of them that are sanctified by it, and it will utterly put an end to the institution of *Egypt's* religious error, silencing that spirit in to the dust, which is why it says, "The beast was taken, and with him the false prophet that wrought miracles before him...These both were cast alive into a lake of fire."[1787]

10. The third woe of the seventh trumpet presents a vision of complete harmony between heaven and earth's men by way of an earth-shaking dispute. The living God will defend His name against the serpent's host; "these shall make war with the Lamb, and the Lamb shall overcome them."[1788] Where "the Lamb" is preached, all "sin" against the LORD His Father is ushered in to the light, for this is that doctrine teaching, "Behold the Lamb of God, which taketh away the sin of the world."[1789] "When he ariseth to shake terribly the earth,"[1790] it will be "against all ungodliness and unrighteousness of men, who hold the truth in unrighteousness,"[1791] and "all unrighteousness is sin."[1792] Seeing as how "the strength of sin is the law,"[1793] when "the Lord Jesus Christ our Saviour";[1794] which "Lord" and "Savior" is "the doctrine of God our Saviour";[1795] is revealed to the eyes of men, this doctrine is come to rip the strength of "sin" from the heart of every "body" of faith. The Lamb will make a complete end of religious error against His LORD's name by piercing through the thoughts and intentions of every

---

1785 Revelation 5:10
1786 Isaiah 28:6
1787 Revelation 19:20
1788 Revelation 17:14
1789 John 1:29
1790 Isaiah 2:19
1791 Romans 1:18
1792 1 John 5:17
1793 1 Corinthians 15:56
1794 Titus 1:4
1795 Titus 2:10

one contrary to His sword, and the serpent's host will, in the midst of heaven's apostles, burn within their person at the revelation of self by the unmixed light of the Spirit's wrath, which is why it says, "And he shall be tormented with fire and brimstone in the presence of the holy angels, and in the presence of the Lamb."[1796]

11. This is that lot assigned to them that would not learn of and do repentance's course during the seven last plagues, "for if we sin wilfully after that we have received the knowledge of the truth, there remaineth no more sacrifice for sins, but a certain fearful looking for of judgment and fiery indignation, which shall devour the adversaries."[1797]

12. Today, this fire of the LORD's Word is to devour our inward parts; isn't it written, "He shall baptize you with the Holy Ghost and with fire"?[1798] The conscience of our conversation is "to be strengthened with might by his Spirit in the inner man,"[1799] which is why it says, "Thou desirest truth in the inward parts: and in the hidden part thou shalt make me to know wisdom."[1800] Right baptism, according to the living God's Spirit, is within the heart of the conversation's mind by His Spirit's wisdom, which is why it says, "Let the word of Christ dwell in you richly in all wisdom."[1801] Such a baptism cannot commence until the mind examines and proves His Spirit's will and law, which is why it says, "Sanctify them through thy truth,"[1802] and, "Ye are clean through the word which I have spoken,"[1803] and, "Be ye transformed by the renewing of your mind, that ye may prove what is that good, and acceptable, and perfect, will of God."[1804] The Lamb is come in vengeful fury to overthrow them that speak against the counsel, "Be renewed in the spirit of your mind,"[1805] for the nature of the priest is in a course

---

1796 Revelation 14:10
1797 Hebrews 10:26,27
1798 Luke 3:16
1799 Ephesians 3:16
1800 Psalm 51:6
1801 Colossians 3:16
1802 John 17:17
1803 John 15:3
1804 Romans 12:2
1805 Ephesians 4:23

halting faith's exercise to magnify "sin" against heaven's judgment, and "whatsoever is not of faith is sin,"[1806] "and the law is not of faith."[1807]

13. It is because priests and elders rule by the religious law and doctrine, and while saying it is of *the living God's Christ* for them to do so, that the Word must come to pronounce His Father's face, and the face of His Spirit's High Priest, angrily. Ministers and elders have reached the height of their wickedness against His name, and at this time, "her sins have reached unto heaven, and God hath remembered her iniquities."[1808] At this time "he cometh, for he cometh to judge the earth: he shall judge the world with righteousness, and the people with his truth."[1809] "The slain of the LORD shall be at that day from one end of the earth even unto the other end of the earth: they shall not be lamented, neither gathered, nor buried; they shall be dung upon the ground...the shepherds shall have no way to flee, nor the principal of the flock to escape."[1810] "The sword shall come upon Egypt, and great pain shall be in Ethio'pia, when the slain shall fall in Egypt, and they shall take away her multitude, and her foundations shall be broken down."[1811] "Thus will I execute judgments in Egypt: and they shall know that I am the LORD,"[1812] says the Spirit.

1806 Romans 14:23
1807 Galatians 3:12
1808 Revelation 18:5
1809 Psalm 96:13
1810 Jeremiah 25:33-35
1811 Ezekiel 30:4
1812 Ezekiel 30:19

32

The Figure Of His Impression

1. When hearing how it is said, "The Lord Jesus shall be revealed from heaven,"[1813] and, "The Son of man shall come in his glory,"[1814] it is that we are learning of the appearing of "the glory of the Father."[1815] If it is written, "Christ was raised up from the dead by the glory of the Father,"[1816] and, "The Spirit of him that raised up Jesus from the dead,"[1817] it is evident that the "glory" of the Father is the Spirit of the Father. What is to be revealed, and what is to "come," is no literal or physical appearing, but rather "the appearance of the likeness of the glory of the LORD."[1818] It is therefore well to comprehend what the LORD's "glory" is so that we may soberly understand what likeness of that glory is to appear "in flaming fire taking vengeance on them that know not God."[1819] The "glory" of God is the image, likeness, or

---

1813 2 Thessalonians 1:7
1814 Matthew 25:31
1815 Romans 6:4
1816 Romans 6:4
1817 Romans 8:11
1818 Ezekiel 1:28
1819 2 Thessalonians 1:8

fashion of God, as it says, "The image and glory,"[1820] and, "The brightness of his glory, and the express image of his person."[1821] What is to be revealed, at the time appointed, in wrath, is the image of God's person, making it necessary for us to understand what "God" is. It is written, "God is a Spirit,"[1822] and since "the Spirit of life"[1823] is "the Word of life,"[1824] "God" is the Word of the LORD's Spirit. The likeness of God is therefore understood as the likeness of the Word's Spirit, and seeing as how "a spirit hath not flesh and bones,"[1825] the appearance of the likeness of the LORD's glory in fire can be no physical or tangible thing.

2. The LORD's "glory" is His Word's righteousness, which is why it says, "In righteousness he doth judge and make war."[1826] To war in righteousness is to war according to the Word's stature, and that righteousness is "the kindness and love of God our Saviour toward man."[1827] This good kindness is according to the saying, "Thou desirest truth in the inward parts: and in the hidden part thou shalt make me to know wisdom," [1828] which is why it says, "Let the word of Christ dwell in you richly in all wisdom."[1829] The engrafting of His Christ's wisdom on the conversation's heart is the Word's righteousness, for the end of this wisdom is liberty from sin against the LORD and Word of this commandment, moving the person to confess, "The law of the Spirit of life in Christ Jesus hath made me free from the law of sin and death."[1830] This allows us to understand that the Spirit's law and wisdom, because this engrafting is not physical or natural, is that "commandment of God our Saviour"[1831] called, "The Lord Jesus Christ our Saviour";[1832]

1820 1 Corinthians 11:7
1821 Hebrews 1:3
1822 John 4:24
1823 Revelation 11:11
1824 1 John 1:1
1825 Luke 24:39
1826 Revelation 19:11
1827 Titus 3:4
1828 Psalm 51:6
1829 Colossians 3:16
1830 Romans 8:2
1831 Titus 1:3
1832 Titus 1:4

"the law is spiritual."[1833] To hear of "Jesus Christ" appearing in "fire" is to hear of the appearing of the likeness of the living God's glory and praise, which glory is the righteousness of the LORD's name, which "name" appears in the likeness or fashion of a commandment. "Jesus Christ" is a term or moniker used to express the Word's law and righteousness, and to hear of its appearing in "glory" and "fire" is to hear of the Word's Faith executing the Spirit's judgment of righteousness in a wrath most omnipotent.

3. Isn't this what is written? Doesn't it say, "The Lord cometh with ten thousands of his saints, to execute judgment upon all, and to convince all that are ungodly"?[1834] Who is this "Lord"? This "Lord" is the same "God" spoken of in the saying, "Sing unto God, ye kingdoms of the earth; O sing praises unto the Lord,"[1835] and, "Blessed be the Lord, who daily loadeth us with benefits, even the God of our salvation."[1836] This "Lord" and "God" are the same entity representing the same Word, for "the Lord gave the word."[1837] This "Lord" is the same Word of whom, in the beginning, it says, "All things were made by him; and without him was not any thing made that was made."[1838] At this time of creation, "the Word was God,"[1839] and with this same Word come in to the spirit of the LORD's Christ, when once this man said, before his passing, "Father, into thy hands I commend my spirit,"[1840] it is that the Word of creation is become that "Lord" and "God" of every spirit of every conversation hopeful to know the living God. For even the LORD's Christ allowed the Word of His Father's throne to be that Lord and God of His faith's body, saying, "I know him, and keep his saying."[1841] Thus, it is that the "Lord" to appear in glory, and that "God" to appear in vengeance, is the Wisdom and Saying of the LORD's Word, the law and commandment of the LORD's Spirit. It is

---

1833   Romans 7:14
1834   Jude 1:14,15
1835   Psalm 68:32
1836   Psalm 68:19
1837   Psalm 68:11
1838   John 1:3
1839   John 1:1
1840   Luke 23:46
1841   John 8:55

only in this fashion that "all ungodliness and unrighteousness of men, who hold the truth in unrighteousness,"[1842] can finally be settled.

4. This is why, at the time appointed, priests and ministers will say, "Hide us from the face of him that sitteth on the throne, and from the wrath of the Lamb,"[1843] for the likeness of the face of the living God is "the knowledge of the glory of God in the face of Jesus Christ."[1844] The face of the LORD's Christ is the doctrine of the Lamb, which doctrine is a law ordained to "purge your conscience from dead works to serve the living God."[1845] Where the Lamb is preached, knowledge of "sin" for right repentance from "sin" and "death" is fallen upon the conversation's conscience, which is why it says, "Behold the Lamb of God, which taketh away the sin of the world."[1846] With the LORD's Christ "having abolished in his flesh the enmity, even the law of commandments contained in ordinances,"[1847] we today have a very clear definition of "sin" relayed to us, for "the sting of death is sin; and the strength of sin is the law."[1848] The "law" spoken of by Paul is the religious "handwriting of ordinances"[1849] by the pen of priests and elders. The passing of the LORD's Christ on the tree perpetually condemns the religious law and tradition of men as "sin," for it is written, "He that is hanged is accursed of God."[1850]

5. As we observe this LORD's Christ on the tree, it is not that we are seeing the condemnation of a man, but rather the cursing of what the illustration of this man's flesh represents. Being "made under the law,"[1851] this Christ's flesh, when on the tree, is representative of a religious spirit and ideology. With this flesh passed away on the tree, it is that the spirit and philosophy of what this body represents; which is a religious conversation ruled by the religious law and tradition of

---

1842 Romans 1:18
1843 Revelation 6:16
1844 2 Corinthians 4:6
1845 Hebrews 9:14
1846 John 1:29
1847 Ephesians 2:15
1848 1 Corinthians 15:56
1849 Colossians 2:14
1850 Deuteronomy 21:23
1851 Galatians 4:4

priests and elders; is passed away not only from the spirit or mind of that conversation, but also from the Faith of the LORD's Word, which Word and Wisdom is that "Lord" and "God" of creation's present science. Therefore, with the LORD's Christ saying, "Father, into thy hands I commend my spirit,"[1852] what is preached is the resurrection and reformation of the conversation through the strengthening of the spirit of the mind, which is why it says, "Put off concerning the former conversation...and be renewed in the spirit of your mind,"[1853] because "wisdom strengtheneth";[1854] this is the kingdom and righteousness of the Word's Spirit. In order to experience the Word's righteousness, or the glory of creation's God, it is that the mind must take in the Word's wisdom and knowledge, to do it, which is why it says, "Of his own will begat he us with the word of truth, that we should be a kind of firstfruits of his creatures";[1855] this is the kingdom and righteousness of God. Being slain on the tree, it is that a conscience bound to the religious law is abolished from heaven's will and wisdom, opening up the person to learn the definition of "sin" for mentally and spiritually chasing redemption's prosperity.

6. It is therefore well to understand that "all unrighteousness is sin," and if "all unrighteousness is sin,"[1856] and if "the strength of sin is the law,"[1857] then "unrighteousness," being "sin," is the religious law. The Lamb's doctrine is preached where "sin" abounds against the name and face of the LORD God's throne, meaning that it is preached to them whose confidence is in a "vain conversation received by tradition."[1858] The Lamb appears to annihilate all confidence in "philosophy and vain deceit, after the tradition of men, after the rudiments of the world,"[1859] which system is built upon "the handwriting of ordinances."[1860] This is how we may know we reverence that coun-

---

1852 Luke 23:46
1853 Ephesians 4:23
1854 Ecclesiastes 7:19
1855 James 1:18
1856 1 John 5:17
1857 1 Corinthians 15:56
1858 1 Peter 1:18
1859 Colossians 2:8
1860 Colossians 2:14

terfeit *Christ*, even by our subscription to "the enmity, even the law of commandments contained in ordinances."[1861] Therefore if we honor a *Christ* preaching, "Righteousness come by the law,"[1862] when it is that, in reality, the LORD's Christ "hath redeemed us from the curse of the law,"[1863] when encouraged by him to worship an image of his own concoction; whether it be of a ceremony and baptism of his own fame, or a *sabbath* of his own person; we may understand that this is that spirit and philosophy nailed to the tree, and that we, by our service to it, are become partakers of them owning the rebuke, "And for this cause God shall send them strong delusion, that they should believe a lie: that they all might be damned who believed not the truth, but had pleasure in unrighteousness."[1864]

7. To be "damned" is to be "accursed," and if our conversation is accursed, it is because our eyes are upon that which is accursed, even upon the cursed tree and that religious persuasion nailed to it. The tree, and what is represented by it, is no image of salvation, "for he that is hanged is accursed of God."[1865] To worship the tree is to unlawfully laud the annihilation preached by it, becoming "the enemies of the cross of Christ: whose end is destruction, whose God is their belly, and whose glory is in their shame, who mind earthly things."[1866] The tree of the LORD's Christ represents a doctrine that, if not soberly examined and experienced, will be turned upside down by the lazy and self-complacent. That tree is an illustration of what not to presently keep and do for a religious conversation, which is why its illustration also preaches absolute division from what is nailed to it, moving the careful observer to say, "God forbid that I should glory, save in the cross of our Lord Jesus Christ, by whom the world is crucified unto me, and I unto the world."[1867] The doctrine of that *Christ* of falsehood

---

1861 Ephesians 2:15
1862 Galatians 2:21
1863 Galatians 3:13
1864 2 Thessalonians 2:11,12
1865 Deuteronomy 21:23
1866 Philippians 3:18,19
1867 Galatians 6:14

saying, "You are justified by the law,"[1868] is a clear turning of the Word's Faith upside down, for an illustration made to inform the conscience of "sin" is mysteriously made to encourage "sin" against heaven's higher education.

8. The LORD's Christ on the tree and passed away is the confession that the manners of the religious world are passed away from His LORD's doctrine, and from whosoever is inclined to learn of and do that doctrine. The wisdom of the religious world is based upon a rule through religious laws and doctrines of priests and elders, and with this Christ's spirit secured to the Word's hands, it is that every spirit is encouraged to quit the religious earth to pass in to the Building of those hands to know the benevolence of those hands, which is why our conversation is to "have escaped the pollutions of the world through the knowledge of the Lord and Saviour Jesus Christ."[1869] Again, it is well to remember that "the Lord Jesus Christ our Saviour"[1870] is "the commandment of God our Saviour."[1871] The "escape" mentioned by Peter is no literal escape, seeing as how our conversation's conscience is "to be strengthened with might by his Spirit in the inner man."[1872] Because "wisdom strengtheneth,"[1873] the inwards of our faith's conversation is to be filled with the wisdom and knowledge of the Word's Spirit, to the end we may be able to comprehend "sin" for learning how to better cultivate faith in heaven's right and sober understanding. When the Lamb's doctrine is correctly preached, the conscience will know its wrong before its face to thoughtfully reform the conversation in confidence of the hope to be received, which hope is by a "faith which worketh by love"[1874] and sound knowledge.

9. Today, the doctrine of the Lamb is to personally regenerate "the eyes of your understanding,"[1875] but when this wisdom is, at the time

---

1868 Galatians 5:4
1869 2 Peter 2:20
1870 Titus 1:4
1871 Titus 1:3
1872 Ephesians 3:16
1873 Ecclesiastes 7:19
1874 Galatians 5:6
1875 Ephesians 1:18

appointed, poured forth upon the then ungodly, it will slay a mass of soul temples collectively. For "he shall judge among the heathen, he shall fill the places with the dead bodies; he shall wound the heads over many countries."[1876]

10. This wrath is specifically ordained for the heads and chief priests of religious denominations holding the LORD God's will and doctrine in unrighteousness; we cannot forget that this war is "against the rulers of the darkness of this world, against spiritual wickedness in high places."[1877] This "war" is a war of God, who is the LORD's Spirit, who is the Word of His Spirit's mouth. This is not, on the Godhead's part, a literal or physical war. The Revelation is a vision from the Spirit's perspective and is not based upon the perspective and superstition of human beings, for, seeing as how "a spirit hath not flesh and bones,"[1878] and that "that which is born of the Spirit is spirit,"[1879] it is that the wrath of the appearance of the LORD God's likeness in glory is a vengeful pouring out of words upon the inwards of the conversation's conscience. This is a battle of hosts and armies of priesthoods, and the only way to combat spiritual error is to proclaim spiritual right to the mind, even as it says, "By manifestation of the truth commending ourselves to every man's conscience in the sight of God."[1880]

11. Therefore when hearing, "The Lord Jesus shall be revealed from heaven with his mighty angels,"[1881] it is that we are hearing of the complete end of that institution holding the Word's name in unrighteousness, "whom the Lord shall consume with the spirit of his mouth."[1882] If this consumption is by the spirit of His mouth, then this consumption is by "the spirit of wisdom and understanding, the spirit of counsel and might, the spirit of knowledge and of the fear of the LORD,"[1883] making the "Lord" of this consumption no literal or

---

1876   Psalm 110:6
1877   Ephesians 6:12
1878   Luke 24:39
1879   John 3:6
1880   2 Corinthians 4:2
1881   2 Thessalonians 1:7
1882   2 Thessalonians 2:8
1883   Isaiah 11:2

physical figure, but rather "the commandment of God our Saviour,"[1884] which spiritual law and commandment is called, "The Lord Jesus Christ our Saviour,"[1885] which "Lord" and "Savior" is "the doctrine of God our Saviour."[1886] This commandment is, seeing as how "God is a Spirit,"[1887] "the appearance of the likeness of the glory of the LORD."[1888] When that year of the Lamb's wrath should appear, "the law of the Spirit of life";[1889] which law is "the doctrine of Christ,"[1890] "the word of righteousness,"[1891] "the law of Christ,"[1892] "the law of truth,"[1893] "the word of truth,"[1894] "the truth of God";[1895] will pour out upon the inwards of them reverencing unrighteousness "by the spirit of judgment, and by the spirit of burning."[1896]

12. This "burning" is not literal, but is a consumption according to how it says, "My soul melteth for heaviness";[1897] because this wrath wholly belongs to the Word, it is well to remember how it says, "The word of God is quick, and powerful, and sharper than any twoedged sword, piercing even to the dividing asunder of soul and spirit, and of the joints and marrow, and is a discerner of the thoughts and intents of the heart."[1898] The intention of the Word's wrath is "to convince all that are ungodly among them of all their ungodly deeds which they have ungodly committed, and of all their hard speeches which ungodly sinners have spoken against him,"[1899] and this correction and re-education occurring against "the imagination of the thoughts of

---

1884   Titus 1:3
1885   Titus 1:4
1886   Titus 2:10
1887   John 4:24
1888   Ezekiel 1:28
1889   Romans 8:2
1890   2 John 1:9
1891   Hebrews 5:13
1892   Galatians 6:2
1893   Malachi 2:2
1894   Ephesians 1:13
1895   Romans 3:7
1896   Isaiah 4:4
1897   Psalm 119:28
1898   Hebrews 4:12
1899   Jude 1:15

the heart."[1900] The Lamb's face is ordained to execute just what the LORD's Spirit intends for the spirit of the conversation, and when this wisdom is found heightened in wrath, it is that "the slain of the LORD shall be at that day from one end of the earth even unto the other end of the earth: they shall not be lamented, neither gathered, nor buried; they shall be dung upon the ground."[1901]

13. At that day, creation's knowledge will hold earth's men when the revelation of the LORD God's name and glory is remorselessly impressed upon their conscience, then "with the voice together shall they sing: for they shall see eye to eye, when the LORD shall bring again Zion."[1902]

1900 1 Chronicles 29:18
1901 Jeremiah 25:33
1902 Isaiah 52:8

33

A Thoughtful End

1. There is no greater illustration explaining the manner in which that anticipated revelation of the Lamb's wrath will appear than when "they brought the colt to Jesus, and cast their garments on him; and he sat upon him. And many spread their garments in the way: and others cut down branches off the trees, and strawed them in the way. And they that went before, and they that followed, cried, saying, Hosanna; Blessed is he that cometh in the name of the Lord."[1903]

2. This image would lead the mind to perceive a free celebration of some sort, wherefore to get the full gist of that age to come, we read: "Rejoice greatly, O daughter of Zion; shout, O daughter of Jerusalem: behold, thy King cometh unto thee: he is just, and having salvation; lowly, and riding upon an ass, and upon a colt the foal of an ass. And I will cut off the chariot from E'phraim, and the horse from Jerusalem, and the battle bow shall be cut off: and he shall speak peace unto the heathen: and his dominion shall be from sea even to sea, and from the river even to the ends of the earth. As for thee also, by the blood of thy covenant I have sent forth thy prisoners out of the pit wherein is no water."[1904]

1903   Mark 11:7-9
1904   Zechariah 9:9-11

3. It may not seem like it, but both Mark and Zechariah do relay the same event. In Zechariah, there is a work to accomplish by the one on the horse, and that work is to "speak peace unto the heathen."[1905] Zechariah's language and imagery does not provoke any sentiment for a literal battle, for if the mission is to speak "peace," and by that peace will cut off the army of the opposing force, then this warfare is accomplished by one who is "just, and having salvation,"[1906] and it is well to know that it is "the grace of God that bringeth salvation."[1907] The living God's grace is no literal or physical instrument, but is that gift or aid to the Spirit's manner of righteousness. To hear that this one on the horse appears with salvation is to hear that "in righteousness he doth judge and make war,"[1908] and all righteousness is accomplished through "the grace of life."[1909] Now, all grace is "shed on us abundantly through Jesus Christ our Saviour,"[1910] and it is well to understand that, in right context of language, "the Lord Jesus Christ our Saviour"[1911] is "the commandment of God our Saviour."[1912] Thus, the illustration of the LORD's Christ on the horse is but a vision of the doctrine of the Word's righteousness appearing by a specific horse, and concerning this "horse," it is written, "The LORD of hosts hath visited his flock the house of Judah, and hath made them as his goodly horse in the battle."[1913]

4. "The horse is prepared against the day of battle,"[1914] and although Mark presents to us a scene of warmth and congratulations, Zechariah presents to us that task leading up to such a celebration. Both Mark and Zechariah preach warfare in their doctrine, but they both pronounce it from different angles.

1905 Zechariah 9:10
1906 Zechariah 9:9
1907 Titus 2:11
1908 Revelation 19:11
1909 1 Peter 3:7
1910 Titus 3:6
1911 Titus 1:4
1912 Titus 1:3
1913 Zechariah 10:3
1914 Proverbs 21:31

5. That horse used in the battle is, as Zechariah tells us, the then sanctified household of the Spirit's name, even as He says, "I have commanded my sanctified ones, I have also called my mighty ones for mine anger."[1915] This horse, in both versions of this vision, is no literal animal, but is a religious tribe of people under the yoke of the name of the one seated on top of them, and "name" means "faith" or "doctrine," as it says, "And hast kept my word, and hast not denied my name,"[1916] and, "Thou holdest fast my name, and hast not denied my faith."[1917] The illustration of the LORD's Christ, seeing as how that horse is representative of a church under heaven's banner, is no literal illustration of a man appearing in any literal or physical likeness or form. The one on the horse represents the Word's commandment, which is why they said, "Blessed is he that cometh in the name of the Lord."[1918] What appears by the living God's then tribe is the knowledge of the revelation of the LORD God's name in omnipotent glory, for this warfare, being "against the rulers of the darkness of this world, against spiritual wickedness in high places,"[1919] must find itself spiritually settled. This why it says, "He shall speak peace";[1920] this fight is won "with the spirit of his mouth."[1921]

6. This speech is not literally given by some man on a horse parting the actual sky, but it says, "Out of his mouth goeth a sharp sword, that with it he should smite the nations."[1922]

7. This "sword" is "the sword of the Spirit, which is the word of God,"[1923] and it is against the then heathen or Gentile religious denominations that will not accept or experience salvation's science. This Word or Saying of heaven's Spirit will overthrow the armies of that contrary tribe by the doctrine of the LORD God's throne in unguarded tones. The Spirit's host will fully pronounce the living God's name through

---

1915 Isaiah 13:3
1916 Revelation 3:8
1917 Revelation 2:13
1918 Mark 11:9,10
1919 Ephesians 6:12
1920 Zechariah 9:10
1921 2 Thessalonians 2:8
1922 Revelation 19:15
1923 Ephesians 6:17

the face of His Son, preaching the reign of heaven's throne against the spirit and philosophy of "sin." Through the testimony of heaven's host, the inwards of that contrary host will be devoured by the speech of the heavenly Sanctuary, leading to the reign of the Spirit's Faith "from sea even to sea, and from the river even to the ends of the earth."[1924] At this time of "rest," the host of the serpent's philosophy have put off their former conversation to pick up heaven's testimony, which is why they all shout, "Blessed is he that cometh in the name of the Lord: blessed be the kingdom of our father David, that cometh in the name of the Lord: Hosanna in the highest."[1925] Thus, with earth now honoring the living God's throne with heaven, the reign of His Spirit's name, through the knowledge of His Son's mediation, is become the song of the age; it is fulfilled, "I have sent forth thy prisoners out of the pit wherein is no water."[1926]

8. The Revelation is like as a manifestation "in a dream, in a vision of the night,"[1927] even like "as when an hungry man dreameth, and, behold, he eateth; but he awaketh, and his soul is empty: or as when a thirsty man dreameth, and, behold, he drinketh; but he awaketh, and, behold, he is faint, and his soul hath appetite."[1928]

9. There is no real thing about the illustration of a vision other than the real meaning behind its projection. When once the illustration is discerned, then the meaning behind the picture will make sense, but to take the illustration to be a literal representation of the image is to commit error in interpretation. How did Joseph translate the dreams of those men? After he heard one man tell his dream, did Joseph give off the impression that the dream was literally factual? Didn't Joseph take the dream and translate it in to reality? Didn't he say, "This is the interpretation of it: The three branches are three days: yet within three days shall Pharaoh lift up thine head"?[1929] If Joseph translated the spiritual revelation given to the chief butler, must we not, above

---
1924 Zechariah 9:10
1925 Mark 11:9,10
1926 Zechariah 9:11
1927 Job 33:15
1928 Isaiah 29:8
1929 Genesis 40:12,13

literally reading the vision, also soberly translate the Revelation given to John? Did Daniel take that golden statue of the king to be a literal thing? Did he not interpret the illustration of that statue? Didn't he break down the body of that statue for the king? The revelation meant some thing above the vision, and must not that vision given to John mean more than colorful words?

10. That scene stating, "I saw heaven opened, and behold a white horse,"[1930] connotes no literal image. That horse, and its rider, is the then purified tribe of salvation's science bringing knowledge of creation's present Faith to the then ministers of the religious world; both small and great. Mark and Zechariah speak on this scene presented to us in the nineteenth division of the Revelation, and the victory will go to that horse and rider on the Spirit's side, leaving that contrary host in shame, so much so that John heard "as it were the voice of a great multitude, and as the voice of many waters, and as the voice of mighty thunderings, saying, Allelu'ia: for the Lord God omnipotent reigneth. Let us be glad and rejoice, and give honour to him."[1931] A collective exclamation, at the end of the controversy, is given by both the earth's ministers and heaven's apostles, which is what that revelation, according to Mark's account, means. Both heaven and earth; the stewards of heaven and the ministers of earth; will abide by the same heavenly throne and banner, for the *earth* purchased by the Son to His LORD's throne on the tree now acknowledges its service to the ministry that purchased them, and to the Spirit of whom they belong.

11. Although the language of the nineteenth division of the Revelation is colorful, it is but a figurative representation of a battle of religious hosts, where one would have the doctrine of the Spirit's righteousness govern their mind, and where the other would have the philosophy of the serpent rule their conversation. This clash is over the name of the living God, and its misrepresentation, and when them that are stout to "peace" do hear the correct interpretation of salvation's science, and of salvation's Word and God, the bodies of the ministers of the earth will fall to the ground and pray for death, for this consumption is without

---

1930   Revelation 19:11
1931   Revelation 19:6,7

mercy upon their conversation's inwards. The end of this controversy, although uttered by ministers, will be won by the Word, for many spirits will be slaughtered, and that burning will initiate the greatest reformatory movement ever recorded in ecclesiastical history; this is why it says, "And there was a great earthquake, such as was not since men were upon the earth, so mighty an earthquake, and so great."[1932] The doctrine and institution of error will come to a complete end, for when once the earth's ministers truly understand their wrong, "these shall hate the whore, and shall make her desolate and naked, and shall eat her flesh, and burn her with fire."[1933] The earth will then experience the greatest regeneration ever witnessed, leading to them fulfilling the saying, "The whole earth is at rest, and is quiet: they break forth into singing."[1934]

12. That doctrine of a *Christ* literally appearing from the sky is no revelation of the Spirit's mind, but we read of Lu'cifer, that counterfeit "son of the morning":[1935] "Hell from beneath is moved for thee to meet thee at thy coming: it stirreth up the dead for thee, even all the chief ones of the earth; it hath raised up from their thrones all the kings of the nations."[1936]

13. This language should sound familiar, for it is written, "Which go forth unto the kings of the earth and of the whole world, to gather them to the battle of that great day of God Almighty."[1937] The doctrine of religious error preaches a *Christ* contrary to that Christ of the Bible, for this *Christ* of Lu'cifer is born to meet the chief priests and elders of the religious world, to support their cause for physically destroying them contrary to "death's" religion. Because "the sting of death is sin; and the strength of sin is the law";[1938] the religion of "death" is a creed supported by the religious law of priests and elders. Seeing as how the LORD's Christ, "having abolished in his flesh the enmity, even the law

---

1932   Revelation 16:18
1933   Revelation 17:16
1934   Isaiah 14:7
1935   Isaiah 14:9
1936   Isaiah 14:12
1937   Revelation 16:14
1938   1 Corinthians 15:56

of commandments contained in ordinances,"[1939] defines the religious law as "sin" against heaven's will and doctrine, them that are against the illustration of what the Spirit wrought by His Christ on the tree pick up service to a conversation fastened by a *sabbath*, baptisms, ceremonies, traditions, and doctrines, after "the handwriting of ordinances."[1940]

14. "Death's" *Christ* is come to savagely and inhumanely destroy them that will not reverence "sin's" "God," which "God" preaches, "Righteousness come by the law."[1941] Thus, the spirit of their institution leads them to confront heaven's host with the doctrine of their *Christ*, but they are disappointed, for it is again fulfilled, "They took the bullock which was given them, and they dressed it, and called on the name of Ba'al from morning even until noon, saying, O Ba'al, hear us. But there was no voice, nor any that answered. And they leaped upon the altar which was made. And it came to pass at noon, that Eli'jah mocked them, and said, Cry aloud: for he is a god; either he is talking, or he is pursuing, or he is in a journey, or peradventure he sleepeth, and must be awaked. And they cried aloud, and cut themselves after their manner with knives and lancets, till the blood gushed out upon them. And it came to pass, when midday was past, and they prophesied until the time of the offering of the evening sacrifice, that there was neither voice, nor any to answer, nor any that regarded."[1942]

15. The failure of their *Christ* to appear opens up the opportunity for their slaughter, which is why it says of their *Christ*, "He gathered them together into a place called in the Hebrew tongue Armaged'don."[1943] This is no literal location, but is rather the *place* of a state or condition; this people of spiritual error will have their conversation ruthlessly slaughtered by the Word of the living God.

16. This slaughter is, again, no physical slaughter. "The Word of life"[1944] is "the Spirit of life,"[1945] and because "a spirit hath not flesh and

---

1939 Ephesians 2:15
1940 Colossians 2:14
1941 Galatians 2:21
1942 1 Kings 18:26-29
1943 Revelation 16:16
1944 1 John 1:1
1945 Revelation 11:11

bones,"[1946] it is that we are "to be strengthened with might by his Spirit in the inner man,"[1947] and "wisdom strengtheneth."[1948] The Word's Spirit can only consume the inwards of the religious conversation, allowing us to understand that it is His intention to "purge your conscience from dead works to serve the living God."[1949] When the Lamb's wrath is unsealed, the conscience of every conversation still holding dear to the institution of error, its name, and its sign, will experience excruciating agony within the spirit of their mind, for, "that which is born of the Spirit is spirit."[1950] Because this is the Spirit's wrath, only the Spirit's manner of consumption applies, and seeing as how the Spirit does not care for the flesh, but rather to correct the flesh by blessing the inwards of the conversation, the greatest shower of blessing ever recorded among men will fall on them. And concerning how the Spirit "blesses," we read, "I will pour my spirit upon thy seed, and my blessing upon thine offspring,"[1951] and, "I will pour out my spirit unto you, I will make known my words unto you."[1952] The Spirit blesses by pouring out the words of His name and doctrine to the conversation's conscience, which is why He says, "My doctrine shall drop as the rain."[1953]

17. Herein we may understand that the illustration of one on a horse, whether discerned by Mark, John, or Zechariah is, in reality, a sure revelation of the living God's doctrine fallen upon the conscience of priests and elders. Heaven's stewards will give this revelation, but the Word will accomplish its slaughter within the inwards of the serpent's host. We today are blessed by the heavenly mediation of the LORD's Christ to receive an outpouring of understanding in measure, then at the appointed age, without measure, filling our hearts with absolute joy, comfort, and gladness. But when this year of the Lamb's wrath is born, it is that all under the banner of "sin's" *Christ* "shall drink of the

---

1946 Luke 24:39
1947 Ephesians 3:16
1948 Ecclesiastes 7:19
1949 Hebrews 9:14
1950 John 3:6
1951 Isaiah 44:3
1952 Proverbs 1:23
1953 Deuteronomy 32:2

wine of the wrath of God, which is poured out without mixture into the cup of his indignation."[1954] "Wine" is language denoting doctrine, and this wrath is executed by the Word's doctrine of creation, but it is given without mixture. We today know only a tempered mixture of blessing, but when the time is come, heaven's will and doctrine will appear without mixture, and in hard comforting tones. The end of this consumption will convince "sin's" men of their violation against heaven's name and throne, and this is the point of the Lamb's wrath, even "to convince all that are ungodly among them of all their ungodly deeds which they have ungodly committed, and of all their hard speeches which ungodly sinners have spoken against him."[1955]

1954 Revelation 14:10
1955 Jude 1:15

34

He Will Come

1. With a sober perception of the form that the living God will take when finally appearing in glory, we today can better apply the heart of our conversation to the revelation of His name, and for the promise of that name. Therefore when hearing how it is written, "The LORD my God shall come, and all the saints with thee,"[1956] it is well to know how Scripture defines "God," for it is "God" that will come to act on behalf of His LORD and Father. Thus, to better grasp the definition of "God," we read, "The house of David shall be as God, as the angel of the LORD before them."[1957]

2. "God" is defined as that "angel" of the living God, and an "angel" is defined for us in the Revelation as a "star," for it says, "The seven stars are the angels of the seven churches."[1958] An "angel" is a "star," and a star, being a bright body of light, is a messenger of the living God's Faith, even as it is said of John, "He was a burning and a shining light: and ye were willing for a season to rejoice in his light."[1959] The man John was not that light, for if they loved his light, then the man is

---

1956 Zechariah 14:5
1957 Zechariah 12:8
1958 Revelation 1:20
1959 John 5:35

not the subject of their love, but rather the flame that made the man worthy to be observed, which flame says, "John came unto you in the way of righteousness."[1960] John's doctrine was that burning and shining star for the living God, wherefore when hearing that this LORD God will appear, and with His host, it is well to know that He will come in the form of His "star," or of His "angel."

3. Seeing as how "God is a Spirit,"[1961] the "angel" or "star" of the living God can be no tangible thing, for what doctrine is physical? When that great revelation of His star finally dawns, it will be His Faith that appears, even as it says, "But received me as an angel of God, even as Christ Jesus."[1962] The "angel" to appear at the appointed time will be "Jesus Christ," which is why, even though it says, "The LORD my God shall come, and all the saints with thee,"[1963] the reality is according to the saying, "The Lord Jesus shall be revealed from heaven with his mighty angels."[1964] That "God" to appear is "the Lord Jesus," and it is well to know that "Jesus Christ" is a name or moniker for the living God's Faith. In all actuality, "the Lord Jesus Christ our Saviour"[1965] is "the commandment of God our Saviour";[1966] what is scheduled to appear in omnipotent glory is no physical revelation of a man, but rather a spiritual revelation of the Spirit's commandment, which is why it plainly states, "He sendeth forth his commandment upon earth."[1967] With unsanctified eyes, it is easy to misunderstand or misinterpret Scripture without thinking, "What vision is literal?" There is no such thing as a literal revelation, but every vision is understood by the figures within it when once "comparing spiritual things with spiritual."[1968]

4. It is true that "God" will appear in glory, and it is absolutely true that "Jesus Christ" will come with heaven's host, but when understanding Scripture's language, that "Jesus Christ" is the name of

---

1960 Matthew 21:32
1961 John 4:24
1962 Galatians 4:14
1963 Zechariah 14:5
1964 2 Thessalonians 1:7
1965 Titus 1:4
1966 Titus 1:3
1967 Psalm 147:15
1968 1 Corinthians 2:13

salvation's science, the portrait becomes clearer, allowing us to observe the greatest spiritual reformatory movement ever witnessed among priests and elders professing *the living God's name*. In the context of the saying, "He cometh with clouds; and every eye shall see him,"[1969] no physical celestial event is spoken of, for this demonstration is not before natural eyes, but rather "the eyes of your understanding."[1970] These "clouds" are the same saints and angels, or who are the Spirit's sanctified hosts, previously mentioned, for "the chariots of God are twenty thousand, even thousands of angels."[1971] The "angels" are, in proper context, chariots, which is imagery denoting an army, as it says, "The chariot and horse, the army and the power,"[1972] and, "The horses and chariots of Pharaoh, and his horsemen, and his army."[1973] These "angels" are "the armies which were in heaven,"[1974] who honor the counsel, "Set your affection on things above, not on things on the earth."[1975] The saints and angels appearing with "Jesus Christ" are apostles sanctified by the heavenly Sanctuary's Faith. These ministers "give the light of the knowledge of the glory of God in the face of Jesus Christ"[1976] "to convince all that are ungodly among them of all their ungodly deeds,"[1977] and herein is the correct interpretation of that anticipated appearing.

5. Therefore, like as it says, "Behold, he cometh with clouds,"[1978] so the illustration is explained by how it says, "Behold, I will send and take Nebuchadrez'zar the king of Babylon, my servant, and will set his throne upon these stones that I have hid; and he shall spread his royal pavilion over them. And when he cometh, he shall smite the land of Egypt, and deliver such as are for death to death; and such as are for captivity to captivity; and such as are for the sword to the sword. And I

1969   Revelation 1:7
1970   Ephesians 1:18
1971   Psalm 68:17
1972   Isaiah 43:17
1973   Exodus 14:9
1974   Revelation 19:14
1975   Colossians 3:2
1976   2 Corinthians 4:6
1977   Jude 1:15
1978   Revelation 1:7

will kindle a fire in the houses of the gods of Egypt; and he shall burn them, and carry them away captives: and he shall array himself with the land of Egypt, as a shepherd putteth on his garment; and he shall go forth from thence in peace. He shall break also the images of Beth-she'mesh, that is in the land of Egypt; and the houses of the gods of the Egyptians shall he burn with fire."[1979]

6. *Nebuchadnez'zar* is a figurative illustration of the living God's "star" and "angel," or of "the Lord Jesus Christ our Saviour,"[1980] which "Lord" and "Savior" is "the commandment of God our Saviour."[1981] As Nebuchadnez'zar was supported by the living God against Egypt and Pharaoh; He says, "I will strengthen the arms of the king of Babylon, and put my sword in his hand: but I will break Pharaoh's arms, and he shall groan before him";[1982] so the living God will labor against that great Egyptian Babylon through His Spirit's commandment. This is a spiritual campaign "not against flesh and blood, but against principalities, against powers, against the rulers of the darkness of this world, against spiritual wickedness in high places";[1983] must we believe that what should be spiritually settled can only find an end by physical means? Physical means were once believed to quench spiritual error; what was the outcome? We read of Nimrod after the flood, "He was a mighty hunter before the LORD."[1984] It is not that Nimrod was a hunter for the living God, but was a hunter against the LORD God's Faith, for no physical act can quench mental and spiritual stubbornness. A greater act than that naturally performed against the antediluvians will take place, which is why it says of this commandment at the time appointed, "In righteousness he doth judge and make war."[1985]

7. This war will be fought, on the part of heaven's host, by the righteousness of "God" through the wisdom of heaven's commandment. The Revelation is a vision telling only the living God's perspective of

---

1979 Jeremiah 43:10-13
1980 Titus 1:4
1981 Titus 1:3
1982 Ezekiel 30:24
1983 Ephesians 6:12
1984 Genesis 10:9
1985 Revelation 19:11

events; no other perspective matters. To the Spirit, it is necessary that the one hearing this vision understand that He will get the victory by righteousness, and righteousness is no physical act. The Spirit's righteousness is the creation of a perfect conversation before His voice, and "perfect, as pertaining to the conscience."[1986] An omnipotent wrath is become necessary because priests and elders of *Egypt* are preaching *His* name through unlawful means, which is why it is well to know that "the wrath of God is revealed from heaven against all ungodliness and unrighteousness of men, who hold the truth in unrighteousness."[1987] Now, "all unrighteousness is sin,"[1988] "and the strength of sin is the law,"[1989] making righteousness' course without "the law of commandments contained in ordinances."[1990] Because the Spirit's aim is to "purge your conscience from dead works to serve the living God,"[1991] the conversation must refrain from "sin" in order to know right blessing, "for whatsoever is not of faith is sin,"[1992] "and the law is not of faith."[1993]

8. The religious law halts faith's right experimental course with the Spirit's voice for knowledge to live by, and this is what makes it "sin" to heaven's Faith, for whatsoever should retard the will and righteousness of the Word's Spirit, it is "sin" and religious error. We therefore understand the Spirit's wisdom and righteousness by the confession: "The law of the Spirit of life in Christ Jesus hath made me free from the law of sin and death."[1994] Resurrection and reformation of the conversation's conscience from "sin" is the end of heaven's Faith, and no physical or literal war is sufficient for this end, which is why "that which is born of the Spirit is spirit,"[1995] and why, concerning *Egypt's* consumption, it says, "Whom the Lord shall consume with the spirit

---

1986   Hebrews 9:9
1987   Romans 1:18
1988   1 John 5:17
1989   1 Corinthians 15:56
1990   Ephesians 2:15
1991   Hebrews 9:14
1992   Romans 15:23
1993   Galatians 3:12
1994   Romans 8:2
1995   John 3:6

of his mouth."[1996] As Nebuchadnez'zar physically injured Egypt, so the Spirit's commandment will mentally and spiritually devour the inwards of *Egypt's* men to fulfill the saying, "These shall hate the whore, and shall make her desolate and naked, and shall eat her flesh, and burn her with fire."[1997] Heaven's then apostles will pronounce the living God's star to the conscience of *Egypt's* priests and ministers, and the revelation will plague the spirit of their mind, so much so that "their flesh shall consume away while they stand upon their feet."[1998]

9. Because "God is a Spirit,"[1999] the Spirit can only devour those parts of the human being born to receive it, which is why our conversation's mind is "to be strengthened with might by his Spirit in the inner man."[2000] It is therefore well to understand that "wisdom strengtheneth,"[2001] and that when hearing, "I can do all things through Christ which strengtheneth me,"[2002] Paul is actually saying that the heart of his conversation is blessed by the living God's wisdom, which is why he says, "Let the word of Christ dwell in you richly in all wisdom."[2003] The Spirit's wisdom is the means whereby the Spirit's righteousness is witnessed and experienced, and because wisdom is not physical, it is that this righteousness is for the inward parts of the conversation's conscience, which is why it says, "Thou desirest truth in the inward parts: and in the hidden part thou shalt make me to know wisdom."[2004] When once "the Lord Jesus Christ our Saviour";[2005] which "Lord" and "Savior" is "the doctrine of God our Saviour";[2006] appears in terrible glory, *Egypt's* men will fully discern their hardheartedness to say, "My soul melteth for heaviness."[2007] The soul of the spiritually negligent will

---

1996 2 Thessalonians 2:8
1997 Revelation 17:16
1998 Zechariah 14:12
1999 John 4:24
2000 Ephesians 3:16
2001 Ecclesiastes 7:19
2002 Philippians 4:13
2003 Colossians 3:16
2004 Psalm 51:6
2005 Titus 1:4
2006 Titus 2:10
2007 Psalm 119:28

melt because "he sendeth out his word, and melteth them,"[2008] seeing as how "in righteousness he doth judge and make war."[2009]

10. What is appointed to consume the "unrighteous" is a word; there is no thing more or less than this. Them that suffer "the sword of the Spirit, which is the word of God,"[2010] at this time, are the willingly impenitent and stubbornly hardhearted to salvation's science. Creation's commandment will so slay the understanding of these priests and ministers that "their infants shall be dashed in pieces, and their women with child shall be ripped up."[2011] The Spirit's judgment and commandment will be preached in the fullness of the LORD God's glory, causing every man's "body" to fall for sorrow, moving them to pray, "I have borne chastisement, I will not offend any more: that which I see not teach thou me: if I have done iniquity, I will do no more."[2012] And we understand that *Egypt's* men do repent for their manner of worship and service because John saw them standing before heaven's throne with heaven's apostles. He writes, "I heard as it were the voice of a great multitude, and as the voice of many waters, and as the voice of mighty thunderings, saying, Allelu'ia: for the Lord God omnipotent reigneth. Let us be glad and rejoice, and give honour to him."[2013]

11. *Nebuchadnez'zar*, the "angel" of the living God, will get the victory for His name. At this time, the wrath of the Lamb is come to annihilate that institution forwarding "sin" by *His* name, "to execute judgment upon all, and to convince all that are ungodly among them of all their ungodly deeds which they have ungodly committed, and of all their hard speeches which ungodly sinners have spoken against him."[2014] This "judgment" is the same commandment of the Spirit, who, for our consolation, states, "A law shall proceed from me, and I will make my judgment to rest for a light of the people."[2015] This law

---

2008 Psalm 147:18
2009 Revelation 19:11
2010 Ephesians 6:17
2011 Hosea 13:16
2012 Job 34:31,32
2013 Revelation 19:6,7
2014 Jude 1:15
2015 Isaiah 51:4

and judgment is the doctrine that the Spirit's Christ preaches, saying, "I know him, and keep his saying,"[2016] and, "For judgment I am come into this world."[2017] To execute "judgment" is to execute the Spirit's law and saying, and the heavenly Sanctuary's then host will perform this judgment upon the conscience of Egypt's men. The Spirit's Word will get the complete victory over spiritual negligence, so much so that *Egypt* will find the spirit and philosophy of its institution for ever silenced, which is why it says, "These both were cast alive into a lake of fire burning with brimstone."[2018]

2016 John 8:55
2017 John 9:39
2018 Revelation 19:20

www.ingramcontent.com/pod-product-compliance
Lightning Source LLC
Chambersburg PA
CBHW060042230426
43661CB00004B/620